God So Loved *the* World

God So Loved the World

A Christology for Disciples

Jonathan R. Wilson

Baker Academic
A Division of Baker Book House Co
Grand Rapids, Michigan 49516

Published by Baker Academic
a division of Baker Book House Company
P.O. Box 6287, Grand Rapids, MI 49516-6287

Printed in the United States of America

Library of Congress Cataloging-in-Publication Data

Wilson, Jonathan R.
God so loved the world : a christology for disciples / Jonathan R. Wilson.
p. cm.
Includes bibliographical references and index.
ISBN 0-8010-2277-0 (pbk.)
1. Jesus Christ—Person and offices. 2. Christian life. I. Title.
BT203.W55 2001
232—dc21 00-068006

For current information about all releases from Baker Book House, visit our web site:
http://www.bakerbooks.com

For two who have taught me so much about Jesus Christ:
Julian Hartt
and
Marti Wilson

CONTENTS

ACKNOWLEDGMENTS

Several of my colleagues at Westmont College, past and present, have read portions of this book: Michael McClymond, Russ Howell, Thomas Schmidt, Telford Work, Tremper Longman, and Bruce Fisk. I am grateful for their encouragement and comments. Over the years, students in my classes at Westmont have read drafts of various portions of the book. I am indebted to them for their help in clarifying several passages.

This work is deeply indebted to my study of Julian Hartt. Though my work is of a very different order from his, my best ideas come from the christological center of his book *A Christian Critique of American Culture: An Essay in Practical Theology* (Harper & Row, 1967). In his most recent letter to me, he asked, "What are you going to make of the kingdom of God? That's what Jesus seemed to care about. What difference does it make to your theology?" This book is inadequate as a response to his question, but I hope that it at least begins to give an answer.

My wife, Marti, and our daughter, Leah, not only tolerate but celebrate my writing. For their love and prayers, I am deeply grateful. They are signs of the kingdom for me.

INTRODUCTION

> For God so loved the world, that he gave his only begotten Son, that whosoever believeth in him should not perish, but have everlasting life.
>
> John 3:16 KJV

This verse from the fourth Gospel, the Gospel according to John, is one of the best-known passages in the Bible. Christians have long considered John 3:16 to be a good summary of the good news brought by Jesus Christ. These days we see "John 3:16" held up on big signs at football games, golf tournaments, and even World Cup Soccer matches in Italy! Many know the reference—and can even quote the verse. But how many of us know the meaning of the verse?

A few years ago, I discovered how easy it is to miss the meaning of a biblical passage. I was in a university classroom listening to a speaker who was trained in English literature, law, and the art of communication. In order to illustrate a point, the speaker referred to all the "John 3:16" signs at sports events. "I finally got so annoyed by those signs," he said, "I dug out a Bible and looked up the reference. It's some obscure, trivial claim about the end of the world."

But John 3:16 is not a trivial verse; it's the very heart of the good news of Jesus Christ. Obviously, in order to understand and communicate the good news brought to the world by Jesus Christ, Christians have to do more than memorize and refer to Bible verses. We must be able to say why we have news that is good for our world—for today. In order to do that, we must be able to say how God's love is shown in the gift of Jesus Christ and we must be able to show that love in the way we live our lives.

I have written this book to help you understand the love of God in Jesus Christ and to live in ways that participate in that love and witness to it more faithfully. Since what we are talking about in this book is "good news," we should expect two things:

1. What we discover in God's gift of love in Jesus Christ will be surprising: It will be *news*.
2. What we discover in God's gift of love in Jesus Christ will meet needs we didn't know we had: It will be *good*.

God's gift in Jesus Christ is *news*. My wife, Marti, is the best gift giver I know. (Of course, when she reads this, she'll have to outdo herself to protect her reputation. I can't wait for my next birthday!) She puts a great deal of thought into buying a gift. She is alert to little clues about what a person is interested in, and she always cares about the person to whom she is giving a gift. No matter how creative I am in anticipating her gifts, she always surprises me. What is true of Marti is infinitely true of God. No matter how much we think we know, Jesus Christ is continually news. I hope to show you some of the surprises that we can hear even in the old, old story of Jesus Christ.

God's gift of Jesus Christ is *good*. Lost in a world full of death, fueled by longings and desires, we expend our energies seeking life in all the wrong directions. God's love in Jesus Christ is good because it shows us both the lies by which we are dying and the truth by which we may find life.

This book, then, is an attempt to describe how the love that God demonstrates in Jesus Christ is good news and how we can live that good news in our lives. There are many possible beginning points for an explanation of the good news; none is necessarily better than any other. But all approaches have to find their center in God's gift of Jesus.

Since the focus of this work is Jesus Christ, it is a study in "Christology," one of the traditional Christian doctrines. Today, many Christians avoid theology. Theologians seem to have their own vocabulary. Many works of theology seem to be written only for other theologians. There's nothing wrong with specialized vocabularies. Most of us learn several in our lives—the vocabulary of football (touchdown, forward pass), or cooking (saute, mince), or the vocabulary of computers (hard drive, internet). And we often use those languages to communicate efficiently with other experts in those fields. At the same time, however, we need people who can simplify a specialized vocabulary so we can begin to understand football, learn to cook, and use a computer.

In this book, I try to address the subject matter of theology, specifically Christology, for people who are just beginning to learn the specialized vocabulary of theology. I know the language of theology and the debates that theologians have among themselves, but I am not writing for them. I am writing for beginners in theology.

I am concerned that the gap between theology and the church has become so great that most Christians actually know more about sports, hobbies, and national politics than they know about Christian doctrine. As a result, Christians often explain their faith in terms of their own experiences or political stances that they hold as Christians. They don't know much about the gospel, and their knowledge of the gospel isn't nearly as profound as their knowledge of other areas of life.

I write this book for beginners, but I also write it for disciples of Jesus Christ. I am not primarily addressing those who reject the gospel or those who may be considering the gospel. Instead, I intend primarily to explain the significance of the gospel to those who have committed themselves to following Jesus Christ. I hope by my explanation to help Christ's disciples know the gospel more fully and live it more faithfully. Of course, I will also be delighted if this explanation removes objections and leads readers to Christ.

The approach I have just described is guided by two convictions about the work of theology. First, I am convinced that theology needs the church. The church is the community that God calls to bear witness to Jesus Christ. The work of theology is to serve the mission of the church. The primary task of the church is to preach the gospel not produce theology. Second, I am convinced that the church needs good doctrine. If the church does not have intellectually rigorous theology, then its preaching of the gospel is vulnerable. It may be blown off course by the demands of contemporary culture and by the sin that is still in us.

God so loved the world that he gave his one and only Son, Jesus Christ. That love is active in the world today to redeem all who believe in Jesus Christ. The proclamation of the gospel by the church makes known to the world the good news of God's love. Theology should help the church learn the language of the gospel so that we may faithfully proclaim it. Theology should also help us learn how to live in faithfulness to the gospel so that not only our words but also our lives bear witness to the reality of God's love.

This book is a work of "Christology," but it is different from many other Christologies in its structure and in some of its content. The book is divided into three parts: stories, images, and practices.

In part 1, we look at the way God's love is revealed in the biblical stories that find their center in Jesus Christ—what he said and did, how he responded to the "role expectations" of his day, and what these stories mean for God and for us. I am convinced by recent arguments that there is a basic narrative structure to the gospel. Of course, not all of the New Testament is presented in story form. But to understand the New Testament we must know the story that gives it meaning. This is not to say that the story of Jesus Christ is make-believe. It is to say that we best understand what God does in Jesus Christ by knowing the story. Christian doctrine is not simply a retelling of the story. Rather, doctrine gives us rules for understanding and living the story faithfully.

In part 2, we examine three "images" (or families of images) that serve as lenses through which we look in order to understand further the meaning of the stories of God's love. We will look at Jesus' life, death, and resurrection through the lenses of victory, sacrifice, and example. These images teach us that to see what God is doing in the world through Jesus Christ, we need to have our eyes trained. In this section I am guided by the conviction that the world teaches us how to see ourselves and our lives. If Christ's disciples are to proclaim faithfully the gospel, then we need to have our vision corrected by the teaching of the Bible.

In part 3, we consider how the stories and images of God's love in Jesus Christ continue in our lives today through the practices in which we engage in the kingdom, the world, and the church. Christology does not come to an end with the Bible. Christ's work continues today. When we are "in Christ" and he is "in us," we continue to learn about him. By faith, we are made participants in the redemption identified by the story of the gospel. The gospel is not an idea; it is a life that Christ's disciples live today. To know that life and live it, we must learn the practices of Christ in the world today.

Together, these three parts cover the traditional subjects of Christology in a slightly different way. Traditionally, theology has presented the doctrine of Jesus Christ in such a way that his life, work, and person seem to be discrete, separate parts of the story. In this book I seek to cover the same ground but in a way that allows us to see how his life, work, and person are intertwined. How I do this can best be understood by considering the chapters of each part.

Part 1 focuses on Jesus' life so that we can see how questions about his person—who he is—arise from the story of the gospel. At the same time, we see how his work is his life and his person. In chapter 1, I consider what Jesus said and did in his proclamation of the kingdom of God. This is not a usual topic for theologians; it is typically left to New Testament studies to consider the role of the four Gospels. I include this material here because I do not believe we can adequately understand the questions about who Jesus is without considering his life. My approach in this chapter is not that of a historian trying to figure out "what really happened" but of a disciple trying to learn how the one I follow lived—and calls me to live.

In chapter 2, I continue with the story of Jesus by considering his fulfillment of messianic expectations. Often, we talk as if the New Testament is the beginning of the story of Jesus Christ. In this chapter, I show that the story begins in the Old Testament by considering the development of messianic expectations and their fulfillment in Jesus as the Messiah. By considering Jesus as Messiah, I also show how the way he lived lead to his death and resurrection. Often, we talk about Jesus' life and death as if there were no connection between the two. My study of Jesus as Messiah attempts to erase this separation by showing that his life, death, and resurrection are parts of one coherent story.

In chapter 3, I turn to questions about who Jesus is. This chapter considers the historic controversies about the person of Jesus Christ that result in the church's confession that he is "fully human, fully divine." By placing this chapter after our study of Jesus' life, I seek to show that the seemingly esoteric debates of the church are of utmost importance. Questions about who Jesus is are not the invention of theologians removed from the mission and life of the church. Rather, these questions are necessary for a church seeking to understand what God has done in Jesus Christ.

Part 2 focuses on the death of Jesus Christ. In its teaching about the death of Jesus Christ, the church has used three basic themes. These themes may be identified in different ways. In this book, I use the images of victory, sacrifice, and example. Each chapter explores the biblical basis for an image and its historical development. To these I add a third, less traditional, section of systematic reflection. I am convinced that these images not only help us to describe the meaning of Jesus' death but also his life. In other words, the cross of Christ shines a light on his life as well, helping us to understand from the cross the significance of what he said and did leading up to the cross. I also believe that these images shine a light on our life in the world today. The sections on systematic reflection, therefore, explore these images as they form our knowledge of God, humankind, sin, and salvation.

Part 3 focuses on the practices of Christology today. This is the least like traditional treatments of Christology. In the chapters in this section, I explore the significance of Christ's resurrection, ascension, and sending of the Spirit. If he is risen, ascended, and present through the Spirit, then the gospel is alive and active in the world today. Our knowledge of Jesus Christ and our life in him does not end with the New Testament; it continues in the world today. The exploration in these chapters of Christ's continuing work is guided by our previous study and deepens our understanding of God's love for the world in Jesus Christ. In successive chapters on the kingdom, world, and church, I recall our previous study to show how we participate in the story of the gospel that we learn from the Old and New Testaments.

Does "God so loved the world" have any significance for this world, for us today? I believe it does. The stories I consider in Part 1 continue even today, and we are invited to become part of those stories. The images of victory, sacrifice, and example teach us how to see beyond and to see through what our culture teaches us in order to see rightly God, humankind, sin, and salvation. The practices by which we live are our participation in God's love that will one day be completed when Jesus Christ returns to bring to its close the story of "God so loved the world."

P A R T O N E

STORY

INTRODUCTION

"For God so loved the world that he gave his one and only Son, that whoever believes in him should not perish but have eternal life" (John 3:16). This verse summarizes a story. Sometimes a story summary is all we need. Especially in our culture, we are used to others summarizing a story for us. "Get to the point!" we exclaim. But often the story itself is the point. Imagine how impoverished our understanding and our lives would be if, rather than reading *Romeo and Juliet,* we simply skimmed a one-paragraph summary:

> Boy and girl meet. Boy and girl fall in love. Parents hate each other. Boy and girl still love each other. Parents object. Boy and girl disobey parents. Boy dies. Girl dies.

The same is even more true of the good news of Jesus Christ. We don't need a plot summary; we need to know the story.

Indeed, we need to learn the story so well that we live in the story. Perhaps you know a child who was so taken with a fairy tale that she lived out that fairy tale and assigned everyone in her life a role in it. As long as this fairy-tale living doesn't go on for too long or become too obtrusive, we are amused and entertained by it.

Like a child with a fairy tale, we need to become so immersed in the gospel story that we are continually living it out in our lives. However, just at this point we need to recognize that the gospel of Jesus Christ is a story—but it is not a fairy tale.[1] If the gospel were a fairy tale, then living by the gospel would be a refusal to grow up, a refusal to face life and live according to the truth of human existence. In this case, Christianity would be a religion for the immature.

Far from being a fairy tale, however, the gospel is the story of truth. As the story of truth, the gospel teaches us what the real world is and how to live in that real world.[2] The gospel story challenges us to consider that all our "realities" are half-truths, distorted truths, or lies. The story of the gospel presents us with the truth that we dared not believe existed. The gospel is the story of a reality more real, more truthful than our wildest dreams, our most extravagant desires. The truth of this story shows us how weak and misdirected our desires and dreams are and shows us what we were created for. This story invites us into the reality it proclaims. Living in this reality is something we can never outgrow. On the contrary, "growing up" means living in the gospel story more and more completely all the time.[3]

The story of the gospel concerns Jesus Christ. We may even say that the gospel is Jesus Christ. In the story of Jesus Christ, another reality—the reality of God's love for the world—is identified and established. Since the story of Jesus Christ is the gospel, nothing else can be substituted for that story.[4] That is, the story of the gospel is not just about sacrificial love or forgiveness or simple living as it happens to be exemplified in Jesus of Nazareth but could be exemplified in some other story. The gospel is the story of Jesus Christ.

Since it is the story of this person, Jesus Christ, and not some abstract principle or concept, the story of the gospel cannot be replaced by some other story. That is, we cannot substitute another story for the story of Jesus Christ just because some other story also talks about love or forgiveness. Christians believe that the story of Jesus Christ is the unique story of the gift of God's love for this world. Therefore, all our thinking about God's love for the world must begin with this story.[5]

An enormous number of questions could be asked at this point about the story of Jesus Christ as we have it in the New Testament. How much do we really know about what Jesus said and did? Do the Gospels report what Jesus actually said and did, or are they accounts of what the early church wished Jesus had said and done? Some people engage in historical and literary research and argument in order to prove something one way or another about the accuracy of the Gospels. Many of their efforts are commendable, but in this book I invite you to another kind of research and proof.

In this book, I will try to lay out, as clearly as I can, the reality of God's love in Jesus Christ. I ask you to consider whether that story makes sense to you. Does it reveal to you something you have not seen before? Is it a reality you would like to live in? If so, then you can prove the truth of the gospel in Jesus Christ in your life not by historical investigation or philosophical argument but by participating in the love of God made real through Jesus

Christ. This is possible because, although the story of the gospel begins thousands of years ago, it continues today.[6] The reality which is the good news of Jesus Christ is an everlasting story; it is eternal life through God's Son, Jesus Christ.

In the next three chapters, we will explore together the story of Jesus Christ as the story of God's love. I am not going to retell the story; remember, there is no substitute for the story. I will, however, draw your attention to particular features of the story in the New Testament and highlight ways that the story is continuing among us today.

In the first chapter, we will explore the words and deeds of Jesus in the four Gospels. This beginning point allows us to follow along with the memory of the early church and the way they told the story of Jesus. In the second chapter, we will continue our exploration of the story of Jesus Christ by examining the roles he played in establishing God's love in the world. This approach allows us to see the story of Christ as a coherent whole rather than as a series of isolated incidents. In the third chapter, we will look back over the story and our explorations in order to consider why and how Christians believe the story of Jesus Christ is the story of truth and reality.

ONE

THE STORY OF THE KINGDOM

The Words and Deeds of Jesus

Today, many people question the continuing relevance of Jesus. After all, he was a first-century Jewish male. What did he know about life in the twenty-first century? He knew nothing about our culture and the challenges we face. Does he have anything to say about nuclear and biological weapons, AIDS, mass starvation, or genocide? He had less education than most of us in North America. What can he teach us? Did he study quantum mechanics, much less Newton's law? He never traveled outside a very small region, so what can he teach us about living in a global society?

If we think these are the questions that need answering, then we will find very little that is initially satisfying in the things Jesus taught. But if we are willing to begin with Jesus' teaching, seek to understand it, and shape our lives by it, then we will find enormous, cosmic, redemptive help. And in the end, even these questions may find the proper response from those who have allowed themselves to become "learners-followers-disciples" of Jesus Christ.

What we will discover in this chapter is that Jesus came to teach us reality. The reality that he teaches us is the reality of God's love. That love cannot be twisted to mean whatever we want it to mean; rather, the love that Jesus reveals takes the shape of his own life. Moreover, that life and that love are present and powerful today. What Jesus taught in his earthly life, therefore, remains as relevant today as it was two thousand years ago. Jesus never goes out of date.

In John 3:16, we read of the love of God, which leads to eternal life. This eternal life is God's gift to us through God's Son, Jesus Christ. As we explore God's gift of eternal life through Jesus Christ, we discover Jesus' own proclamation of that gift recorded in the first four books of the New Testament. These books are the church's memory of what Jesus Christ said and did. For several years, the disciples had been trained and taught by Jesus. Now, as the Holy Spirit brought the disciples into eternal life, the Spirit also guided them so that they faithfully remembered and understood what Jesus taught about God's love for the world.[1]

In John's Gospel, God's love for the world leads to "eternal life." In Matthew, Mark, and Luke, the same reality is conveyed by the phrases "kingdom of God" and "kingdom of heaven." Some have argued that the kingdom of God (which Mark and Luke use) is something different from the kingdom of heaven (which Matthew uses), but I think the difference is simply due to the authors choosing language familiar to their audiences. We can find instances of this in our own lives. For example, North Americans would call the game my daughter plays every Saturday in the fall "soccer," but in Great Britain the game would be called "football."

Whether "kingdom of God" or "kingdom of heaven" or "eternal life," the Gospel writers are reporting one reality: God's love for the world in Jesus Christ. They may have different emphases and perspectives, but taken together their accounts give us a portrait of the reality of God's relationship to the world according to Christian convictions. For the sake of consistency, throughout this chapter I will use the phrase "kingdom of God" for that reality.[2]

Using the phrase "kingdom of God" is a bit risky. We are not familiar with kingdoms today, and for many the language of kingdom and kingship carries with it ideas of oppression, domination, and slavery.[3] However, when we look at the kingdom of God in Jesus' life, we find that he defines what the kingdom is rather than being defined by our ideas of the kingdom. The kingdom he establishes is unlike our oppressive human kingdoms. Our calling is not to abandon the term because it has been misused but to rediscover the good news of the kingdom that Jesus proclaimed and enter into it so our lives bear witness to it.

The difference between our kingdoms and God's kingdom is stated clearly by Jesus in Mark 10:42–45:

> You know that those who are regarded as rulers of the Gentiles lord it over them, and their high officials exercise authority over them. Not so with you. Instead, whoever wants to become great among you must be your servant, and whoever wants to be first must be slave of all. For even the Son of man did not come to be served, but to serve, and to give his life as a ransom for many.

Apart from Christ, our ideas of the kingdom of God are upside down; he comes to turn them right side up.[4]

Since Jesus comes to turn our world right side up, his coming is good news. Often, because we are used to living in an upside-down world, Jesus looks like bad news. When I was a boy, I loved standing on my head and imagining what the world would be like if everything were turned upside down. I would get so lost in that other world that when my father walked into the room, he looked out of place. He was walking on the ceiling!

That is what happens when Jesus brings the kingdom of God. When he fellowships with outcasts, forgives his enemies, and turns the other cheek, he looks upside down and out of place, but in truth he is the only one walking and living right side up. That is why his coming is good news. And that is why his coming is the gift of eternal life—he shows us how to live the way God intended us to live in this world. Faced with a world in which "kingdom of God" sounds oppressive, followers of Jesus Christ need to relearn and live the story of the kingdom that Jesus proclaimed.

We can begin to learn and live the good news of the kingdom of God by looking at four characteristics of the kingdom in Jesus' words and deeds: the reality, perfection, value, and openness of the kingdom.[5] Of course, these characteristics are an interpretation of what Jesus said and did concerning the kingdom. They are meant to give you some structure and some rules for learning and living the good news of God's love for the world in Jesus Christ. My hope is that this presentation will drive you back to Scripture to see whether these things are so.

This chapter is no substitute for reading the New Testament. But the New Testament is not meant to be read by an individual for himself or herself; it is meant to be read by the church for the church. When Philip met the Ethiopian eunuch in Acts 8, the Ethiopian recognized that he needed an explanation in order to understand Scripture. Philip represented the church's understanding of Jesus Christ as the fulfillment of what the Ethiopian was reading. The Ethiopian's understanding was enlarged by Philip's explanation so that he became a believer in Jesus Christ. My exposition in this chapter is my way of participating with you in the life of the church and offering to you an explanation that has enlarged my understanding and deepened my life as a believer and as a participant in the kingdom of God.

The Reality of the Kingdom

In Jesus' words and deeds, the kingdom is not an ideal for which we are to strive; it is not an ideology by which we are to live; nor is it a promise for which we are to hope. Rather, in Jesus' words and deeds the kingdom of God is a reality in which we are to live.

If the kingdom were an ideal, an ideology, or a promise, then Jesus' message would not be the good news that it is. An ideal, although it may cause us to work hard, ultimately oppresses us, due to its very nature of being ideal rather than real. An ideal is beyond our grasp, always teasing us and always far from us. An ideology, although it may give meaning to a life, depersonalizes its followers; they become mere instruments of the ideology. Ideologies are not made to fulfill human beings; rather, human beings are made to fulfill ideologies. Therefore, ideologies are fundamentally antihuman; they are bad news. A promise, although it may be a source of hope and a way of life, does not make that way of life possible; it merely makes it desirable. And so we may live by a promise until it is fulfilled. In Jesus Christ we have more than an ideal, an ideology, or a promise. In him we have the kingdom of God made real, the redemption of humanity made actual, the promise of God fulfilled.

The reality of the kingdom of God is shown by Jesus to be present *here and now*.[6] The kingdom of God is present *here*—in the human community, not apart from it—and it is present *now*—at this time, not some future time. Jesus hints at this in Mark's first report of his preaching:

> After John [the Baptist] was put in prison, Jesus went into Galilee, proclaiming the good news of God. "The time has come," he said. "The kingdom of God is near. Repent and believe the good news!"
>
> Mark 1:14–15

The nearness of the kingdom becomes its clear presence in Luke 11:20: "But if I drive out demons by the finger of God, then the kingdom of God has come to you."

In the larger context of this passage—Jesus' ability to defeat Satan by driving out demons—he connects the work that he does with the coming of the kingdom of God. Time and again, the presence of the kingdom here in the human community is not merely announced by Jesus' words; it is also powerfully proclaimed by his deeds.

Jesus' miracles are thus signs of the kingdom and of Jesus' authority to bring the kingdom. We see this combination of word and deed in the healing of the paralytic in Mark 2. There Jesus declares the kingdom of God to be present by saying to the paralytic, "Son, your sins are forgiven" (Mark 2:5). In this declaration, Jesus brings the paralytic into a proper relationship with God—he brings the paralytic into the kingdom. This forgiveness is a proclamation of the kingdom. But so that his authority will be clear to everyone, Jesus says to the paralytic, "'I tell you, get up, take your mat and go home.' He got up, took his mat and walked out in full view of them all. This amazed everyone and they praised God, saying, 'We have never seen anything like this!'" (Mark 2:11–12).

Jesus also shows the kingdom to be present here by his participation in the human community. The story of the gospel is the story of Jesus eating and drinking, going to weddings, walking in the marketplace, hiking in the country, fishing in the lakes, worshiping in the synagogue. Jesus shows that the kingdom is present here, in this place—and in every human place. We do not have to go out into the desert to find the kingdom, though it is present there. We do not have to retreat behind high walls to find the kingdom. We do not have to protect ourselves from everyday life to find the kingdom. Jesus shows us that the kingdom is present here—where we are.

The reality of the kingdom is shown not merely by its presence here and now but also by its *actuality*—the kingdom of God is activity. We tend to think of "kingdom" as defined by geographical boundaries; a kingdom is a place. The actuality of the kingdom calls us to recognize that the kingdom of God refers first not to place but to power—to God's rule or reign. As actuality, the kingdom is not potential but real. As activity, God's kingdom is more than an idea or concept. Here we may simply look again at how Jesus declares and enacts the presence of the kingdom of God in order to see that the kingdom is not potential or promise or concept. We may say of a person, "She has great potential as a scholar." Or we may say of an athletic team, "They are having a great season, but they haven't reached their potential." Such statements look to the future and hold out the possibility of great things, but nothing is yet realized and nothing is certain.

In the Gospels, Jesus establishes and reveals the actuality of the kingdom: The ideal is made real, the promise is fulfilled, the potential is realized. Jesus' miracles of healing, his feeding of four thousand and five thousand, his fellowship with all people, his forgiveness of sins—these *acts* reveal the *actuality* of the kingdom.

As actuality, the kingdom has a concreteness to which we are accountable. The kingdom is not a conceptuality with which we merely think; it is an actuality in which we must live (and living includes thinking).[7] The actuality of the kingdom, as Jesus lives it out, is far from the spiritualized interiority that is often our obsession. The kingdom may begin with an interior work of God (we consider this later in the chapter), but it cannot end there. In its actuality in Jesus' life, the kingdom calls us into relationships: We cannot be content with "peace of mind"; we must seek out peace with our neighbor, even our enemy.

Finally, in the words and deeds of Jesus, the reality of the kingdom is established and revealed as *everlasting*. The kingdom is not something present only during Jesus' bodily presence here on earth, either in the past or in the future. Nor is the kingdom merely a memory upon which we live. The kingdom is everlasting reality. Once established by Jesus Christ, the kingdom cannot be dislodged from the world.

Since the kingdom is everlasting, Jesus' call in the New Testament to enter the kingdom is a call also to us. The kingdom is not something we must conjure up out of the past, nor is it something we must anticipate in the future. The kingdom, in its everlasting actuality, is a present reality, rooted in the past and moving toward the future, which we must learn to see and to participate in.

Since the kingdom is everlasting, no present actuality of the kingdom exhausts its power or its meaning. Although everything else in our world is subject to finitude, decay, and death, the kingdom of God is subject to none of these. In the kingdom, we do not have a fading reality; we have an inexhaustible, everlasting reality. Neither the passage of time, nor human resistance, nor demonic strategem can wear down the kingdom of God.[8]

Since the kingdom is everlasting, it has a future. Here a great deal of theological energy has been expended. As we look to the future of the kingdom, we look for the second coming of Jesus Christ and the consummation of the work he has already begun. In the past few centuries, many people set dates for the return of Christ. This date setting and how one views the manner of Christ's return shape the identity of many churches.[9]

But date setting and preoccupation with the future miss the very things that Jesus himself proclaimed about the kingdom of God. Certainly, there is great joy for humanity in knowing that our present struggles with the sin and evil of this world have a termination date set by God. But if that time is going to be glorious, then we should be concerned with living like that time here and now. That life is what Jesus Christ makes a reality here and now. The life of the kingdom has already begun in this world. God's love in Christ establishes that life and calls us to it. The future is now, even though the present does not contain all that the future holds.

There are two great difficulties in our believing and practicing the reality of the kingdom. First, the kingdom Jesus Christ establishes and reveals does not look very much like the kingdom we want. This was true in New Testament times and it is true today. Back then, the people wanted God to establish a kingdom that would liberate them by destroying others, especially other human kingdoms. However, the kingdom Jesus teaches and establishes does not come in that way. Rather, it comes as the fulfillment and perfection of all creation and is, therefore, open to all.

Since the kingdom of God, which comes in Jesus Christ, does not fit our expectations, its reality is often hidden from us. We cannot see it because we are looking for the wrong thing. Looking for the kingdom that fits our expectations is like looking on a shelf for a book that I am sure has a blue cover. I cannot find the book. Where has it gone? Did I loan it to someone? I'm sure it was right there. Then, I look more closely and discover the book right where it is supposed to be—with a brown cover. My erroneous expectation caused me to overlook it several times.

The same thing happens with the kingdom of God. As we will see in the next chapter, this disappointment of the people's expectations played a significant role in their call for Jesus' crucifixion. The same disappointed expectations are present today. If the kingdom of God is really present, then why is there so much sin and evil? How can the Holocaust happen in a world in which God's kingdom is present? Surely the only sane conclusion to draw from all of this is that the kingdom of God is not a present actuality. But such a conclusion repeats the error of Jesus' executioners.

Jesus establishes and reveals the kingdom in the midst of spiritual and material poverty, in the midst of suffering, in the midst of evil. Moreover, Jesus proclaimed the presence of the kingdom in the midst of this world. If we believe the good news of the kingdom in Jesus Christ, then none of the conditions or events in our world can count against the present reality of the kingdom of God. Do not misunderstand: These conditions and events are not the kingdom, but neither do they count against the kingdom. The kingdom is present and actual wherever and whenever someone is restored to relationship with God, the enemy is loved, the hungry fed, the sick healed.

The second reason we have difficulty with the reality of the kingdom is that we have untrained eyes and have not submitted ourselves to the discipline necessary for learning to see the kingdom that is present and active in our world. When I was a child I loved the hidden picture puzzle in *Highlights* magazine. One page would contain, for example, a large picture of a farm scene. Within that drawing many common farm objects would be concealed. Today's equivalent are the Waldo books in which Waldo is "concealed" somewhere in an intricately drawn, finely detailed scene. Waldo is there and he is not really hiding, but it takes concentration and attention to detail to find him in the middle of everything else.

The same may be said of the kingdom. Jesus proclaims the reality of the kingdom. The kingdom is present and actual in our world, but we have difficulty seeing it. We need to have our eyes trained. We need to learn what distracts us from seeing and living in the kingdom. This is the purpose of Scripture: to teach us what the kingdom of God looks like and how to look for it. And often we need others to point us in the right direction, to say, not "there's Waldo," but "there's the kingdom." Others have done that for me, and that is what I hope to do for you.

The Perfection of the Kingdom

In his establishment of the kingdom of God, Jesus Christ shows us what human life is supposed to be. In so doing he exposes the corruption of human longings that distort and destroy our lives. He shows us that life is not meant to be a mixture of good and bad, a little more good than evil, or a struggle against all odds. Life is meant for perfection, but that perfection is not a moral faultlessness achieved by human effort. Rather, the perfection of the kingdom is life as God intended it to be lived and as God makes possible that life.

In Matthew, Jesus says:

> Therefore I tell you, do not worry about your life, what you will eat or drink; or about your body, what you will wear. Is not life more important than food, and the body more important than clothes? Look at the birds of the air; they do not sow or reap or store away in barns, and yet your heavenly Father feeds them. Are you not much more valuable than they? Who of you by worrying can add a single hour to his life?
>
> And why do you worry about clothes? See how the lilies of the field grow. They do not labor or spin. Yet I tell you that not even Solomon in all his splendor was dressed like one of these. If that is how God clothes the grass of the field, which is here today and tomorrow is thrown into the fire, will he not much more clothe you, O you of little faith? So do not worry, saying "What shall we eat?" or "What shall we drink?" or "What shall we wear?" For the pagans run after all these things, and your heavenly Father knows that you need them. But seek first his kingdom and his righteousness, and all these things will be given to you as well. Therefore do not worry about tomorrow, for tomorrow will worry about itself. Each day has enough trouble of its own.
>
> 6:25–34

In this passage, Jesus shows how our longings for security and necessities of life become corrupted. Jesus does not say the longings are bad in themselves; he does not say, "Seek first the kingdom and then you won't need these things." Rather, he says, "Direct your longings in the right way, long for, seek the kingdom of God, then these other longings will find their proper place and direction." In this way, the perfection of the kingdom brings good news to humanity.

Frederick Buechner, a contemporary author, has exposed the corruption of our longings in a striking statement. In *Wishful Thinking*, Buechner writes: "Lust is the craving for salt of one who is dying of thirst."[10] Do you get the picture? Here is someone lost in the desert for days without water, face raw and bleeding, lips swollen and cracked. And as he crawls along the sand, he croaks in a broken voice, "Salt, please, someone, give me salt." And as a mirage forms in the distance, he imagines rising there in the desert as his salvation, a four-story-tall box of table salt. That, Buechner says, is what our lust is. We who are dying because of our need for love, cry out, in the corruption of our longings, for lust.

In the kingdom, Jesus shows us what perfected human longing seeks. Thereby, Jesus also exposes and condemns our corrupt human longings. But he does so not to destroy us but to destroy our corruptions. Therefore, we must say that the perfection of the kingdom is also the redemption of creation.

In Jesus Christ, therefore, the kingdom comes as the perfection of creation. God comes in Jesus Christ, not to rescue us from creation but to redeem creation—and we who believe as part of that creation. Jesus shows God's concern for creation in the miracles that correct what has gone wrong in creation, such as healing the deaf and the blind. Deafness and blindness are not God's intention for creation; Jesus' miracles are the revelation and restoration of God's intention for creation.

Other acts of Jesus should be seen in the same context. For example, his feeding of the five thousand was certainly an expression of his compassion and his power, but both Jesus' compassion and his power establish and reveal the perfection of the kingdom that is the perfection of creation. We must recognize that Jesus' miracles are not arbitrary displays of power or the ultimate marketing strategy. Rather, his miracles are signs of the restoration of a creation that is God's kingdom.

This same concern for the perfection of creation may also be seen in our description of Jesus as fully human—the claim by the church that in Jesus Christ God became a human being. To be more concrete, God became flesh.[11] In taking on flesh, becoming incarnate, that is, "enfleshed," God began to heal the breach between God and creation. Our flesh, our materiality, is not something to be despised and escaped.[12] By taking our flesh, the matter of which we are made, God honored and sanctified that which had already been declared "very good" (Gen. 1:31).

This same conviction is reflected in our belief that Christ's body died and was raised from the dead. In the crucifixion, Christ suffered bodily in our place so that our bodies may be made righteous.[13] And after his death, Christ's body was raised from the dead. We sometimes think incorrectly about the resurrection by thinking that Christ's spirit was set free from his body. In this way of thinking, the risen Lord is some kind of apparition that occasionally materializes.

But what the church has long meant and what the Bible teaches by "the resurrection" is that Jesus' *body* was made alive again. Certainly there were some differences between his pre-resurrection and his resurrection body. But there was also enough continuity that the disciples (with some difficulty) could recognize him, Thomas could feel the wounds of the crucifixion, and Jesus could eat with them. So without getting into other issues at this point, we can note that in the resurrection of Christ's body we once again see that God's kingdom is the perfection of creation.

If the kingdom is the perfection of creation, then we cannot be content with any interpretation of Christian life and faith that restricts them to an interior spirituality that has no concern for the whole of creation. Our life and our faith concern the whole person and the whole of life. If God cares about our bodies enough to raise them from the dead, then we too should care about our own bodies and the bodies of others. But we should care for them in a way appropriate to the perfection of the kingdom of God.

What we often do in our culture, with disastrous consequences, is think that God cares only about our "spirits" or our "souls."[14] When we restrict God's concern to spirits or souls, we end up drawing our ways of caring for our bodies from our culture. And we become obsessed with appearance and physical fitness. Jesus exposes the corruption of these longings and perfects them by calling us to seek first the kingdom of God (even with our *bodies*), and the other things will be added.

What is true of our bodies in this perfection is true of creation as a whole. One of the corollaries of the resurrection of our bodies is that God will also give us a place to live in those resurrected bodies. Jesus' miracles that restore creation are signs of God's ultimate restoration of creation, when, as the Revelation of John tells us, there will be "a new heaven and *a new earth*" (Rev. 21:1, emphasis added). If God cares for this world so much that God is going to remake it, then we must care for it now in order to reflect the character of God and the kingdom of God.

Of course, once again we must be careful of corrupt longings. Many today are involved in environmental concerns, not because they serve the kingdom of God and worship the Creator but because they serve the kingdom of humanity and worship creatures and the creation. When our longings for creation are corrupt, we seek to preserve creation, not out of the peace and joy that come from participating in the work of God's kingdom but out of fear that human survival depends on our power and ability. In fact, it is human power and ability that have brought us to the point of destruction. Only our participation in the kingdom of God can save us.

One of the marks of our humanity involves our tendency and willingness to live by illusions. God created us with many powers. Our sin corrupts those powers, distorting our vision and leading us into death. In Jesus Christ, the kingdom comes in its perfection to expose our illusions, transform our longings, and renew God's creation. Only through the kingdom are we properly dis-illusioned so that we may see the reality of God in our world and live rightly.

The Value of the Kingdom

The value of the kingdom is announced explicitly by Jesus in the very beginning of his ministry: "The time has come, . . . the kingdom of God is near. Repent and believe the *good* news!" (Mark 1:15). "Good news" is simply the translation of the Greek word that we also translate as "gospel." The news of the kingdom that Jesus announces is gospel; it is good.

Jesus' proclamation of the kingdom is good news not bad news, because he proclaims it as a reality, as something present, actual, and everlasting. Jesus' proclamation is also good news because the kingdom is revealed to be a gift, a work of God, not an achievement of humanity. Jesus does not announce a new demand to be met or a postponement of the fulfillment of the promise. Rather, he announces that God's own action has met the old demand and fulfilled the promise.

Time and again, Jesus shows how we have reduced God's demands to a standard we can meet. He reveals our work for what it is: a reduction of God's demands upon our lives. Then, after restoring the radical demands of God, Jesus announces that those demands have been met by his own life of obedience.

This is good news for two reasons. First, it tells us that God will not tolerate the least thing that is destructive of our lives and relationships with God and one another. In our quest to achieve at least *some* goodness, we often lower the standards of goodness to a level we believe we can reach. Such a compromise would merely perpetuate something like the world we already have, a world in which there is a mixture of good and evil. So the good news is that God, in love for us, refuses the compromise that would simply perpetuate or readmit sin into our world. Second, Jesus' reaffirmation of God's standards tells us that God meets them through God's own action. When we might think that Jesus has doomed us by reasserting God's demands, we hear the good news that rather than being doomed we are saved.

If God allowed us the compromise, the lowering of standards, we would be doomed to the eternal presence of sin. God, however, does not allow the compromise. But if God does not allow the compromise, then we must meet God's demands. If God's demands are not met, we are doomed by God's holiness. But God in Jesus Christ meets the demands. Here is the value of the kingdom—Jesus Christ proclaims the absolute demand of God's holiness and announces that the demand has been met in himself.

The news of the kingdom is also good because it is the announcement of the fulfillment of God's promises. In the Old Testament, we have many promises from God. In Luke, Jesus reads one of those promises from Isaiah 61:

> The Spirit of the Lord is on me, because he has anointed me to preach good news to the poor. He has sent me to proclaim freedom for the prisoners and recovery of sight for the blind, to release the oppressed, to proclaim the year of the Lord's favor.
>
> Luke 4:18–19, quoting Isaiah 61:1–2

After reading this, Jesus announces, "Today this scripture is fulfilled in your hearing" (Luke 4:21). The news is good: Those who have been waiting, longing for the coming of God and the fulfillment of God's promises, will have their longings met. The promises are fulfilled in the establishment and revelation of the kingdom of God through Jesus Christ.

Throughout his ministry, Jesus appears as the fulfillment of God's promises. In the next chapter, we will see how this is true of Jesus in his role as Messiah. Here we will consider an exchange between Jesus and John the Baptist. John is in prison and Jesus is performing many wonderful deeds:

> John's disciples told him about all these things. Calling two of them, he sent them to the Lord to ask, "Are you the one who was to come, or should we expect someone else?" When the men came to Jesus, they said, "John the Baptist sent us to you to ask, 'Are you the one who was to come, or should we expect someone else?'"
>
> At that very time Jesus cured many who had diseases, sicknesses and evil spirits, and gave sight to many who were blind. So he replied to the messengers, "Go back and report to John what you have seen and heard: The blind receive sight, the lame walk, those who have leprosy are cured, the deaf hear, the dead are raised, and the good news is preached to the poor. Blessed is the man who does not fall away on account of me."
>
> Luke 7:18–23

The question asked by John and his disciples is exactly this: "Are you the fulfillment of all that God has promised?" And Jesus' reply is a resounding, "Yes." In his words and deeds, and ultimately in his person, Jesus is the fulfillment of God's promises.

We must recognize an important difference, however, between Jesus as the fulfillment of God's promises and Jesus as the fulfillment of our expectations. On the basis of God's promises, we develop expectations of what God is going to do and how God is going to do it. But when God works, God does not come to fit into our preconceived notions. God comes in Jesus to fulfill God's own promise, that is, to fulfill God's promise with God's own meaning and purpose, not to meet our expectations. The kingdom of God is not the fulfillment of any human political vision; it is not the achievement of economic aspiration; it is not the attainment of psychological stability. It is the fulfillment of God's promises. This is one reason why followers of Jesus can never become so secure that we lose our sense of wonder, our awe at the surprises of God.

In addition to seeing the value of the kingdom in the fulfillment of God's demand and promise, we may also see the value of the kingdom from another angle: its *costliness*. Jesus describes this in two parables:

> The kingdom of heaven is like treasure hidden in a field. When a man found it, he hid it again, and then in his joy went and sold all he had and bought that field.
>
> Again, the kingdom of heaven is like a merchant looking for fine pearls. When he found one of great value, he went away and sold everything he had and bought it.
>
> Matthew 13:44–46

In these parables, Jesus makes it clear that the kingdom costs everything a human being has. As Jesus says in Luke:

> If anyone would come after me, he must deny himself and take up his cross daily and follow me. For whoever wants to save his life will lose it, but whoever loses his life for me will save it. What good is it for a man to gain the whole world, and yet lose or forfeit his very self?
>
> 9:23–25

Here again the cost of the kingdom is evident. We must give up our lives in order to live in the kingdom. This makes sense only if we recognize that there is another kingdom, against the kingdom of God, into which we are born and in which we live. We are born into the kingdom of "this world," a kingdom of sin and death. We can only enter the kingdom of God by giving up our lives in that other kingdom. Thus, we must die to ourselves—the "selves" that live in that other kingdom. That is the cost of the kingdom.

This means that we cannot add the kingdom of God to a list of other things we belong to or own. We cannot belong to God's kingdom *and* another kingdom. We cannot love and serve the kingdom of God alongside other things. As Jesus says, "No one can serve two masters. Either he will hate the one and love the other, or he will be devoted to the one and despise the other. You cannot serve both God and Money" (Matt. 6:24).

When we enter the kingdom of God, we die to that other kingdom, whether it is money or sex or power or self-righteousness or something else, and begin the lifelong process of erasing the habits and memories of that other life. Such a process, however, is not something by which we earn the kingdom. Rather, it simply *is* the way we live in the kingdom.

To some the costliness of the kingdom sounds like an invitation to self-extinction. In this understanding, to "deny myself" in order to enter the kingdom is the same as ending my life, denying myself any worth or fulfillment as a human being. Thus, in order to be in the kingdom of God, I have to become something not human. To others the costliness of the kingdom sounds like a surrender of the freedom of the individual, the autonomy that we cherish and guard in our society.

If either of these views is correct, then God's love in Jesus Christ would be bad news for humanity. But both of these views are shaped by illusion. The first view confuses the denial of the self that is sinful and dead with the denial of our humanity. In contrast to this, the kingdom is the good news that our humanity, which is shriveled and dead in the world, is fulfilled in the kingdom of God. The kingdom is about living the way Jesus lived—in his love, and joy, and peace. And this way of life is what it means to be fully human. The kingdom is not the denial of our humanity but its fulfillment—

as God intended it. As our lives in the "world" die, we are raised to life in the kingdom.

The second view, which sees the costliness of the kingdom as a surrender of our autonomy, misjudges the human situation. This view assumes that humans are free to choose our own destiny and that no one should be granted authority over our freedom as individuals. In contrast to this, the kingdom reveals that we are not free to choose our destiny. Far from being free, outside the kingdom of God we are corrupted and fated for death and judgment. The kingdom of God is the good news that God overcomes our fate in Jesus Christ. To become participants in God's kingdom is not to surrender our freedom but to be granted the freedom to become what we are intended to be.

Even with these clarifications, some find the kingdom a horror and turn away from it to the lives they live in the kingdom of death. But others see in the kingdom of God the deepest longings of their hearts, the fulfillment of their dreams, the offer of life in the midst of death. To them the kingdom is open.

The Openness of the Kingdom

The openness of the kingdom is announced in Jesus' preaching and demonstrated in his life. Anyone who will come to the kingdom is welcome:

> Jesus replied, "Let us go somewhere else—to the nearby villages—so I can preach there also. That is why I have come."
>
> Mark 1:38

> Come to me, all you who are weary and burdened, and I will give you rest.
>
> Matthew 11:28

> I tell you the truth, whoever hears my word and believes him who sent me has eternal life and will not be condemned; he has crossed over from death to life.
>
> John 5:24

> On the last and greatest day of the Feast, Jesus stood and said in a loud voice, "If anyone is thirsty, let him come to me and drink. Whoever believes in me, as the Scripture has said, streams of living water will flow from within him."
>
> John 7:37–38

Together, these passages announce the openness of the kingdom to those in villages, to all who believe, to all who will come to Christ. But surely Jesus draws some boundaries. What about sinners, social misfits, political renegades? Does Jesus really mean to say that social outcasts are welcome in the kingdom? What about tax collectors—Jews who collaborated with the Roman government? Surely Jesus does not mean that the kingdom is open to such traitors and sinners. Jesus' words and deeds make clear the welcoming openness of the kingdom:

> As Jesus went on from there, he saw a man named Matthew sitting at the tax collector's booth. "Follow me," he told him, and Matthew got up and followed him.
>
> While Jesus was having dinner at Matthew's house, many tax collectors and "sinners" came and ate with him and his disciples. When the Pharisees saw this, they asked his disciples, "Why does your teacher eat with tax collectors and 'sinners'?"
>
> On hearing this, Jesus said, "It is not the healthy who need a doctor, but the sick. But go and learn what this means: 'I desire mercy, not sacrifice.' For I have not come to call the righteous, but sinners."
>
> Matthew 9:9–13

By having dinner with Matthew and other sinners, Jesus makes clear that the kingdom is open to them.

Jesus also clearly welcomes another kind of social outcast into the kingdom:

> As Jesus was on his way, the crowds almost crushed him. And a woman was there who had been subject to bleeding for twelve years, but no one could heal her. She came up behind him and touched the edge of his cloak, and immediately her bleeding stopped.
>
> "Who touched me?" Jesus asked.
>
> When they all denied it, Peter said, "Master, the people are crowding and pressing against you."
>
> But Jesus said, "Someone touched me; I know that power has gone out from me."
>
> Then the woman, seeing that she could not go unnoticed, came trembling and fell at his feet. In the presence of all the people, she told why she had touched him and how she had been instantly healed. Then he said to her, "Daughter, your faith has healed you. Go in peace."
>
> Luke 8:42–48

In this and many other incidents, Jesus responds to women in ways completely unacceptable to his society.[15] Women were considered dangerous to the purity of men. And a woman who was bleeding made unclean anything that she touched. According to the righteousness of his society, Jesus should have shrunk back from the woman and rebuked her for touching him. Instead, he commended her for her faith. Such an act was utterly revolutionary; it overturned the social stigma attached to women and revealed the full and welcoming openness of the kingdom to them.

Another incident in Jesus' life reveals the depth of this revolution:

> As Jesus and his disciples were on their way, he came to a village where a woman named Martha opened her home to him. She had a sister called Mary, who sat at the Lord's feet listening to what he said. But Martha was distracted by all the prepa-

> rations that had to be made. She came to him and asked, "Lord, don't you care that my sister has left me to do the work by myself? Tell her to help me!"
>
> "Martha, Martha," the Lord answered, "you are worried and upset about many things, but only one thing is needed. Mary has chosen what is better, and it will not be taken away from her."
>
> Luke 10:38–42

In Jesus' day, women as a whole were generally considered incapable of intellectual or spiritual achievements. Trying to teach a woman to reason was widely regarded a waste of time. But here Jesus gladly teaches Mary and commends her attention to his teaching.

In an often misunderstood passage, Jesus reaches out to another group:

> Then little children were brought to Jesus for him to place his hands on them and pray for them. But the disciples rebuked those who brought them.
>
> Jesus said, "Let the little children come to me, and do not hinder them, for the kingdom of heaven belongs to such as these." When he had placed his hands on them, he went on from there.
>
> Matthew 19:13–15

In Jewish culture, as in many cultures, children were sometimes viewed as a nuisance, a distraction from the main business of life. In this brief passage, Jesus first demonstrates that children are participants in God's reality, not a distraction from it. Second, his "such as these" comment warns us that if we become members of the kingdom, then the world may view us as marginal to life and a distraction. The openness of the kingdom is inseparable from its costliness.

So Jesus welcomes the sinners, the traitors, the women, and the children of Israel into the kingdom. Such a welcome is radical in itself. But Jesus goes one step further to lay the foundation for the spread of the kingdom beyond "Israel," that is, beyond the physical descendants of Abraham. In two encounters, Jesus lodges in the memory of the disciples an openness to Samaritans and Gentiles, which eventually bears fruit in the Book of Acts (see Acts 8 and 10).

In John 4, Jesus encounters the Samaritan woman at the well. The New Testament and other records make it clear that Samaritans, who were probably the descendants of interracial marriage between Jews and Gentiles, were despised by Jews. In contrast to that attitude, we find Jesus openly sharing the kingdom—eternal life—with a Samaritan. And she and other Samaritans believe. Similarly, in the parable of the good Samaritan, one of the most significant aspects of the story is not just that someone stopped to help the victim but that the someone was a Samaritan. When Jesus makes a Samaritan the hero of a story that he tells to Jews, he opens the kingdom to Samaritans.

In two other encounters of Jesus, we see Gentiles displaying the faith of the kingdom. In Matthew, Jesus meets a Canaanite (Gentile) woman:

> Leaving that place, Jesus withdrew to the region of Tyre and Sidon. A Canaanite woman from that vicinity came to him, crying out, "Lord, Son of David, have mercy on me! My daughter is suffering terribly from demon-possession."
>
> Jesus did not answer a word. So his disciples came to him and urged him, "Send her away, for she keeps crying out after us."
>
> He answered, "I was sent only to the lost sheep of Israel."
>
> The woman came and knelt before him. "Lord, help me!" she said.
>
> He said, "It is not right to take the children's bread and toss it to their dogs."
>
> "Yes, Lord," she said, "but even the dogs eat the crumbs that fall from their masters' table."
>
> Then Jesus answered, "Woman, you have great faith! Your request is granted." And her daughter was healed from that very hour.
>
> 15:21–28

We often read this story as Jesus' resistance to Gentiles, because we concentrate on his statement rather than on the story. However, the structure of the story and the woman's response to Jesus show us, not Jesus' rejection of Gentiles, but the great faith of a Gentile. The surprise of the story is that a Gentile believes that the kingdom has come in Jesus. The same theme shapes the story in Luke 7 of Jesus' encounter with the Roman centurion. Once again, the encounter emphasizes the faith of the Gentile so that Jesus comments, "I tell you, I have not found such great faith even in Israel" (Luke 7:9).

Rich and poor, traitors and sinners, women and men, Jew, Samaritan, Gentile, the kingdom of God is open to all. While we might like his inclusion of one or another of these groups, we might want to exclude others. Jesus' kingdom, by contrast, is open to all. Just when some may be cheering his inclusion of a political revolutionary like Simon the Zealot, he calls a political collaborator like Matthew. And as we applaud Jesus' love for the poor, he gladly dines at the table of a rich man.

The kingdom is open to all—but this does not mean that all are in the kingdom. Jesus' mission was to announce the good news of the kingdom and invite humanity into the life of the kingdom. The reality of the kingdom demands a response: Will we give up our ideas and our ideals for God's reality? The perfection of the kingdom demands a response: Will we give up our pretensions to perfection and accept God's gift of righteousness through believing in Jesus Christ? The value of the kingdom demands a response: Will we surrender our expectations, our achievements, our very selves and allow God to sustain our lives? The openness of the kingdom demands a response: Will we admit the emptiness of our excuses for not living as God calls us to live and enter into the kingdom, which is the joy of all desiring? In his words and deeds, Jesus establishes and reveals the reality, perfection, value, and openness of the kingdom of God. In this kingdom God transforms a fallen creation. The story has begun. Will we be participants in it?

TWO

THE STORY OF THE MESSIAH

Some of the most challenging aspects of life involve the role expectations people have of us. I grew up as a preacher's kid—a "PK." And I well remember my mother continually correcting church members' expectations: "Jonathan is to be good, not because he's the preacher's son, but because every child should be taught to be good." As I moved into the multiple role expectations of my adult years, I began to struggle with changing from one role to another and sorting out the conflicts between those roles. I would arrive home from a difficult meeting still in my "chairperson's role," and I wouldn't be ready for the change to husband or father. Or our family day—Saturday—would arrive, and I would feel guilty about taking the day off because I had left some task undone at work. Role expectations and role conflicts—they are a part of our lives.

In order to explore the good news of Jesus Christ, we need to look at the role expectations and conflicts he faced as he enacted the kingdom of God. For many years, what we are going to call "roles" the church called the "offices" of Christ.[1] But to us, "offices" may sound like Jesus was in the commercial real estate business. What are often called the offices of Christ, therefore, I will call the roles of Christ.

The offices (or roles) the church talks about are prophet, priest, and king.[2] If we consider the name Jesus Christ, we see where these roles came from. Jesus Christ is actually a combination of a name, "Jesus," given to him by his mother and father under the direction of an angel, and a title, "Christ," given to him . . . from where? "Christ," of course, is the Greek word for "Messiah," which is the Hebrew word for "anointed," that is, the "divinely appointed one." When we talk about Jesus *Christ*, we are saying that Jesus, that man from Nazareth who lived and taught and died and rose again, is the *Messiah*.

Now we are ready to see where prophet, priest, and king come from. If Jesus is the Messiah, and we get that term from the Old Testament, then when we look for those who were "anointed" in the Old Testament, we find three offices with continuing significance—prophet, priest, and king. The Christian conviction is that Jesus of Nazareth, the Christ, fulfills these roles and in so doing enacts the kingdom of God.

Fulfills is an important word here. The more natural way for us to talk is to say that Jesus "plays" these roles or "fills" these roles. But such language suggests that the roles were already there and Jesus just came along and fit into roles that were already established. The roles were already established, but what we will see is that Jesus surprises and remakes our "role expectations." Through the way he lives, Jesus shows us what those roles are supposed to be. Rather than prophet, priest, and king defining or describing Jesus, Jesus defines them, and the stories of his life describe what those roles are meant to be. In other words, Jesus, the Christ, *fulfills* the roles of prophet, priest, and king.

In addition to the role expectations that Jesus fulfills, we will also see that there are role conflicts between prophet, priest, and king that Jesus overcomes. In the Old Testament, these three roles often conflicted severely. Jesus comes not merely to bring harmony among the three but also to unite them in his one person.

In the history of theology, the threefold office of Jesus as Messiah has played a significant role. However, its treatment has tended to be conceptual, oriented toward ideas rather than toward story. Certainly, the offices of prophet, priest, and king have been located in the context of Israel and the Old Testament. But even then, the offices have not been located within a narrative, the story of Israel and the coming of the Messiah.[3] In this chapter I will display the story of the kingdom in the coming of the Messiah, Jesus of Nazareth.

I have three aims in telling this story. First, I want to bring the Old and New Testaments together in narrative continuity. In other words, I want to remove the pages between the two testaments in our Bible so that we see them as one continuing story. This does not mean that my account is anti-Semitic. It does mean, however, that I recognize a difference between Christianity and Judaism. For Christianity, the story of the "Old" Testament continues in Jesus of Nazareth; for Judaism, it does not. My narrative, then, is an attempt to be clear about the Christian conviction that Jesus of Nazareth is the Messiah—the fulfillment of the Old Testament hope and thus the enactment of the kingdom of God. Along this same line, I should make clear that my narrative of failure in the Old Testament is not a special indictment of Israel but an indictment of all humankind of which Israel is exemplary as the people chosen by God. It is a wonderful and fearful thing to be God's people.

The second thing I aim to accomplish is to unite Jesus' life, death, and resurrection in one story. Often in our churches, Jesus' life, death, and resurrection are treated in watertight compartments, as if one has nothing to do with the others. In this chapter, I will tell the story of Jesus as Messiah so that we may be able to see how his life led to his death, and how his life and death led to his resurrection. In a complex way, we need to recognize that the Jesus who was raised is the one who lived in a particular way and died a particular death. The Jesus who died is the one who lived in a particular way and was raised from the dead. And the Jesus who lived in this particular way is the one who was crucified and raised. Each only gains its full meaning from the others. We do not know what it means to say that Jesus was raised from the dead unless we know how he lived and why he died. We do not know the meaning of his life unless we know that he was crucified and raised. And we do not know the meaning of his death unless we know how he lived and that he was raised.

My third aim is to provide a story within which our own lives may be lived. Only Jesus is Messiah, but he calls us to follow him. To follow Jesus is to journey with him; to journey with Jesus is to share the same story. As we share in that story, we become the messianic community. The story of the Messiah teaches us how to fulfill the roles to which we are called as we participate in the kingdom enacted by Jesus Christ.

Christ as Prophet

In the Old Testament, we can see how the role of prophet developed and what people's expectations were of a prophet. To find the basic expectation of a prophet, we look in the Book of Deuteronomy. This book is really the heart of the Old Testament. It represents the fundamental convictions of the people of God.

The Book of Deuteronomy enshrines the agreement, the "covenant," between God and Israel as Israel entered the land God was giving them. All the books prior to Deuteronomy look forward to this time, and all the books and history that come after Deuteronomy look back to it for guidance.[4] So when we want to know about prophet, priest, or king in the Old Testament, the first place we look is in Deuteronomy.

In Deuteronomy we read these words about the prophets:

> The nations you will dispossess listen to those who practice sorcery or divination. But as for you, the Lord your God has not permitted you to do so. The Lord your God will raise up for you a prophet like me from among your own brothers. You must listen to him. For this is what you asked of the Lord your God at Horeb on

> the day of the assembly when you said, "Let us not hear the voice of the LORD our God nor see this great fire anymore, or we will die."
>
> The LORD said to me: "What they say is good. I will raise up for them a prophet like you from among their brothers; I will put my words in his mouth, and he will tell them everything I command him. If anyone does not listen to my words that the prophet speaks in my name, I myself will call him to account. But a prophet who presumes to speak in my name anything I have not commanded him to say, or a prophet who speaks in the name of other gods, must be put to death."
>
> You may say to yourselves, "How can we know when a message has not been spoken by the LORD?" If what a prophet proclaims in the name of the LORD does not take place or come true, that is a message the LORD has not spoken. That prophet has spoken presumptuously. Do not be afraid of him.
>
> 18:14–22

Many things in this passage could occupy us, but we want to concentrate on the expectations concerning a prophet. The general description is that a prophet will be "like" Moses. The passage goes on to say what this "likeness" will be: (1) He will be chosen by God; (2) he will speak for God; (3) his work will be enforced by God; (4) what he declares will come true.

In the midst of this description of a true prophet like Moses, there is also an indication that there will be false prophets. These false prophets will speak words that are not from the Lord and will lead the people to serve other gods. These false prophets are to be put to death.

The history of the Old Testament contains continual conflicts between true and false prophets. Two early instances of this conflict are Elijah's confrontation with the prophets of Baal on Mount Carmel (1 Kings 18) and Micaiah's prophecies against King Ahab (1 Kings 22). Then during the time of the later prophets (the ones who have books named after them, such as Amos, Joel, and Isaiah), we find an enormous gulf between true and false prophecy.

Hosea speaks about the people of God stumbling around without direction from the Lord, and stumbling around with the people are "the prophets" (Hosea 4:4–6). In this stumbling, the Lord's people are "destroyed from lack of knowledge." Micah exposes one motivation for these false prophets: "[Israel's] leaders judge for a bribe, her priests teach for a price, and her prophets tell fortunes for money. Yet they lean upon the LORD and say, 'Is not the LORD among us? No disaster will come upon us'" (3:11). In these passages, prophets whom Israel has come to recognize as true prophets describe the work of false prophets: False prophets speak out of ignorance and greed. That is, false prophets prophesy even when they have no word from the Lord, and they do it for financial gain.

Jeremiah contains the clearest description of the confrontation between true and false prophets. Jeremiah continually attacks prophets who prophesy by Baal, who are greedy and prophesy, "Peace, peace, when there is no peace" (Jer. 6:14; 8:11). Jeremiah himself is attacked by these (false) prophets and their collaborators (Jeremiah 11; 26; 28; 37–38). In these confrontations, Jeremiah remains faithful to the Lord, but the false prophets are the ones honored by the kings, priests, and people. God judges the false prophets, but the people judge Jeremiah. They prefer the lies of the false prophets to the truths of Jeremiah. Thus, although Jeremiah's prophecies were preserved and cherished by later generations who saw their truth, his words and his ministry were rejected by his contemporaries.

True and false prophets—in this conflict we see the corruption of humanity, which leads to the practice of false prophecy and its acceptance by the people. But we also see the faithfulness of God in raising up prophets and sending them to God's people so that they might know the truth.

At the close of the history that is told in the Old Testament, Israel has within its prophetic tradition the promise from the Lord of a "new covenant":

> "This is the covenant I will make with the house of Israel
> after that time," declares the LORD.
> "I will put my law in their minds
> and write it on their hearts.
> I will be their God,
> and they will be my people.
> No longer will a man teach his neighbor,
> or a man his brother, saying, 'Know the LORD,'
> because they will all know me,
> from the least of them to the greatest," declares the LORD.
> "For I will forgive their wickedness
> and will remember their sins no more."
>
> Jeremiah 31:33–34

And in the concluding verses of the Old Testament, the prophecy of Malachi records God's promise to send the prophet Elijah. For more than three hundred years after the last of the Old Testament prophecies, Israel waited and longed for God to once again send God's prophets to God's people.

When John the Baptist and then Jesus appear, announcing the coming of the kingdom of God, the people immediately begin to wonder if John or Jesus is the "prophet Elijah" promised by God in Malachi. John soon disappears from the scene, and Jesus becomes the center of questions and hopes. Is Jesus a prophet? Has God broken the silence? Is the Lord once again guiding God's people? Is Jesus the one we have longed and watched for?

Indeed, the people did declare him to be a prophet. When Herod asks the people who this Jesus is, some say he is Elijah, while others say he is a prophet like the prophets of old (Mark 6:15). When Jesus enters Jerusalem on what we call Palm Sunday, visitors to Jerusalem who ask what all the fuss is about are told that it's about "Jesus, the prophet from Nazareth in Galilee" (Matt. 21:11). And when some begin plotting to kill Jesus, we are told that "they looked for a way to arrest him, but they were afraid of the crowd because the people held that he was a prophet" (Matt. 21:46).

As the people identified Jesus as a prophet, he accepted the role. Indirectly, we see this in his comment in the Gospel of Mark: "Only in his hometown, among his relatives and in his own house is a prophet without honor" (6:4). Jesus says this in the context of a visit to his hometown, when the people there rejected his teaching and his ministry. In commenting on their rejection, Jesus identifies himself as a prophet.

In many passages in the Gospels, Jesus furthers his identity as a prophet by claiming to speak God's truth. The old phrase from the King James translation of the Bible, "verily, verily," states Jesus' claim to the truth. Today the NIV translates this same phrase as, "I tell you the truth." With either phrase, the important thing to note is that Jesus claims the role of true prophet.

This claim comes into fierce conflict with those in John 5–8 who see Jesus as a false prophet. In these chapters Jesus claims to be sent by "the Father"; he claims that Moses wrote about him; he claims to be fulfilling the promise of Jeremiah 31; he claims that the words he speaks are "spirit and life"; he claims that the words he speaks are from God. These claims fit precisely the description of the true prophet in Deuteronomy.

If Jesus' claims had gone only this far, he probably would have faced opposition but not a plot to kill him. If he had claimed only to be a prophet like Moses, we would probably revere his memory but not claim him as Lord. But, in fact, Jesus' claims do not stop here.

In John 5–8, Jesus claims not only to be a prophet sent by God but to have come down from heaven. He claims not merely to teach words of life but to be in his own self the word of life and the bread of life. He claims to have been in the Father's presence, and he says, "Before Abraham was born, I am!" After this last claim, many "picked up stones to stone him" (John 8:58–59). Their reaction is understandable and from one perspective commendable. Remember the anticipation in Deuteronomy of false prophets who would lead the people after other gods? To many, particularly to the leaders charged with protecting the truth of religious teaching, Jesus seems to be teaching another god—one who has come to them in human flesh. In their view then, their religious responsibilities required that they execute the judgment due a false prophet—death.

So in many ways Jesus fills the role of prophet. But he also *fulfills* the role of prophet. He does not merely bring the truth of God, he is the truth of God. He does not merely direct God's people along the way, he is the way. He does not merely point them to life, he is the life.

As Jesus fulfills the role of prophet, he faces the same fate that many true prophets face. He speaks of this as he continues toward Jerusalem even though he has been warned that Herod wants to kill him:

> He replied, "Go tell that fox, 'I will drive out demons and heal people today and tomorrow, and on the third day I will reach my goal.' In any case, I must keep going today and tomorrow and the next day—for surely no prophet can die outside Jerusalem.
>
> "O Jerusalem, Jerusalem, you who killed the prophets and stone those sent to you, how often I have longed to gather your children together, as a hen gathers her chicks under her wings, but you were not willing! Look, your house is left to you desolate. I tell you, you will not see me again until you say, 'Blessed is he who comes in the name of the Lord.'"
>
> Luke 13:32–35

Jesus knows that as a prophet he is going to Jerusalem to die.

What then shall we say of Jesus' teaching about the kingdom of God and his fulfillment of the role of prophet? He died as a false prophet, as one guilty of blasphemy and false teaching. His death is precisely what God calls for if Jesus' claims are false. Seen in this light, the leaders of Israel acted just as they should have. How shall we respond to that judgment?

Jesus' disciples faced precisely this hope-destroying, faith-defeating, love-dispelling conclusion after Jesus' execution: The one whom they had seen as Messiah, as the fulfillment of God's promise and their longings, was a charlatan, a false prophet. But this failure of hope, faith, and love was overwhelmed by the raising of Jesus. The resurrection of Jesus overturned the verdict of humanity. In the crucifixion, we declared Jesus to be a false prophet and a blasphemer; in the resurrection, God declared him to be the true prophet, the righteous one, the Son of God. What is the sign of a true prophet according to Deuteronomy? That his words come true. What did Jesus prophesy? What sign did he offer of his messiahship? The resurrection (Matt. 12:38–40; Mark 9:9–10; John 2:18–21). In his resurrection, Jesus is shown to be the way, the truth, and the life.

When we today seek direction, when we look for truth, when we search for life, we are looking for a prophet. That search is corrupted time and again by lies and illusions, by our own selfishness, by our dependence on our own abilities. When Jesus tells us that the way, the truth, and the life come to us as gifts from God the Father, we reject him even as his contemporaries did. We don't want to give up on our own abilities—in biblical terms, we hold on to what we think of as our own righteousness. But in reality we are stumbling around in darkness, clothed in filthy rags. When Jesus as prophet declares that truth to us, may we accept it and enter into the kingdom of truth and life.

Christ as Priest

In the Old Testament, no passage describes the work of priests as thoroughly as Deuteronomy 18 describes the work of prophets. References to the priesthood and instructions for its work are scattered throughout the Old Testament.

In Deuteronomy 18, however, we do have a brief description of the priesthood:

> The priests, who are the Levites—indeed the whole tribe of Levi—are to have no allotment or inheritance with Israel. They shall live on offerings made to the LORD by fire, for that is their inheritance. They shall have no inheritance among their brothers; the LORD is their inheritance, as he promised them.
>
> This is the share due the priests from the people who sacrifice a bull or a sheep: the shoulder, the jowls and the inner parts. You are to give them the firstfruits of your grain, new wine and oil, and the first wool from the shearing of your sheep, for the LORD your God has chosen them and their descendants out of all your tribes to stand and minister in the LORD's name always.
>
> verses 1–5

This passage reveals a few things about the priesthood. It refers to one element that we generally think of as the work of priests: sacrifice. But if we read closely, we find that although sacrifices are mentioned, it is not the priests who are sacrificing but the people. Now, eventually in the Old Testament, sacrifice certainly becomes the work of the priests, but we are wrong to think that it is the only work of priests.

Moses' description of the Levites in Deuteronomy 33 reveals other priestly responsibilities:

> About Levi he said: "Your Thummim and Urim belong to the man you favored. You tested him at Massah; you contended with him at the waters of Meribah. He said of his father and mother, 'I have no regard for them.' He did not recognize his brothers or acknowledge his own children, but he watched over your word and guarded your covenant. He teaches your precepts to Jacob and your law to Israel. He offers incense before you and whole burnt offerings on your altar. Bless all his skills, O LORD, and be pleased with the work of his hands. Smite the loins of those who rise up against him; strike his foes till they rise no more."
>
> verses 8–11

In this passage we get a much fuller description of the work of the priests. First, we are reminded that through the Thummim and the Urim (though we do not know exactly what these were), the priests were able to discern God's guidance. Second, we are reminded that the Levitical priests were totally consecrated to the Lord. Third, we are told that the Levites were responsible for guarding and teaching the covenant and the law. Only after this are we told, fourth, that the priests offered sacrifices to God.

Now we have a fuller picture of the priestly role in Israel. They are responsible not only for the sacrifices Israel offered in worship, but they are also responsible for the covenant and the law. Indeed, this latter responsibility may have been primary.

So we are missing half the story if we only think of priests as offering sacrifices. If we have the whole story—priests charged with the sacrificial system *and* with teaching covenant and law keeping—then we can more easily make sense of the failure of the priesthood in the Old Testament. This failure is most obvious in the later prophets, where we see persistent and profound conflicts between (true) prophets and priests:

> From the least to the greatest,
> all are greedy for gain;
> prophets and priests alike,
> all practice deceit.
> They dress the wound of my people
> as though it were not serious.
> "Peace, peace," they say,
> when there is no peace.
>
> Jeremiah 8:10–11

> Because you have rejected knowledge,
> I also reject you as my priests;
> because you have ignored the law of your God,
> I also will ignore your children.
> The more the priests increased,
> the more they sinned against me;
> they exchanged their Glory for something disgraceful.
> They feed on the sins of my people
> and relish their wickedness.
> And it will be: Like people, like priests.
> I will punish both of them for their ways
> and repay them for their deeds.
>
> Hosea 4:6–9

In both of these passages, the priesthood is condemned because they have corrupted the worship practices of Israel. Hosea and Jeremiah condemn the priests because they lead Israel in worshiping "foreign idols" (Jer. 8:19) and they allow worship to be perverted by prostitution (Hosea 4:10–14).

Isaiah adds another condemnation of the priesthood:

> Hear the word of the Lord,
> you rulers of Sodom;
> listen to the law of our God,
> you people of Gomorrah!
> "The multitude of your sacrifices—
> what are they to me?" says the Lord.

"I have more than enough of burnt offerings,
    or rams and the fat of fattened animals;
I have no pleasure
    in the blood of bulls and lambs and goats.
When you come to appear before me,
    who has asked this of you,
    this trampling of my courts?
Stop bringing meaningless offerings!
    Your incense is detestable to me.
New Moons, Sabbaths and convocations—
    I cannot bear your evil assemblies.
Your New Moon festivals and your appointed feasts
    my soul hates.
They have become a burden to me;
    I am weary of bearing them.
When you spread out your hands in prayer,
    I will hide my eyes from you;
even if you offer many prayers,
    I will not listen."

1:10–15

This is a disturbing passage. It is difficult to imagine a more religious people than those described here. They are zealous for worship: Their sacrifices are multitudinous. The language used to describe their sacrificial animals ("fattened animals") indicates that they are not cheating by bringing substandard sacrifices. They are so enthusiastic about their worship that they seem to have added new meeting times. They are people of prayer.

But the words of the Lord in the mouth of Isaiah speak condemnation of these zealously religious people. How is it that they are under God's condemnation? The answer comes in the following verses:

Your hands are full of blood;
    wash and make yourselves clean.
Take your evil deeds
    out of my sight!
Stop doing wrong,
    learn to do right!
Seek justice,
    encourage the oppressed.
Defend the cause of the fatherless,
    plead the case of the widow.

Isaiah 1:15–17

In this condemnation, Isaiah draws on the law and covenant to pronounce judgment on Israel's worship. The work of the priest is not simply to keep worship going in the prescribed manner; the priest is also charged with teaching law and guarding the covenant. Isaiah's oracle shows that the priests were not fulfilling their responsibilities.

The prophetic condemnations of the priesthood for idolatry, immorality, and injustice show us that in the Old Testament the priests, like the prophets, failed in their mission. Yet the Old Testament still looks forward to a time when the mission of the priest will be fulfilled. In Zechariah 6:9–14, the prophecy of a righteous ruler who will build the temple and sit on the throne is also a prophecy of a priest approved by God: "And he will be a priest on his throne" (6:13). In this prophecy, priest and king are seen in harmony. But before we look at the king, we must see how Jesus comes as priest.

Since we usually think of priests as offering sacrifices, we may be tempted to overlook Jesus' life as an expression of his priesthood and go straight to his death as a sacrifice. However, if we look at Jesus' life in light of the larger responsibilities of the priesthood, then we see Jesus as priest in much of his preaching and in many of his actions.

One of the most powerful revelations of Jesus' fulfillment of the priesthood is his cleansing of the temple:

> On reaching Jerusalem, Jesus entered the temple area and began driving out those who were buying and selling there. He overturned the tables of the money changers and the benches of those selling doves, and would not allow anyone to carry merchandise through the temple courts. And as he taught them, he said, "Is it not written: 'My house will be called a house of prayer for all nations'? But you have made it a 'den of robbers.'"
>
> Mark 11:15–17

His condemnation, drawn from Jeremiah 7:11 and Isaiah 56:7, may certainly be understood as prophetic condemnation. But the actual cleansing of the temple is the action of a priest establishing righteousness in his sphere of responsibility. And as Luke adds, following the cleansing of the temple, Jesus continued daily to teach there. In cleansing the temple and teaching there, Jesus reveals himself as a righteous priest.

Many other actions and sayings of Jesus should also be understood not as prophetic condemnation of "priestly" religion but as righteous priestly fulfillment of religion. In his healing on the Sabbath, Jesus reveals the proper order of things: Humanity is not made for the Sabbath, but the Sabbath for humanity. In Jesus' table fellowship—his meals with those who were excluded from temple worship—Jesus fulfills the purpose of the law and the covenant. They are meant not to exclude but to include by overcoming sin with holiness. In other words, the role of the priest as fulfilled by Jesus is not to exclude or separate from all that might taint one's holiness. Rather, the priestly role is to overcome evil with good.

Jesus' work as priest is a significant factor in the plot that leads, humanly speaking, to his death. After the cleansing of the temple, we are told, the leaders of the people began to seek a way to kill him (Mark 11:18; Luke 19:47–48). To be the righteous priest in a corrupt world is to give up one's life.

But Jesus' sacrifice is more than just our sinful rejection of his righteousness. It is also the overcoming of our evil and the fulfillment of our longings. The letter to the Hebrews tells us quite clearly and forcefully that Jesus' sacrifice makes us righteous and ends the need for any other ritual sacrifice. Another more subtle fulfillment may also be seen in Jesus' work as priest by again looking back at his cleansing of the temple. Jesus' words on that occasion reflect an inclusive understanding of the priesthood that goes beyond the sinners of Israel to include the Gentiles—the temple is "a house of prayer for all nations." Here Jesus quotes from Isaiah 56, which looks forward to a time when eunuchs and foreigners will be God's people.

The fulfillment of the longing expressed prophetically by Isaiah is found in the New Testament as Jesus Christ becomes the temple of God. In John, we are told:

> Jesus answered them, "Destroy this temple, and I will raise it again in three days." The Jews replied, "It has taken forty-six years to build this temple, and you are going to raise it in three days?" But the temple he had spoken of was his body.
>
> 2:19–21

Here we see the final fulfillment of the priesthood in Jesus. As he calls Israel to a new understanding of the priesthood by challenging their understanding of the law, covenant, and sacrifice, he faces death.[5] Where the priests brought sacrifices to God, Jesus as priest is himself the sacrifice.

And in Ephesians 2, Paul argues that in Jesus Christ the promise of Isaiah 56 has been fulfilled:

> Remember that at that time you [Gentiles] were separate from Christ, excluded from citizenship in Israel and foreigners to the covenants of the promise, without hope and without God in the world. But now in Christ Jesus you who once were far away have been brought near through the blood of Christ.
>
> verses 12–13

Throughout the rest of chapter 2 and into chapter 3, Paul continues this argument: Through Christ, both Jew and Gentile have been reconciled to God and thus to one another.

Thus, the role of the priest in teaching the law, guarding the covenant, and offering sacrifices has reached its fulfillment in Jesus Christ. What we in our sinfulness were unable to do, God accomplished by sending God's

Son, Jesus Christ, as the fulfillment of the priesthood. In so doing, Jesus fulfills the law, opens the covenant to all who will come, and offers the final sacrifice for our sins. In him as priestly Messiah the kingdom is enacted.

We humans long for acceptance before God. Time and again we seek that acceptance by excluding those whom we judge to be unacceptable to God, by seeking to make ourselves righteous, and by attempting to please God with our rituals. Through Jesus' fulfillment of the priesthood, our illusions are exposed, our self-righteousness judged, and our rituals purified. By the gift of Jesus Christ we are accepted by the loving God who overcomes our exclusiveness, our self-righteousness, and our rituals in order to make us those who welcome others, who practice Christ's righteousness, and whose lives are wholly serving God's kingdom.

Christ as King

In the Old Testament, Yahweh is to be Israel's king. But eventually the people of Israel, wanting to be like other people, ask for a human king. Although their request falls short of the ideal, it is granted by God. However, in granting Israel's request, Yahweh does not set them free to follow the pattern of kingship among their neighbors.

In Deuteronomy 17, we find Yahweh's criteria for Israel's king:

> When you enter the land the LORD your God is giving you and have taken possession of it and settled in it, and you say, "Let us set a king over us like all the nations around us," be sure to appoint over you the king the LORD your God chooses. He must be from among your own brothers. Do not place a foreigner over you, one who is not a brother Israelite. The king, moreover, must not acquire great numbers of horses for himself or make the people return to Egypt to get more of them, for the LORD has told you, "You are not to go back that way again." He must not take many wives or his heart will be led astray. He must not accumulate large amounts of silver and gold.
>
> When he takes the throne of his kingdom, he is to write for himself on a scroll a copy of this law, taken from that of the priests, who are Levites. It is to be with him, and he is to read it all the days of his life so that he may learn to revere the LORD his God and follow carefully all the words of this law and these decrees and not consider himself better than his brothers and turn from the law to the right or to the left. Then he and his descendants will reign a long time over his kingdom in Israel.
>
> verses 14–20

In this lengthy passage, we are given a number of criteria by which a king is to live and by which he is to be judged. (1) He is not to gain his position through personal popularity or military strength but by appointment from

God. (2) The injunction against acquiring great numbers of horses is a way of saying that the king is not to build his own army (warfare was the primary use for large numbers of horses). In contemporary terms we would say that the king is not to build up an arsenal or engage in an arms race. (3) The injunction against taking many wives has behind it the conviction that some of those many wives would be foreigners who worship other gods and would lead the king into idolatry. (4) The king is not to accumulate personal wealth. (5) He is to live by God's law. (6) He is to be humble, to consider himself as one of his brother Israelites.

As a whole these requirements describe a king unlike any other king—one who seeks nothing for himself, is entirely dependent on Yahweh, and seeks only to obey Yahweh. If the king does these things, we are told, then his kingdom will last. But the Old Testament history of Israel's kings is full of failure. In the Books of Samuel and Kings, the monarchs of Israel and (after the nation divided) Judah are measured not by the prosperity of their reigns, their military victories, or their political successes but by their (lack of) faithfulness to the criteria laid out in Deuteronomy. From the perspective of these books, the history of the kings of Israel (the northern kingdom) was one of unceasing failure. Time after time, a king of Israel is named, the period of his reign is identified, and we are told that "he did evil in the eyes of the LORD." When Hoshea, king of Israel, is defeated by Shalmaneser, king of Assyria, and the northern kingdom is led into exile by Assyria, this story reaches its end:

> All this took place because the Israelites had sinned against the LORD their God, who had brought them up out of Egypt from under the power of Pharaoh king of Egypt. They worshiped other gods and followed the practices of the nations the LORD had driven out before them, as well as the practices that the kings of Israel had introduced.
>
> 2 Kings 17:7–8

In the overlapping histories of Israel and Judah, Judah, the southern kingdom, fares much better. Many of their kings did "what was right in the eyes of the LORD." But after many righteous kings, Judah suffers from a series of evil kings. In succession, Jehoahaz, Jehoiakim, Jehoiachin, and Zedekiah "did what was evil in the eyes of the LORD" (2 Kings 23:32, 37; 24:9, 19). And when the fall of Jerusalem and the exile of Judah are narrated, the story is introduced with the comment that "it was because of the LORD's anger that all this happened to Jerusalem and Judah, and in the end he thrust them from his presence" (2 Kings 24:20).

So the story of the Old Testament is in part the story of the sinful failure of Israel's monarchy. Through this story, we see Israel's longing for a leader, a ruler. And we are confronted by the corruption that prevents the human fulfillment of that longing.

Nevertheless, the Old Testament reflects the persistent longing for a righteous king, reflected in the Old Testament prophecies of the righteous king. These are the passages we usually think of when we talk about the "Messiah." Indeed, these passages form the substance of Handel's *Messiah*. One of the most famous and powerful passages declares:

> For to us a child is born,
> to us a son is given,
> and the government shall be on his shoulders.
> And he will be called
> Wonderful Counselor, Mighty God,
> Everlasting Father, Prince of Peace.
> Of the increase of his government and peace
> there will be no end.
> He will reign on David's throne
> and over his kingdom,
> establishing and upholding it
> with justice and righteousness
> from that time on and forever.
> The zeal of the LORD Almighty
> will accomplish this.
>
> Isaiah 9:6–7

This passage looks forward to the fulfillment of Deuteronomy 17. And in the New Testament, this prophecy and others like it find their fulfillment in Jesus Christ.

At the beginning of the story of Jesus, when the Holy Spirit brings about his conception, Jesus is portrayed as king:

> But the angel said to her, "Do not be afraid, Mary, you have found favor with God. You will be with child and give birth to a son, and you are to give him the name Jesus. He will be great and will be called the Son of the Most High. The Lord God will give him the throne of his father David, and he will reign over the house of Jacob forever; his kingdom will never end."
>
> Luke 1:30–33

This portrayal continues throughout the Gospels. The Magi come seeking "the one who has been born king of the Jews" (Matt. 2:2). In the midst of Jesus' exorcisms and healings, which the Gospels portray as signs of the kingdom of God, the people wonder, "Could this be the Son of David?" (Matt. 12:23).

Perhaps the clearest expression of Jesus as king is his entry into Jerusalem on what we now celebrate as Palm Sunday:

> As they approached Jerusalem and came to Bethphage on the Mount of Olives, Jesus sent two disciples, saying to them, "Go to the village ahead of you, and at once you will find a donkey tied there, with her colt by her. Untie them and bring them to me. If anyone says anything to you, tell him that the Lord needs them, and he will send them right away." This took place to fulfill what was spoken through the prophet: "Say to the Daughter of Zion, 'See your king comes to you, gentle and riding on a donkey, on a colt, the foal of a donkey.'"
>
> The disciples went and did as Jesus had instructed them. They brought the donkey and the colt, placed their cloaks on them, and Jesus sat on them. A very large crowd spread their cloaks on the road, while others cut branches from the trees and spread them on the road. The crowds that went ahead of him and those that followed shouted, "Hosanna to the Son of David!" "Blessed is he who comes in the name of the Lord!" "Hosanna in the highest!"
>
> Matthew 21:1–9

But if Jesus comes as messianic king and is welcomed into Jerusalem, how is it that only a few days later he is executed on a cross? Pursuing the answer to this question ultimately reveals to us Jesus' fulfillment of the role of king.

In the Old Testament, the king was to depend on Yahweh, follow the law, and serve his fellow Israelites. In the New Testament, Jesus as messianic king fulfills each of these expectations. Jesus' dependence on Yahweh is shown in his refusal to defend himself. Just as Israel's king was not to rule by his own power but depend on Yahweh to fight for him, so Jesus also refuses to defend himself.[6] In fulfillment of the Old Testament prophecy, Jesus is the king who knows that if he is truly appointed by God, then God will fight for him and reveal the righteousness of the king. Our natural expectation of a king is that he will be a mighty warrior who leads his side to victory. Jesus is victorious by his dependence on God.

As messianic king, Jesus also follows the law. He is the righteous king. He is perfectly obedient to the Father. He does only what the Father tells him. He fulfills the law rather than abolishing it. As priest he teaches the law; as king he lives the law. As prophet he proclaims the will of God; as king he lives the will of God.

As messianic king, Jesus serves his brothers and sisters. Once, two of Jesus' followers, James and John, came to him seeking places of honor in the kingdom.

> When the ten [other disciples] heard about this, they became indignant with James and John. Jesus called them together and said, "You know that those who are regarded as rulers of the Gentiles lord it over them, and their high officials exercise authority over them. Not so with you. Instead, whoever wants to become great among you must be your servant, and whoever wants to be first must be slave of all. For even the Son of Man did not come to be served, but to serve, and to give his life as a ransom for many."
>
> Mark 10:41–45

In this passage, Jesus talks about the true fulfillment of kingship. In God's kingdom, the king is to serve, not be served. Even beyond the Old Testament rule that the king is not to elevate himself above the people, Jesus says that in the kingdom of God the king is to lower himself, to be servant and slave.

Jesus knows how radical this claim is. He knows that for him his kingship means death. As he approaches his death, Jesus is mocked as king:

> Then the governor's soldiers took Jesus into the Praetorium and gathered the whole company of soldiers around him. They stripped him and put a scarlet robe on him, and then twisted together a crown of thorns and set it on his head. They put a staff in his right hand and knelt in front of him and mocked him. "Hail, king of the Jews!" they said. They spit on him, and took the staff and struck him on the head again and again. After they had mocked him, they took off the robe and put his own clothes on him. Then they led him away to crucify him.
>
> Matthew 27:27–31

To reveal true kingship as servanthood, to be obedient to God, and to depend on God, Jesus must humble himself even to death on the cross. In our evil corruption, we humans respond to servanthood and righteousness and nonresistance with rejection, condemnation, and violence.

But what about the sentence that we execute: Servanthood is weakness, righteousness is detestable, nonresistance is to be crushed. How can we claim that Jesus is the messianic king who establishes the kingdom of God in this world when we are able to hang him on a cross and mock him and destroy him?

For the New Testament, the answer to these questions is found in Jesus' resurrection. In raising Jesus from the dead, God reverses our sentence of judgment on Jesus and reveals that the way Jesus fulfilled the role of king is the way approved by God. Jesus depended on the Father to defend and sustain him. And the Father did just that, not by preventing Jesus' death, but through his death. Likewise, Jesus' resurrection demonstrates God's approval of Jesus' way of life—the righteousness of Jesus is the righteousness approved by the One who holds power over life and death. And finally, Jesus' resurrection from the dead shows that the way of servanthood is the life that overcomes death.

We long either for the power of kings so that we may be rulers who control life or for those who have power to be rulers who enhance our lives. In the history of the Old Testament, we see that the corruption of humanity makes impossible the fulfillment of those longings. Because of our sinful corruption, our use of power and our attempts to rule end in death not life.

God so loved the world that he sent his Son to be King. Jesus' kingship did what we could not do. Where we seek life and bring death, Jesus through death brings life. Jesus as Messiah fulfills our longings for a king by bringing the kingdom of God through giving up his life and becoming a servant. He shows us that through giving up our lives to God we enter into life.

Conclusion

In the roles he fulfills as Messiah, Jesus enacts the kingdom of God. His story is the story of a new reality planted in this world by his faithfulness as prophet, priest, and king. It is the story of one life lived in complete, perfect accord with God's intentions for creation. By living in perfect accord with God's intentions, Jesus Christ actualized the kingdom of God.

As Jesus made the kingdom a reality through his actions, he also showed us what our longings are really about. Our longings and expectations are distorted by sin. When we force ourselves and others into those longings and expectations, we destroy them and ourselves. We may even seek to fit God into our preconceptions. In Jesus' fulfillment of the roles of the Messiah, he exposes our sinful distortions and directs us toward truth.

In his revelation of truth, Jesus fulfills God's commitment to creation and God's promise to redeem. In the story of Jesus as Messiah, we see the value of God's love. In him, we also see the costliness of that love. As prophet, priest, and king, he lives in this world to enact the kingdom of God. We who are of this world cannot accept that way of living, and so we kill him. His way of living by the kingdom in this world leads inexorably to his death.

In his life, death, and resurrection, Jesus opens the kingdom to all humanity. He breaks down all the barriers between God and humanity and between all the "ways" of being human. In his way of living out the role of Messiah, Jesus threw open citizenship in the kingdom of God to all who would come to his way of living.

So in the story of the Messiah we also see the story of the kingdom. In Jesus' words and deeds, he proclaims the kingdom of God; in his role as Messiah, he enacts the kingdom of God. Jesus' story is the story of the kingdom of God. In fact, the story of the kingdom is so much the story of Jesus Christ that we may go so far as to say that Jesus Christ *is* the kingdom of God. To be "in Christ" is to be in the kingdom of God. To proclaim Christ is to proclaim the kingdom. Thus, what Jesus proclaimed and enacted—the kingdom of God—is proclaimed and enacted by the church as the presence of Christ himself. In faithfulness to the story of the kingdom of God, the church proclaims the story of Jesus Christ and calls us to faith in him.

THREE

WHOSE STORY IS IT?

Jesus Christ as Fully Human and Fully Divine

In the previous chapters, we looked at the story of the kingdom of God as the expression of God's love in Jesus Christ. We encountered a great deal of drama and surprises. We are now ready to ask a critically important question: Who is the story about? Whose story is it, anyway? In our discussion so far, we have been freely mixing talk about God with talk about humanity. How is it that the story of Jesus involves talking about both God and humanity in such strong, pervasive language?

We can identify five possible ways in which the story of Jesus involves God and humanity: (1) Jesus is a human being, perhaps *the* human being, who sought God most faithfully and successfully; (2) Jesus is a divine being, perhaps *the* divine being, who appeared on earth in search of humans; (3) Jesus is somehow a human being and a divine being who is like God; (4) Jesus is somehow God and a creature who is like a human being; (5) Jesus is both a human being and God—fully human and fully divine.

Each of these answers has been proposed over the centuries to answer the question, "Who is Jesus Christ?" This is not precisely the same question I am asking in this chapter, and the answers to this traditional question have seldom been put in "story" form. But if we recognize that the gospel of the kingdom is the story of Jesus Christ, then my question is the same question. To ask, "Who is Jesus Christ?" is to ask, "Who is the story of the kingdom about?"

The church has traditionally viewed the fifth answer above as the correct answer. As we will see, it is the answer the church arrived at in a series of meetings—church councils—from A.D. 325 to 451, and it is the answer that fits Scripture and guides faithfulness to the gospel today.[1] As church leaders met in these councils over the centuries, three issues were intertwined as they sought to understand the full significance of the gospel of Jesus Christ. They were, of course, concerned with the identity of Jesus Christ—who is he? As they answered this question with the affirmation that he is "fully human and fully divine," they became involved at the same time with two other questions. If Jesus Christ is fully divine, then what does that tell us about God? In reflection on this question, the church affirmed the doctrine of the Trinity—God is three and one.[2] Finally, if Jesus Christ is both fully human and fully divine, how do these two "natures" exist in one "person"?

In the following accounts, I will retrieve this history of the doctrine of Jesus Christ by asking a different question. The early church naturally and rightly asked their questions and pursued their answers in the language and thought forms of their culture. That is what the church must do if we are to proclaim the gospel to the world in which we live. Today, in our culture, the questions about Jesus Christ take a different form and require new answers that enable us to be faithful to the same gospel—the everlasting actuality of the kingdom proclaimed and enacted by Jesus Christ. What are the rules for proclaiming and living the story of Jesus Christ as the kingdom of God? To answer this question, we will consider five possible answers that correspond to the five positions listed above. As we consider these possibilities, we will examine their fit with Scripture as the story of the kingdom, with other Christian doctrines as guides to that story, and with the shape of Christian living as our participation in that story.

The Story of Jesus Christ Is about a Human Being Who Faithfully and Successfully Seeks God

According to this answer, the gospel is about one who was born as (merely) a human being. This man, Jesus of Nazareth, sought and obeyed and loved God so faithfully, persistently, and rightly that God approved of him more than any other human being. At this point, the story can go in two different directions, one that views Jesus as the adopted Son of God, and another that views Jesus as the great, perhaps the greatest, prophet or teacher of religion.

In the first version, God "adopts" Jesus as God's Son in order to show God's special and unique approval of Jesus. Although when Jesus was born he was just another human being, at some point in his life he became God's Son. For many who hold this view, the moment of adoption was at Jesus' baptism, when "a voice from heaven said, 'This is my Son, whom I love; with him I am well pleased'" (Matt. 3:17).

This view, which in its earliest forms was called "Adoptionism" (for obvious reasons), is still with us today.[3] Adoptionists today may talk about Jesus possessing the Spirit of God in greater measure and power than anyone else. Like the early Adoptionists, these people see Jesus' baptism as the time when the Spirit came upon him in the form of a dove (Matt. 3:16) and his crucifixion as the time when the Spirit left, as Jesus "gave up his spirit" (Matt. 27:50).

Another way to work out this first answer, in a way slightly different from Adoptionism, is to say that Jesus is the great prophet or teacher of religion. According to this view, Jesus was born as a human being like us, but he was so dedicated and single-minded in his search for God and for religious truth that he is the great, perhaps the greatest, teacher of religious truth. In this approach, Jesus is compelling as an example and teacher of religion. This view elevates the teaching of Jesus and sees his sayings as wisdom by which we should live.

This view, which in its earliest expression was called "Ebionism," places Jesus in a line with God's other prophets. He may be the last and greatest of the prophets, but he still stands in the same category with them. Today, Ebionism finds expression among those who view Jesus as a great teacher and place him alongside, or sometimes a little above, Buddha, Mohammed, L. Ron Hubbard, and other teachers of religion.

A great deal in these views is attractive. There is a simplicity of logic and an apparent humility about their claims for Jesus. But they do not hold up under close scrutiny, because they do not fit the claims of the Bible about the identity of Jesus Christ or the effect of his work.

The teaching of the New Testament makes it clear that Jesus did not *become* divine sometime during his earthly life by adoption, nor did he live his life as a mere human. Rather, Jesus was marked by divinity from the very beginning of his life. This is emphasized in Matthew and Luke through the story of the virginal conception of Jesus: His very conception was an act of God. But we would be wrong to think of Mary's conception of Jesus as the beginning of his sonship. His sonship describes his relation to the Father, not his birth as a human being. And, as we will see, that relationship of Father and Son did not have a beginning. Moreover, Jesus was conceived not by the Father and Mary but by the Spirit and Mary. In the New Testament, the description of this process is very circumspect. God and Mary do not have intercourse, yet conception and birth resulted from the encounter.

The fourth Gospel and Paul's writings make even clearer the error of the "adopted son" and "great teacher" views. In John, we read:

> In the beginning was the Word, and the Word was with God, and the Word was God. He was with God in the beginning. . . . The Word became flesh and made his

> dwelling among us. We have seen his glory, the glory of the One and Only, who came from the Father, full of grace and truth.
>
> 1:1–2, 14

In this passage, John makes it clear that the story of Jesus begins in eternity, in God's life, not in history, in the life of a human. For John, the story of the gospel is first about the Son who came *from* the Father and returned to him, not the human who became the Son as he was adopted by the Father.[4]

Paul's writings also make clear this claim. In Ephesians 1, Paul talks about God planning our salvation in Jesus Christ before the creation of the world. In Philippians 2, he speaks of Jesus Christ as "being in very nature God." In Colossians 1, the Son is "the image of the invisible God" and "before all things." The author of the letter to the Hebrews writes that "the Son is the radiance of God's glory and the exact representation of his being, sustaining all things by his powerful word. After he had provided purification for sins, he sat down at the right hand of the Majesty in heaven" (Heb. 1:3).

All of this teaching from the New Testament makes clear the conviction that the story of the gospel begins with God not humankind. God does not enter the picture after Jesus' birth; rather, the whole thing begins with God and God's purposes.

This claim fits what we have seen in previous chapters. If the kingdom of God is what Jesus proclaimed it to be in his words and deeds and what he enacted as Messiah, then he cannot be a mere human being. When the church formulates the conviction that Jesus Christ is "fully human and fully divine," we are not adding something to the story. Rather, we are discovering what has to be true if the story is true. One step toward that discovery is the realization that Jesus cannot be merely human. As we saw in chapter 1, the kingdom of God is not the goal we have achieved or the ideal we are to pursue. It is the activity of God, redirecting our corrupt longings, exposing and correcting our illusions, perfecting creation, meeting God's demands, fulfilling God's promises, costing us ourselves, and giving us our humanity. No mere human could do those things. The story of Jesus cannot be true if it is only the story of a human being in search of God.

Likewise, in chapter 2, we saw that the story of Jesus as Messiah is not about a mere human finally getting it right as prophet, priest, and king and thus establishing the kingdom of God. Rather, the story of Jesus as Messiah is the story of our human failure exemplified in the history of Israel and of God through Israel becoming human to do something for us that we cannot do. For those who accept as true the biblical story of Jesus as the Messiah, the story of Jesus cannot be merely the story of a human being.

By making the story of Jesus simply and humbly the story of a human being, therefore, this approach rejects God come to us and dooms humankind to persistent failure and sin. Although we may be attracted to Adoptionism and Ebionism because of our desire for independence and our commitment to deserving what we get, in the end our longing to save ourselves damns us. Our story is the story of the human race sinking in quicksand; the more we struggle and the harder we work to save ourselves and bring the kingdom apart from Christ, the quicker we perish. When we give up the illusion that the story of salvation begins with us, then we may find the story of our salvation in the story of Jesus Christ as fully human, fully divine and enter into the the good news of God's love for our world.

The Story of Jesus Christ Is about God Who Comes in Search of Humanity

Although this view may be given as an attempted correction of the previous view, when suggested as a full description of the gospel, it must be judged inadequate and misleading. A close examination will show why this is the case. According to this view, the gospel is the story of God, but not of a human being. While acknowledging that a creature or being named "Jesus" existed and did and said some of the things attributed to him in the New Testament, this view claims that Jesus was not really human.

The two earliest versions of this view, Docetism and Gnosticism, were rooted in convictions about the world and the nature of God.[5] Docetists believed that God was unchanging in such a way that God could not have "changed" in order to become a human being. Therefore, in order to account for the appearance of Jesus Christ, Docetists claimed that he only "seemed" or "appeared" to be human. Their name, "Docetist," derives from the Greek word *dokein,* meaning "to seem" or "to appear."

The Gnostics had a more comprehensive system of belief than the Docetists. Gnosticism, in fact, was a system of belief that could adapt to many different religions so that there were Jewish Gnostics, Christian Gnostics, Greek Gnostics, and so on. For our concerns, the most important element of Gnostic belief is the view that the world is divided into spirit and matter. Spirit is capable of pleasing God, but matter is not. Spirit may be acceptable to God, but matter can never be acceptable to God. Thus, for Gnostics, we humans are separated from God because of our bodies. Salvation means becoming righteous in our spirits and escaping our bodies forever.

Given these beliefs, the scandal of the gospel for the Gnostics was the claim that in Jesus Christ God has come in the flesh. For Gnostics this cannot be. God cannot become flesh: Flesh is matter, and matter is evil, irredeemably evil. If God became flesh, that would be the fall of God, not the salvation of humankind. So, like the Docetists, the Gnostics claimed that Jesus only seemed to have a human body. In reality, he was an apparition—today we might say a hologram—of God.

Although these views may be strange and scandalous to us, we come very close to them when we refuse to allow Jesus his humanity. Particularly in conservative churches we tend to play up the divinity of Jesus Christ and downplay his humanity. Like the Gnostics, we want a God who is above the turmoil and tragedy of being human. We want a God untouched, unscathed by pain and suffering.[6]

I discovered something like this in my own ministry. About two years into my first pastorate, I was talking with another pastor about my sermon topics. We realized that although I had preached from John, from Paul and the other New Testament letters, and from several Old Testament books, I had not yet preached any sermons from Matthew, Mark, or Luke. As we puzzled over this, I came to the realization that I had trouble with these Gospels because I viewed them as presenting the humanity of Jesus more strongly than the rest of the New Testament. I realized that I had not come to terms with Jesus' humanity. I tended toward Gnosticism in practice, though I rejected it as doctrine. As a result, I really couldn't proclaim the full gospel in my preaching.

When Docetists, Gnostics, and contemporary Christians tell the gospel exclusively as the story of God, they must ignore or reject much of the New Testament. They exchange the good news of Jesus Christ for an emaciated or truncated story that is, finally, the bad news that God loves "us" but not our full humanity and certainly not the rest of creation.

In contrast to these groups and my practical Gnosticism, one of the persistent convictions of the writers of the New Testament is that Jesus Christ was a full human being.[7] In Matthew, Mark, and Luke, the humanity of Jesus, including his embodiment, is clear in the very way they tell the story; to look for a more explicit claim is to miss the forest by looking for a tree. The first chapter of John's Gospel, which has so much to teach about Jesus Christ as God, also teaches that Jesus was human: "The Word became flesh" (John 1:14). John's first letter seems clearly to address the error of Docetism and Gnosticism:

> That which was from the beginning, which we have heard, which we have seen with our eyes, which we have looked at and our hands have touched—this we proclaim concerning the Word of life.
>
> 1 John 1:1

> This is how you can recognize the Spirit of God: Every spirit that acknowledges that Jesus Christ has come in the flesh is from God, but every spirit that does not acknowledge Jesus is not from God.
>
> 1 John 4:2–3

From these passages, we may infer that something such as Gnostic or Docetist beliefs arose early in the church and had to be addressed by the disciples of Jesus.[8] Their answer is clear: Jesus was a human being.

In Paul's writings, the humanity of Jesus is at the very heart of his argument. In Romans 5, the "one human, Jesus Christ," is contrasted to the "one human, Adam." After referring to Adam's sin in verse 14, Paul draws a series of comparisons:

> For if the many died by the trespass of the one man, how much more did God's grace and the gift that came by the grace of the one man, Jesus Christ, overflow to the many! . . . For if, by the trespass of the one man, death reigned through that one man, how much more will those who receive God's abundant provision of grace and of the gift of righteousness reign in life through the one man, Jesus Christ. . . . For just as through the disobedience of the one man the many were made sinners, so also through the obedience of the one man the many will be made righteous.
>
> verses 15, 17, 19

If Adam is fully human, then so also is Jesus Christ. In this way, Jesus does what we cannot do because of our sin.[9]

The same conviction occurs in many other places in Paul's letters. In Romans 8:3, God sends his Son "in the likeness of sinful man," and in Philippians 2:7, Christ Jesus is spoken of as "being made in human likeness." At first glance, the language of these passages may seem to be teaching Docetism. But the word translated "likeness" implies identity not difference; it is a very different concept from Docetism. Thus, in these passages Paul continues to affirm the humanity of Jesus.

Some have suggested that Paul was not really concerned with the life of Jesus or his humanity, because Paul spends so little time telling about Jesus' life. But in fact Paul is deeply convinced of the humanity of Jesus, as we have seen in these passages. And he does not retell the story of Jesus' life because he presumes his readers' familiarity with it. Paul is not writing a Gospel; he is writing letters to those who know the story of the gospel.

Among the books of the New Testament, one other stands out for its emphasis on the humanity of Jesus. The letter to the Hebrews bases a great deal of its argument on the identity of Jesus Christ with humanity. Jesus calls us "brothers"; "he had to be made like his brothers in every way"; he "has been tempted in every way, just as we are—yet was without sin" (Heb. 2:11, 17; 4:15).

This last passage leads directly to one of the problems some people have with the claim that the story of Jesus is not just the story of God but is also the story of humankind. If we accept that Jesus really is God come as a human being, are we not making God sinful? Is not this the very thing that the Gnostics and the Docetists feared—that in our beliefs about Jesus Christ we might compromise God's "Godness"? This fear, however, is rooted in a misconception about humankind. When we look at humankind today, we see our evil, our depravity, our greed, lust, and violence. Surely, then, God cannot become human. But what we see today when we look at humankind is not what we were created to be. Humanity is intended to live in perfect relationships with God, with others, with creation, and with ourselves. With this conviction in mind, we can see that becoming human would not compromise God's goodness or righteousness.

The emphasis of Paul (and of the author of the letter to the Hebrews) is that Jesus identified with us such that he was not born with some kind of natural immunity to sin, which rendered sin powerless in his life. Rather, Jesus was born susceptible to sin, but he did not yield to sin. He came as fully human into a world of sin and showed us that full and true humanity is perfectly righteous and obedient. We cannot achieve that full and true humanity because we are born sinners. Only by God's gift through Jesus Christ can humans, by grace through faith, become fully human, living in unbroken relationship with God. Jesus Christ overcomes sin on behalf of humankind. This cannot be said too strongly: Jesus' victory over sin and his obedience to the Father were not the result of his being non-human; victory and obedience were the accomplishment of his humanity.

The earliest witnesses to the gospel of Jesus Christ told that gospel as the story of a human being. Indeed, the very power of their witness is found in the identity of Jesus Christ with humankind. Those who make Jesus other than human leave humanity without one who has overcome our sin, our suffering, and our alienation from God. In their view, we are not saved through the redemption of our humanity but through escape from our humanity. The good news of the kingdom in Jesus Christ for those who believe is that God saves our humanity. Indeed, the story of the kingdom is the story of our becoming human through Jesus Christ. That story is real because the humanity of Jesus Christ is real.

Our examination of these first two approaches has shown us that the story of the gospel is not the story of one who was merely a human being or merely a divine being. It is the story of God and of humankind in one person, Jesus Christ. However, even after this result there are other possible answers that also ultimately fall short of the truth of God's love in Jesus Christ.

The Story of Jesus Christ Is the Story of a Human Being and a Divine Being Who Is like God

Up to this point, we have the clear conviction that the New Testament teaches that Jesus was human and divine. But there is still some room for variation, and with this statement, we encounter one of the most difficult challenges the church has faced. The challenge represented by this position is found in the words "a divine being who is like God."

According to this view, the Son or Logos ("Word") who became incarnate was divine, but he was from a lower rank than God. This view was first taught in the church in the fourth century by a theologian and leader of the church named Arius.[10] There is a great deal of discussion about what Arius believed, but it seems he thought that a great gulf existed between God and creation. God is timeless and unchanging; creation is subject to time and change. How, then, could God become a participant in creation?

Arius sought to solve this problem by positing a distinction between the divinity of the Father and the divinity of the Son. According to Arius, the Father has existed from all eternity and has no beginning, but the Son was created by the Father and thus has a beginning. The Father is unchanging, but the Son is changeable. Thus, the Son is not divine in the same way that the Father is divine—he is less "God" than the Father. Because the Son is subject to time and to change, he could become a part of creation—he could become human. Although the Son is inferior to the Father, he is superior to the rest of creation because he was created at the beginning of time not in time, he is the only Son of the Father, and all else was created through the Son.[11]

In this proposal, Arius seeks to affirm the humanity of Jesus and his divinity in keeping with the consensus of the church. By locating the divinity of the Son prior to the birth of Jesus, Arius avoids the earlier heresy of Adoptionism. By affirming that the Son became a part of creation, he avoids the heresy of Gnosticism. However, he does not avoid heresy altogether. As Arius describes the Father and the Son, there is a fundamental difference between the Father and the Son. If we use the categories of Creator and creation, the Father belongs on the side of Creator and the Son does not. Thus, for Arius the story of Jesus was the story of a human and divine being who was like God but who, unlike God, could participate in creation because he was a creature.

The most significant opposition to Arius came from a theologian named Athanasius. The views of Arius and Athanasius gave the church one of its most intellectually and politically intriguing debates. The argument lasted for almost 150 years. In the early years of the debate, the church vacillated between the two positions, but it eventually sided with Athanasius and spent a number of years working out the details of Athanasius's understanding of the person of Jesus Christ. The debate was complicated as questions about Jesus as human-divine were intertwined with questions about God as Trinity.[12]

Today, similar questions confront us through "churches" that teach that the divinity of Jesus Christ originates in the life of an angel who through intelligence and devotion attained divinity before he became incarnate in Jesus Christ. We also are moving toward this view when we start thinking of ranks within God. For example, we may think, "Certainly the Father would never subject himself to suffering the way the Son did." Or, "The Son sure got the dirty job, mucking around down here with us sinners." But these views do not accord with Scripture or with our understanding of how God accomplishes our salvation.

The Scripture passages that led us earlier to reject the denial of the divinity of Jesus Christ also lead us to reject the claim that the Son is a little less divine than the Father. Certainly the New Testament and the church see a difference between the Father and the Son: The Father sends and gives the Son; the Son is obedient to the Father. But the New Testament also teaches the equality of the Father and the Son. In John, Jesus says, "Before Abraham was born, I am!" (John 8:58). His use of "I am" clearly repeats the name of God in Exodus 3:14, a name that describes God as always existing. And in John 10:30, Jesus claims, "I and the Father are one." Likewise, the writings of Paul and the letter to the Hebrews, which we looked at earlier, teach the divinity of Jesus Christ.

In the end, the church rejected Arius, not because Scripture says something that clearly and explicitly denies Arius's view, but because the church fathers reflected on the implications of Arius's view and saw that it was at odds with the gospel taught by the Bible. At this point, great demands are placed on the church. First, we are confronting a position that is not clear-cut like the earlier views that explicitly rejected either the humanity or divinity of Jesus. Second, we must reflect on the meaning of the gospel and Arius's view. We cannot just "look it up in the Bible."

When the church reflected on this debate, they realized that Arius's view ultimately denied the good news of the kingdom in Jesus Christ. The gospel proclaims that in Jesus Christ we see the love and forgiveness and mercy and grace of God. In other words, in Christ we see God and come to know God in relationship to us. But if Arius's view is accepted, then in Christ we come to know only the Son, that is, the second rank of God. Since the Son is not fully God in Arius's view, we cannot trust Christ to teach us about the Father. Certainly he has been with the Father, but only from his creation. What about prior to his creation? And if he is not by nature God as the Father is God, then we cannot trust his revelation of the nature of God.

Ultimately, then, Arius leaves our salvation in doubt. For Arius, the story of Jesus Christ is the story of the second rank of God who became human. But if our Creator is God beyond Christ, then we do not know what our standing is before the first rank of God. Where Arian doctrine reigns today, this uncertainty leads humankind to seek salvation not through the grace of God but through the works of humankind. If the Son can achieve divinity, then perhaps we can also.

Against this, Athanasius and the early church recognized that the good news of the kingdom is that the love and forgiveness of our Creator is present in Jesus Christ. In him God has given us the kingdom. We "work," that is, we live by the rule of the kingdom, not to attain the kingdom but because we have already been given it in Jesus Christ. That gift cannot come from one who is less than fully God. In Jesus Christ we do not have the story of a kingdom like God's kingdom; in him we have the kingdom of God. Therefore, we must say that in Jesus Christ we do not have a divine being who is like God; we have the divine being; we have One who is God.

The Story of Jesus Christ Is the Story of God and a Creature like a Human Being

By this time you have probably realized that the history of the church's teachings follows the rule that for every position there is an opposite position. When the church errs to one side, it tends to overcorrect and err by swinging to the opposite extreme. The view we have to consider now is one that errs in the opposite direction from Arius.

According to this view, the gospel is about God, fully God, and a being who is almost completely human. Of course, the key phrase here is "almost completely." Those who held this view found it difficult to conceive of one person, Jesus Christ, having two natures, one fully human and one fully divine. If this were the case, surely one of two things would happen. Either the human nature would corrupt the divine, or the human and divine would be in constant conflict. In the first instance, Jesus Christ would be a sinner; in the second he would be schizophrenic. To solve this apparent difficulty, a theologian named Apollinaris (also spelled Apollinarius) argued that Jesus Christ was fully divine but only partly human. Drawing on Paul's distinction between the body, soul, and spirit of humanity (for example in 1 Thess. 5:23), Apollinaris argued that the divine Logos became flesh, that is, became encapsulated in a human body and soul, but he displaced the human spirit or mind.[13] Thus, for Apollinaris, the gospel is the story of the displacement of human spirit by God in a human body.

This view may sound a bit like Gnosticism and Docetism, which believe that Jesus only appeared to be human, but this view does acknowledge a bit more humanity in Jesus. In contrast to Docetism and Gnosticism, Apollinaris taught that Jesus really did have a human body and soul. But the Logos replaced the spirit of Jesus, in which (according to Apollinaris) the will resides.

For Apollinaris, this position had theological and logical advantages. Theologically, in Apollinaris's scheme of things, this view protected God from sinning. Logically, this view avoided the confusions that attend the claim that Jesus Christ was one person with two natures by claiming that he was one divine nature, clothed (so to speak) in a human body and soul.

Like Arianism, Apollinaris's view is not a clear-cut denial of the church's teaching. But many in the church quickly recognized that this was a subtle denial of Jesus' full humanity. The Gospels and the other writings of the New

Testament give no indication that Jesus was partly human. On the contrary, as we have already seen, they tell the story of Jesus as the story of one who is fully human.

As the church reflected on this biblical teaching in the light of Apollinaris's claim, they also recognized more clearly that if Jesus did not become fully human, he could not redeem our full humanity. That is, they came to recognize more completely that the way in which God redeems us is by becoming one of us. This shocking and unexpected means of redemption caused a great deal of misunderstanding and struggle in the church. But as the early church members confronted the various claims we have noted, the meaning of the gospel of Jesus Christ became clearer to them. In the confrontation with Apollinaris, it became clear that only that which God became could God redeem.

Today, we may commit the same error as Apollinaris if we try too hard to smooth out the logical difficulties of claiming that the story of Jesus is the story of one fully human, fully divine. In our culture we like precision, logical exactitude, and complete explanation. But the story of Jesus is not something that fits into our explanations and schemes. Rather, the story of Jesus, as I have argued, exposes our illusions and sins and perfects our good longings. We cannot judge the gospel; the gospel judges—and redeems—us.

Today, we may also succumb to Apollinaris's view when we think that some aspects of being human must be too horrible, too evil, too fallen for God to be involved with them. For example, what do you think about Jesus' sexuality? The movie *The Last Temptation of Christ* stirred a great deal of controversy when it came out and showed rather explicitly the supposed sexual temptations of Christ. I do not think it is a very good movie, nor do I agree with its theology. But the book from which it is taken, *The Last Temptation of Christ* by Nikos Kanzantzakis, challenged my own view of Jesus when I read it. I had to ask, "How human is my Jesus?"

The irony of fencing off from Jesus some part of our humanity is that we then do not allow him to heal or redeem that area. To continue our example, if Jesus did not experience human sexuality as we do, then he has no knowledge of human sexuality as a human nor can he redeem our sexuality. If this is the case, then we must look elsewhere to understand our sexuality and its perfection. In so doing, we would have to acknowledge that the kingdom of God in Jesus Christ is less than the fulfillment of God's purpose and the perfection of creation.

In the end, then, Apollinaris's view and others like it suggest that God's rule has been established over some aspects of human life, but not all. Such views fall short of the good news of the kingdom of God in Jesus Christ. In him, God has come as fully human to redeem all our humanity and to perfect and fulfill every aspect of our lives. Therefore, we must say that Jesus Christ did not reject some aspect of being human; instead, he became absolutely, fully human. In so doing he establishes and reveals the glory of being human. In him, the kingdom is indeed gospel.

The Story of Jesus Christ Is the Story of One Who Is Fully Human and Fully Divine

In the two previous chapters, we looked at the gospel as the story of the kingdom in the life and work of Jesus Christ. So far in this chapter we have considered four possible answers to the question, "Who is the story of Jesus Christ about?" As we have seen why the church rejected those answers, we have also been moving toward the answer that the church has given to the question: The story of Jesus Christ is the story of one who is fully human and fully divine.

According to this answer, the story of the kingdom is the story of God and a human being. The story begins with God's initiative. The word that describes God as the one who begins the story is *grace*. Grace tells us that the gospel is not something that humankind deserves from God. Jesus is not merely a human being who was so faithful and obedient that he came to deserve God's kingdom. As fully divine, Jesus Christ is God's grace come to us. The story does not end, however, with God's initiative; it is completed only when we see that Jesus Christ is also fully human. The gospel is not just the story of something that happens in God's life. It is also the story of how God's grace happens in human life, how God shares God's life with humankind. The story of the kingdom is the story of Jesus Christ as a human being who manifests God's love in such a way that the possibility is open for all humankind to participate in that love. So the church answers that the story of the kingdom is the good news that God became all that we are so that we might participate in God's life.

The church's answer was worked out over several centuries at four important meetings of the church: the Councils of Nicea, Constantinople, Ephesus, and Chalcedon. These councils worked out the biblical teaching on Jesus Christ in the context of their cultures, languages, and debates. They rejected some positions as unbiblical and incongruent with Christian convictions about Jesus Christ. They affirmed other positions as biblical and congruent with Christian convictions. Most of the councils produced statements, called creeds or definitions, that summarize their conclusions. The church leaders sought to give us not an exhaustive, irreplaceable account of who Jesus Christ is but some clear boundaries within which we are to talk, think about, and follow Jesus Christ.

The church councils do not say everything that has to be said about Jesus Christ, and we cannot be content simply to repeat their conclusions. The creeds and definitions of the councils are the place to begin our theology not the place to end it.

Nevertheless, they are the place to begin. At these councils, leaders of the church sought to be faithful to the gospel. We can learn from them by apprenticing ourselves to them. Indeed, we have already begun that process as we considered the positions that they rejected. Let us now look at their affirmation of Jesus as fully human, fully divine.

In affirming the full divinity of Jesus, the Council of Nicea (A.D. 325) described him as "begotten of the Father as only begotten, that is from the essence of the Father, God from God, Light from Light, true God from true God, begotten not created, of the same essence as the Father." The Council of Constantinople (A.D. 381) basically affirms the Council of Nicea, adding to this section of the creed, "before all time." These phrases affirm the divinity of Jesus Christ. They also set boundaries for talking and thinking about his divinity by adopting some language and rejecting other language.

By adopting the language "begotten of the Father" and "of the same essence as the Father," the councils reject the positions of the Adoptionists, the Ebionites, and Arius. The rejection of the first two is rather clear; the rejection of Arius may need a bit more explanation.

Arius's view of Jesus Christ centered on two claims: The Son was created by the Father, and the Son was a different essence from the Father. Clearly, with their language of "begotten not created" and "same essence," the church rejected Arius's view. To make that unambiguous, the Nicene Creed appends a series of phrases, used by Arius and his supporters, that the church rejects as proper language for Jesus Christ.

In this affirmation of the full divinity of Jesus Christ, the church recognizes that the story of the kingdom is the story of the redemption of the world by God, who created the world. The gospel is not the story of God's abandonment or rejection of the world. It is the story of God's love for the world, established and revealed in Jesus Christ. So the church through great struggle confesses that Jesus Christ is fully divine.

To that confession of the full divinity of Jesus Christ the church adds the confession of his full humanity. The humanity of Jesus is implicit in the creeds of Nicea and Constantinople in the confession that he "was born of the Virgin Mary" and "suffered under Pontius Pilate, was crucified, dead and buried." These phrases imply the real humanity of Jesus, but the challenges of Apollinaris and others forced the church to confess more clearly the fullness of Jesus' humanity at the Council of Chalcedon (A.D. 451).

Chalcedon produced what is called the "Chalcedonian definition":

> Following, then, the holy fathers, we unite in teaching all men to confess the one and only Son, our Lord Jesus Christ. This selfsame one is perfect both in deity and also in humanness; this selfsame one is also actually God and actually man, with

a rational soul and a body. He is of the same reality as God as far as his deity is concerned and of the same reality as we are ourselves as far as his humanness is concerned; thus, like us in all respects, sin only excepted. . . .

We also teach that we apprehend this one and only Christ—Son, Lord, only-begotten—in two natures; without confusing the two natures, without transmuting one nature into the other, without dividing them into two separate categories, without contrasting them according to area or function. The distinctiveness of each nature is not nullified by the union. Instead, the "properties" of each nature are conserved and both natures concur in one "person" and in one subsistence. They are not divided or cut into two persons, but one and the same Son and Only-begotten God the Word, Lord Jesus Christ; even as the prophets from earliest times spoke of him and our Lord Jesus Christ himself taught us, and the creed of the Fathers has handed down to us.[14]

The church came to this definition rather reluctantly, hoping that the Nicene Creed, revised at Constantinople, would be sufficient. But the challenges of Apollinaris and others made necessary a further statement. In this definition, the full humanity of Jesus is affirmed in language that rejects Apollinaris and others whose teaching denies Jesus' humanity.

The definition also rejects one other error that we have not yet examined. Some teachers, after the church had affirmed the divinity and humanity of Jesus Christ, sought to make more logical the story of the kingdom and the union of humanity and divinity in Jesus. They did this by arguing that in Jesus humanity and divinity were, so to speak, crossbred, resulting in a new being. This being was, strictly speaking, neither human nor divine but some hybrid of humanity and divinity. Thus, these teachers claimed that Jesus did not have two natures, human and divine, but one nature, neither human nor divine. Their name, "Monophysites," comes from one *("mono")* and nature *("physis")*.

Since the church had developed a fairly mature understanding of Jesus at this point, they quickly recognized that such a view threatened everything they believed about the gospel. According to such a view, the gospel is not about God or humankind but some alien creature. It has a neat and tidy logic, but it does not fit the story of the kingdom. In a way this is the most serious error of all because it excludes both God and humankind from the good news of the kingdom come in Jesus Christ. Although the language may be unfamiliar to us, Chalcedon clearly rejects this claim that Jesus has one nature and sets clear boundaries for the church's convictions about Jesus Christ.

Conclusion

By affirming the full humanity and full divinity of Jesus Christ, the church recognizes and proclaims the gospel of the kingdom as the story of God and humankind. The story is not about one or the other, nor is it about one then the other; it is always about both God and humankind. As the story of both, the good news of the kingdom in Jesus Christ accomplishes the reconciliation of God and humankind and reveals truly who God is and who we are.

The reconciliation of God and humankind is clearly enacted in the kingdom of God established and revealed by Jesus' words and deeds. The reality of the kingdom is the reality of God and humankind in present and everlasting fellowship. The value of the kingdom is God's gift to humankind and the death of human life apart from God and the beginning of life with God. The perfection of the kingdom is the establishment of God's purposes for humankind and for creation. The openness of the kingdom is the invitation to humankind to enter into relationship with God through the kingdom of Jesus Christ.

In the story of the kingdom, Jesus Christ reveals the true God. That is to say, whatever our language about God and our descriptions of God, they must "fit" the gospel of the kingdom. We cannot impose our ideas of God upon the gospel. Rather, the gospel is about the reality of God. In the gospel, God "imposes" Godself upon us—in order to redeem us. One of the two major errors made by some in the early church was thinking of God in ways that made it impossible for God to act as the church believes God did in Jesus Christ. (In part 2, we will look more closely at who God is revealed to be by the gospel.)

Finally, in the story of the kingdom, Jesus Christ reveals true humanity. Just as Jesus' revelation of God conflicts with our ideas of God, so also Jesus' revelation of humanity conflicts with our views. When we sin or fail at some task, we often say, "Well, after all, I'm only human." But in truth, when we sin we are being less than human. Jesus' revelation of true humanity shows us that to be truly human is to be without sin and perfectly obedient. That is what we are made for, and that is what God makes us into in God's kingdom. In this sense, Jesus is the only fully human being ever to have lived. As we participate in his kingdom, we become like him—we become human for the first time in our lives.

The story of Jesus Christ is the story of one who is fully human, fully divine, who comes to establish and reveal the kingdom of God. In his proclamation, his acts, and his person, Jesus Christ is God and humanity in perfect relationship with one another. Thus, we must say that he is the kingdom of God.

CONCLUSION

In the story of God's love in Jesus Christ, the New Testament proclaims a new reality, the kingdom of God. This kingdom of God is a new way of thinking about things and a new way of looking at the world, but it is not *just* a new way of thinking or seeing. This kingdom of God is also a new way of living, but it is not *just* a new way of living. Ultimately, this kingdom of God is a new reality that God establishes and continuously makes actual.

Therefore, the story we have been exploring is not just a story about the past, it is also a story about the present and the future. This makes it the one universal, never-ending story. Yet at the same time, this story is always the story of Jesus Christ. That is, the story of Jesus Christ does not end with his death, his resurrection, or his ascension. His story continues today in the everlasting, actual presence of the kingdom of God.

To believe this story—to believe the gospel—is to see and participate in the reality it proclaims. In order to see and participate faithfully in that everlasting actuality, we must continually learn and relearn, tell and retell the story of the gospel of Jesus Christ. In this learning and telling, we must always listen and watch for mistakes in our telling of the story. What have we forgotten, what have we neglected, what have we taken for granted, what have we substituted for the story? Since the story is a reality in which we are called to live, we must also take care to identify and acknowledge our failures in living in the story. What have we distorted, neglected, or substituted in our lives?

Those who believe this story have many ways to proclaim its significance and truth. We use language—the creeds, the confessions of the church, and personal testimony. We use the vocabulary of Christian convictions to identify sin and to identify righteousness. In this language, we both identify ourselves with others past, present, and future who believe the story, and we guide our lives through what is and is not the kingdom in our world.

In order to proclaim the significance and truth of the story of the kingdom, we also act in particular ways. We praise God, acknowledging that the kingdom is a gift not an achievement. We celebrate baptism and communion as participation in and proclamation of the kingdom. We proclaim and participate in Christ's kingship by using power to serve rather than dominate.

In our words and deeds, the kingdom of Jesus Christ continues today, not because of our achievement but because of our participation in the kingdom of God. Just as the story of the kingdom come in Christ is the story of God and humanity, so today the continuation of that story is the story of God and humanity. God graciously initiates the presence of the kingdom, but our participation in it makes the kingdom actual here and now.

This is not some new story; it is still the story of the kingdom of God in Jesus Christ. Jesus proclaims this continuation of the story in what we have called "the everlasting actuality of the kingdom." He enacts its continuation in his resurrection. The church acknowledges it in its confession of Jesus Christ as fully human, fully divine.

All of this is possible because the story of the kingdom does not end with the story of Father and Son. The story of the kingdom continues as the story of the Father, Son, and Holy Spirit. As the loving Father sends the Son, so also the Holy Spirit is sent.

This part of the story can and should be told in many different ways. In one way, the story of the Spirit is the story of the church. As the Spirit comes upon the disciples at Pentecost, the church is empowered to fulfill the mission that Jesus gave it. In another way, the story of the Spirit is the story of the continuing reality of the kingdom. As the Spirit works in the world, the kingdom that Jesus established and revealed continues to redeem humanity today. In part 3 of this book, we will look at these ways of telling the story of the gospel of the kingdom. Before we do that, however, in part 2, we will look at another way in which the story of the Spirit must be told.

In John's Gospel, Jesus tells the disciples that they still have much to learn about the kingdom of God and about himself. He tells them that teaching will come to them through the work of the Holy Spirit. The Holy Spirit will take what Jesus has said and done and lead the disciples of Jesus into greater participation in and understanding of the love of God in Jesus Christ. That fuller understanding of the kingdom and of the work of God's love in Jesus Christ is found in the writings of the New Testament that reflect on the meaning and reality of Christ's life, death, and resurrection. In part 2, then, we will explore the story of the kingdom of God's love in Jesus Christ as it continues through the Holy Spirit's guidance of the church's realization that in his life, death, and resurrection, Jesus Christ is victor, sacrifice, and example.

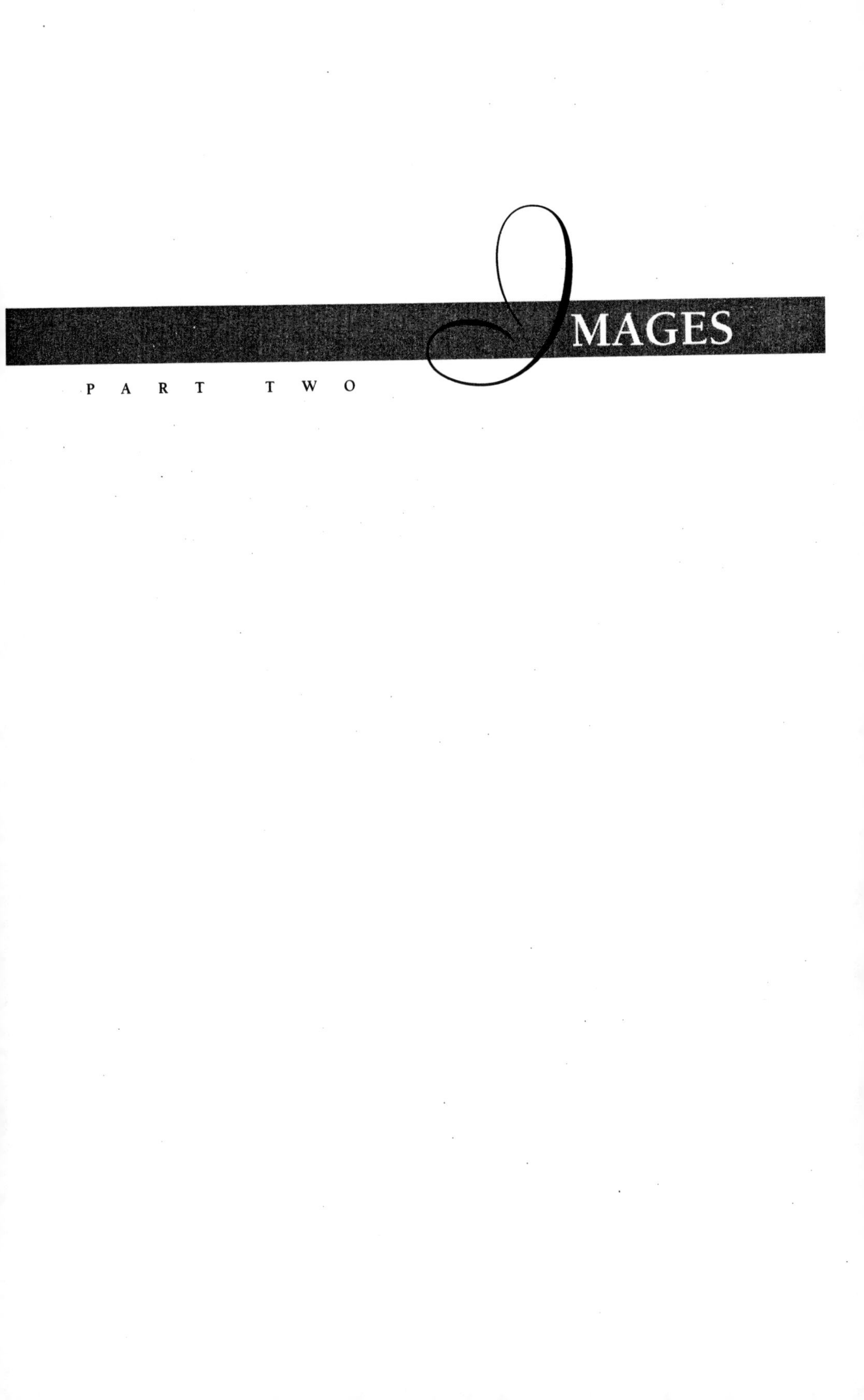

IMAGES

PART TWO

INTRODUCTION

Throughout the history of the church, several themes have been used to attempt to capture the meaning of Christ's death for human life. In order to explain the claim that Christ's death brought God and humanity back together after they were separated by sin, Christians have used the words *reconciliation* and *atonement*. By claiming that Christ's death achieves reconciliation between God and humanity—their at-one-ment—Christians also claim that God's love for the world is climactically revealed in the death of Jesus Christ.

The New Testament supports this emphasis on Christ's death. Roughly one-third of each of the Gospels is dedicated to the events of the last week in Jesus' life leading up to his death. Moreover, Jesus' death is important not just because of the space the Gospel writers give it but also because of its function in the story. For each of the Gospels, Jesus' death is the event toward which the story moves. As we saw in chapter 2, the way in which Jesus fulfilled the roles of prophet, priest, and king led to his death. If we look at the letters of the New Testament, we see the same focus on Christ's death. For Paul, John, Peter, and the other letter writers of the New Testament, Jesus' death is central. Even where that death is not explicitly in view, it is necessarily implicit in their writing.

However, in the way that Christians have talked about Christ's death, we have often given the impression that his death has no real connection to his way of life. That is, we have interpreted Christ's death as if it were a singular event, entirely unrelated to the rest of the gospel story. Thus, for example, when we have interpreted Christ's death as a sacrifice, we have at times ignored the sacrificial character of the rest of his life. When we use this image of sacrifice for Christ's death and ignore his life, we have to draw our understanding of sacrifice from somewhere other than the biblical story. And as we might expect, this procedure has led to some unbiblical interpretations of Christ's sacrifice. Therefore, it is always important to hold together the story of Jesus Christ and the images of that story.

In the next three chapters, we will consider three images the church has used for understanding Christ's death: victory, sacrifice, and example. We will examine the biblical basis for each image and the historical interpretations of each. In this examination, we will seek to *see* both Jesus' life and his death according to each image. Then we will reflect on how each image gives us a vision of God, humanity, sin, and salvation.

This talk about "images" of Jesus Christ may be new and unfamiliar to you.[1] Particularly for those in the Protestant tradition, images are not supposed to play a part in Christian faith. Moreover, in our culture today, we use the term *image* to describe something that has no reality or that appears to be other than it really is. We may say that someone is concerned with his public image. Or we may talk about image makers. In this sense, an image is something a person creates to achieve a particular goal. "She has an image as a caring person, but it is just an act to gain support for her candidacy."

Although we can see in these examples the negative meanings we often give to the notion of image, we can also see two other aspects of image. First, we can see the power of images. Images shape how we look at persons and events. They may even guide which persons and events we pay attention to. Images are a way of creating a reality or of denying a reality. Second, images are inescapable. We escape the power of one image only through the power of another image. When we see through the image that has been manufactured by someone and "see him for what he really is," we use another image to identify that new insight.

Therefore, in spite of the dangers and misuses of images, we must pay attention to them. The solution to their abuse and misuse is not to dispense with images altogether but to use images properly and to be sure that the images we attend to are truthful and real. In fact, the next three chapters are the result of my conviction that in Jesus Christ we find the images that guide us into the truth that is reality. In other words, these images are the most powerful images available to humanity because in them we are not creating or denying reality. In these images of Christ, we participate in the reality of the kingdom that he established and revealed. That kingdom is our redemption; as these images participate in that kingdom, they too are our redemption.

The next three chapters reveal three images of the story of the gospel in Jesus Christ. These images originate in the New Testament; they are not the only New Testament images, but they are the dominant images in the Bible and in the history of theology.[2] As we look at these images, our purpose will be to deepen our understanding of them. We will do this by looking at the New Testament uses of each image. We will see how each image is tied to the story of Jesus Christ. This connection between the image and the story is mutually illuminating and correcting. That is, the images tell us how to understand the story, and the story controls our understanding of the images. So, for example, we will see that the image of victor teaches us that Christ's death is not a disaster or a tragic flaw in God's plan. On the other side, the story of the kingdom come in Jesus teaches us that the image of sacrifice is not something that can be applied to just any act of self-giving. In both cases, the unity of story and image is important for us to understand the reality of God's love in Jesus Christ.

After we have explored the biblical basis for an image, we will examine some ways it has developed in the history of theology. In this section of each chapter, we will sharpen our grasp of the biblical image by analyzing how it has been applied in other times and places. As a result of this analysis, we will be able to identify the strengths of an image and the mistakes to be avoided in our own understanding and development of the image.

Finally, we reflect on the image for our own day. Here we move beyond looking *at* an image in order to look *with* an image. In this section, we will gather up all that we have learned about a particular image of the reality of the kingdom in Jesus Christ and use that image as a means of seeing other things. Every image that has power depends on a "field of meaning" for its power, and a field of meaning must have some connection to the lives of those who encounter an image. For example, the image of ice in the saying "cold as ice" has no meaning or power for someone who has never known or experienced ice. Similarly, to imagine God as my shield has less power for me than for the ancient Israelites who depended on shields in battle. As we consider these images of Jesus Christ, then, we will seek to place them within fields of meaning that have power for us today and are still faithful to the Bible. In particular, we will learn to see God, humanity, sin, and salvation in the light of each image of Jesus Christ.

As we see with these images, we must keep in mind the indissoluble connection between these images and the kingdom of God in Jesus Christ. Because of this connection, these images are not make-believe, or wish-fulfillment, or just the way Christians look at things. Rather, because of their connection with the kingdom in Jesus Christ, these images identify the truth and reality in which Christians participate. Even better, in so far as these images are identified with Jesus Christ, they are the reality in which Christians know God's love and have eternal life.

FOUR

CHRIST AS VICTOR

In the early church, after the close of the New Testament, the meaning of the gospel story was often described as victory. In this description, Christ was seen as victorious over all the forces of evil that threaten to destroy the world and human life along with it. We can find some reasons for this emphasis on victory in the situation of the early church: They were a threatened minority drawing hope for their lives from Christ's victory, and their culture was marked by the language of conquest. But the best reason why they drew on the language of victory is its presence in the Bible. As we look at the biblical basis for the language of victory, we will see how the gospel story gives a particular shape to the hope of the church. We will also see how it reshapes the language of victory that the church learned from its culture.[1]

Biblical Basis

When thinking of Christ as victorious, the natural inclination is to focus on the resurrection: In Christ's resurrection we see victory after the double defeat of his rejection by Israel and his death. Certainly Christ's resurrection is a victory. But when we look at biblical references to Christ as victor, we are taught also to think of his life and death as victories. After we have seen how Jesus' life and death can be viewed as victories, we will look more closely at his resurrection as victory.

In the New Testament, Jesus' work is often described in the language of triumph and victory.[2] Paul, writing about Christ in Colossians, says that "having disarmed the powers and authorities, he made a public spectacle of them, triumphing over them by the cross" (Col. 2:15). In Romans, Paul uses the triumphant cry of "freedom" to describe Christ's victory: "Through Christ Jesus the law of the Spirit of life set me free from the law of sin and death" (Rom. 8:2). The author of Hebrews affirms the full humanity of Jesus and his triumph:

> Since the children have flesh and blood, he too shared in their humanity so that by his death he might destroy him who holds the power of death—that is, the devil—and free those who all their lives were held in slavery by their fear of death.
>
> 2:14–15

And in the most evocative image that combines Christ's death and resurrection, John's Revelation portrays the risen Jesus Christ in a vision:

> When I saw him, I fell at his feet as though dead. Then he placed his right hand on me and said: "Do not be afraid. I am the First and the Last. I am the Living One; I was dead, and behold I am alive for ever and ever! And I hold the keys of death and Hades."
>
> 1:17–18

In this vision, the triumph of Jesus Christ is evoked not only by John's awe but by the keys that Jesus holds. These keys to death and Hades symbolize his victory over them. They are not in control of human existence and creation; Jesus Christ is.

These passages see Christ's victory climactically enacted in his death. But as we have seen in chapter 2, his death fits his way of life and his identity as Messiah. Before we look at Christ's death as victory, therefore, we will see how his life is also a victory.

Jesus is victorious in his life through his faithfulness and obedience to God. Humankind's deepest defeat is our inability to live in proper relationship to God by obeying God. In Romans 5, Paul contrasts the disobedience of the one man, Adam, which makes us all disobedient sinners, with the obedience of the one man, Jesus Christ, which makes righteous those who believe.[3] Through his obedience, Jesus Christ shows us that living in right relationship to God in the kingdom means living obediently. By conquering our disobedience, Christ makes it possible for us to enter the kingdom. As obedient human, Christ is victor.

Another victory Christ achieved in his life is victory over the forces of evil. Of course, our disobedience is a kind of evil, but in the Gospels, there is another evil over which Christ triumphs: the evil of the demonic and the evil within the fallen creation. This evil is a force outside humankind that rules over us and destroys our lives.

Jesus triumphs over this evil in many of his miracles, most clearly seen in Matthew 12:22–29. There, after Jesus heals a "demon-possessed man who was blind and mute," his opponents accuse him of using demonic power to drive out demons. Jesus agrees that he is confronting demons but argues that

> if Satan drives out Satan, he is divided against himself. How then can his kingdom stand? . . . Or again, how can anyone enter a strong man's house and carry off his possessions unless he first ties up the strong man? Then he can rob his house.
> verses 26, 29

Thus, Jesus sees his power to cast out demons as a sign of his triumph over Satan. Sickness, hunger, and distress are all signs of the rule of evil in this age. Jesus' miracles of healing, feeding, and calming disclose the power of his victory over Satan and the evil of this world. As evil's conqueror, Jesus is victor.

Although we must see Jesus' life as a victory, his victory is seen climactically in his death. This may seem a rather odd claim, that Jesus triumphed through his death, but that is what the New Testament continually asserts: The image of victory reveals to us the truth of his death.

Seeing the death of Jesus Christ as victory opens up a whole realm of truth. First, it shows us that his death was an act of obedience. It was, in fact, the deepest act of obedience. As the hymn in Philippians proclaims, "He humbled himself and became obedient to death—even death on the cross!" (Phil. 2:8). This passage announces that Jesus Christ obeyed God even to the point of dying on the cross. This deepest expression of obedience by one who is fully human triumphs over our disobedience and opens the kingdom to us.

Second, Christ's death on the cross defeats Satan and all other powers by exposing them. Remember, humans serve lies and are captive to illusions. We believe that evil is good, that Satan is the source of pleasure, excitement, and life. We believe that the powers of this world—governments, religions, social structures—can give us meaning, purpose, and approval. What the death of Christ exposes is the fallenness, the evil, the impotence of those forces. In Christ's death, the government, the religious and social forces of his day—leaders and people—joined together to crucify him. That decision and Jesus' acceptance of it is their defeat.

We can pursue this theme further by looking at the alternatives open to Jesus. When the verdict was pronounced on him, he could have fought it. He could have argued his case in court. Or he could have appealed to Pilate's political sensibilities. Or he could have called his followers to armed resistance. But he did none of these. He did none of these because by the very act of adopting the means of power held by any of these, he would have been defeated by them.[4] If he had fought by means of pagan law, pagan politics, or military might, he would have been acknowledging their supremacy, their power. But rather than be defeated by them, he trusted himself to God, whom he knew was his deliverer.

And so finally we must see Christ's resurrection as victory. But if what we have already seen in the New Testament is true, then Christ's resurrection is not victory that follows defeat in his life and death. No, in the New Testament, Christ's resurrection is victory that climaxes and discloses the triumph of his life and death. In other words, Christ's resurrection corrects our view of Christ as political criminal, as religious blasphemer, and as social misfit, so that we may see Christ as God sees him: victor over sin, death, and Satan. The resurrection, then, is God's gracious, loving revelation of how we are to regard Jesus Christ. And it is one with the rest of the story of Jesus Christ in his triumphant establishment of the kingdom of God. In Christ's victory, God's love for the world and our redemption are everlastingly set in motion.

Historical Development

This biblical image of victory was developed by several theologians in the history of the church as they sought to communicate the good news of Jesus Christ to others. As we look at some of their accounts, we want to learn from their insights and their errors.

One of the first theologians to reflect on Christ as victor was Irenaeus. Irenaeus argues that Christ came "that he might kill sin, deprive death of its power, and vivify man."[5] In his theology, Irenaeus sees the meaning of sin not so much in individual acts as in a kingdom that controls and destroys humanity. Death is the final destruction worked by sin. Life is given through Christ's defeat of sin and death.

An important question that Irenaeus addresses concerns the identity of the victor. Is the victory of Christ the triumph of a human being whom God then crowns as victor? This question, of course, is the same one we examined in chapter 3: "Whose story is it?" Irenaeus's answer is the same as that given at Nicea and the other councils. The victory is won by God, who became human in Jesus Christ. The disobedience of humanity must be defeated by the obedience of a human. The mortality of humanity must be defeated by the life of a human. But we are all born into disobedience and death. Only through the action of God could these victories be won. In Christ, we have the victor over sin and death who is fully human, fully divine.

As theologians developed this image of Christ as victor, they expounded other biblical passages. One important passage is Paul's description of our freedom from slavery in Romans 6:

> For we know that since Christ was raised from the dead, he cannot die again; death no longer has mastery over him. The death he died, he died to sin once for all; but the life he lives, he lives to God.

> In the same way, count yourselves dead to sin but alive to God in Christ Jesus. Therefore do not let sin reign in your mortal body so that you obey its evil desires. . . . For sin shall not be your master, because you are not under law, but under grace.
>
> verses 9–12, 14

The passage continues with a contrast between slavery to sin, which is death, and slavery to righteousness, which is life. Under the image of victory, theologians drew on this passage to suggest that human freedom from sin's bondage was the chief accomplishment of Christ's victory.

If Christ's victory frees us from slavery, then another question naturally arises: How did Christ free us? Here some theologians drew another biblical notion into the discussion—the idea of "ransom," which Jesus uses to describe his purpose: "For even the Son of Man did not come to be served, but to serve, and to give his life as a ransom for many" (Mark 10:45).

As they developed this notion of Christ as victor who ransoms us from slavery, these theologians were led to ask, "Who is the slave master, and to whom is the ransom paid?" Although a few suggested that Christ paid the ransom to God, most theologians rejected this conclusion because it made God our slave master even in sin and portrayed God paying the ransom to himself. Most theologians, therefore, came to the conclusion that Christ paid the ransom to Satan.

There are problems with this conclusion, however, because it seems to make God subject to Satan. That is, Satan appears to be in control of the situation, telling God what has to be done in order to buy the slaves' freedom. This problem may be resolved in two ways. One way is to view "ransom" as an "incomplete symbol."[6] According to this approach, the New Testament means for only some, not all, of the meaning of ransom to apply to the work of Christ. So we might say that "ransom" tells us that humanity is enslaved and that we are freed by Christ, but "ransom" is not meant to tell us precisely how that freedom was achieved.

Another solution to the problem of ransom may be found if we remember that this discussion is taking place within the image of victory. If Christ is the "victorious ransom," then the whole dynamic of the transaction is changed and the claims make more sense. In this approach, Christ is given as ransom to the powers and the power (Satan) that enslave humanity. But as ransom he is also victor, not only in freeing the slaves but also in being freed himself from that power. By accepting Christ as ransom, Satan is doubly defeated. He not only loses his slaves, he also loses the ransom payment. So the picture of Christ as ransom must be qualified by the image of Christ as victor. He is the victorious ransom.

This notion of Christ as the victorious ransom was given a picturesque concreteness by a fourth-century theologian, Gregory of Nyssa. Gregory pictured Jesus' humanity as the bait that concealed the fishhook of his divinity:

> As we have already observed, the opposing power [Satan] could not, by its nature, come into immediate contact with God's presence and endure the unveiled sight of him. Hence it was that God, in order to make himself easily accessible to him who sought the ransom for us, veiled himself in our nature. In that way, as it is with greedy fish, he might swallow the God head along with the flesh, which was the bait.[7]

In Gregory's development of this picture, the devil sees in Christ something greater and more desirable than the sinners he holds in bondage. So he swallows the bait of Jesus' perfect humanity and is destroyed by his divinity.

A danger with this view is that it could be taken to imply that Jesus was God cloaked in a human body, an error similar to Apollinaris's view. However, a deeper problem with this picture is that its portrayal of Satan as deceived does not fit with the demons' knowledge of who Jesus was (Mark 1:34; Luke 4:34). Moreover, this approach portrays God as freeing us through deception rather than through truth. It seems best, therefore, either to treat ransom as an incomplete symbol or to place it within the context of victory without trying to be too concrete about how the ransom works.

After the sixth century, this image was neglected for several centuries. Then in the sixteenth century, Martin Luther gave it new life. In his ministry, Luther was well aware of spiritual battles and at one point even threw an inkwell at the devil as he tried to distract him from his work. The images of battle and victory shape his great hymn "A Mighty Fortress Is Our God":

> A mighty fortress is our God,
> a bulwark never failing;
> Our helper He amid the flood
> of mortal ills prevailing;
> For still our ancient foe
> doth seek to work us woe;
> His craft and power are great,
> and armed with cruel hate,
> on earth is not his equal. . . .
>
> And though this world, with devils filled,
> should threaten to undo us,
> We will not fear for God hath willed
> His truth to triumph through us;
> The prince of darkness grim,
> we tremble not for him;
> His rage we can endure;
> for lo, his doom is sure;
> one little word shall fell him.

In this hymn and his other works, Luther wrote in much the same terms as the earlier theologians about Jesus' victory over sin, death, and Satan. But he also added other "powers" to the list of those defeated by Christ. As Gustav Aulén points out, Luther, in a long list of powers defeated by Jesus Christ, includes the law and the wrath of God.[8] But should these be included? When Paul speaks of Christ defeating "principalities and powers" (Colossians), he implies that Christ defeated many things. Does that list include the law and the wrath of God?

Although the New Testament clearly speaks of Christ setting us free from the law and from the wrath of God, I think it is wrong to place them under the image of victory as powers that Christ defeated. Rather, as we will see, law and wrath belong under the image of Christ as sacrifice. To anticipate that discussion, we may say that apart from Christ, the law and the wrath of God are dangerous to us, not as enemies to be defeated but as good things to which we cannot properly respond.

An analogy may help us understand this situation. Imagine someone who is extremely allergic to fish, so allergic that if he eats fish he will go into shock and possibly die. In this situation, we would say that fish is a bad thing for him because of his situation—the problem is in him, not in the fish. What needs correction is not something in fish but something in my friend. That, I think, is the situation with humanity and the law and wrath of God. These are not bad things, but because of our condition, sin, we are susceptible to them. Jesus Christ does not defeat law and wrath, he corrects what is wrong in us that makes them dangers to us. We will see how that happens in the next chapter.

We may say, then, that Luther revives the image of Christ as victor in his theology and hymnody. But he extends the image too far at some points in his theology.

In the twentieth century, the image of Christ as victor has given important guidance to the church in its confrontation with the particular injustices of the industrial age. One of those who drew on this image was Walter Rauschenbusch. After many years in a pastorate in the Hell's Kitchen section of New York City, Rauschenbusch saw Christ's work as a struggle with and victory over "religious bigotry, the combination of graft and political power, the corruption of justice, the mob spirit, militarism, and class contempt."[9]

Rauschenbusch's theology has been suspect in some churches because he is seen as a proponent of the "social gospel," which is at odds with the Bible. Reasons given for rejecting the social gospel are many, and the debate is complex. However, the question we must ask here is not whether Rauschenbusch teaches a social gospel but whether his teaching illuminates Scripture and helps us understand better our situation in the light of Scripture. I think he accomplishes both of those things.

First, Rauschenbusch opens our eyes to the social forces that conspired to execute Jesus. Certainly, God's purpose was worked out in Christ's death, but this does not absolve humanity, nor should it obscure the plotting against Christ. As Peter says to the crowd at Pentecost, "You, with the help of wicked men, put [Jesus] to death by nailing him to the cross" (Acts 2:23). Rauschenbusch accurately exposes the evil forces that conspired to kill Jesus.

In addition, Rauschenbusch illuminates our own situation. Writing in 1917, Rauschenbusch describes the world at the end of World War I, but he also portrays with astonishing insight the destructiveness of World War II. At that time, the evils he identifies conspired together in the Holocaust perpetrated by Nazi Germany and the nuclear destruction perpetrated by the United States. We cannot point our finger at those who conspired to crucify Jesus without also indicting our age.

At the same time, there is also a lesson to learn from an error in Rauschenbusch's view and the social gospel movement. In their focus on Christ as victor, they became susceptible to a triumphalism that began to regard the kingdom as something brought by human power and progress rather than as a gift of God's grace.[10] What we must always keep in mind is that we do not win the victory or bring the kingdom; rather, we inherit the victory and receive the kingdom.

Another expression of Christ as victor in the twentieth century may be found in liberation theology.[11] As with the social gospel, when many people hear "liberation theology" they immediately reject it. But if Christ is victor, as we have seen in Scripture, then he is also liberator. In some sense, then, all Christian theology must be liberation theology. The difficulty comes when we try to specify how he is liberator and what he liberates us from.

Here we must return to the story of the gospel for our guidance. The one who is victor is the one who preached the gospel in word and deed and fulfilled the offices of prophet, priest, and king as one who is fully human, fully divine. When liberation theology imports, under the banner of victory, a kingdom other than the one established and revealed by Jesus Christ, then it leads us astray. When liberation theology "fits" the gospel of the kingdom revealed in Christ, then it faithfully and powerfully represents Christ to us, for us, and, often, against us. Since we are slow to recognize our own familiar sin, we must particularly practice the openness of the kingdom toward those who seem most different, most challenging. Of course, we must also remember that it is the openness of the *kingdom*, not just any openness. The kingdom imposes its actuality on every scheme of humanity, especially our own.

Finally, in this century more churches are (re)discovering the reality of "spiritual warfare." By spiritual warfare, I mean the reality of the demonic in our world. As with some of the other ideas we have been considering, the language of "spiritual warfare" may be rejected by some. Our culture has been so shaped by materialist, scientific notions of reality that if our five senses cannot touch, taste, feel, see, or hear something, it does not exist. Or it may exist, but it does not have any reality in this world.

Many Christians in our day, however, are discovering through experience that the demonic in the Bible was not just a cultural prejudice of that day that we have outgrown. For many, conflict with the demonic is a present-day reality. The great danger for many of these Christians is that they come from churches that have not adequately taught them about Christ as victor. In the absence of that teaching, they go out to "win the war." But we do not win the war; Christ the victor has already won it.[12] We fight battles, but if we do not recognize that our power comes from his victory, then we fight in the wrong way, with the wrong weapons. By so doing, we make ourselves vulnerable to defeat and despair and often cause more harm than good to ourselves and others.

The church at the end of the twentieth century and the beginning of the twenty-first century, therefore, needs to live by the image of Christ as victor. We must learn from the failures and dangers, the successes and strengths identified by the church's earlier efforts to see by this image. In so doing, may we see the kingdom more clearly and live in it more faithfully.

Systematic Reflection

In the previous section of this chapter, we examined some instances in the history of the church of the image of Christ as victor. In this section, we will consider how this image illuminates today our vision of God, humanity, sin, and salvation. These four areas shape much of our understanding of God's love for the world in Jesus Christ. By looking at these areas of Christian conviction through the image of Christ as victor, therefore, we may give christological shape and substance to our understanding of the gospel of the kingdom.

If I reverse the image, it may help you begin to understand what we will do in this section. What if we thought of Christ as loser? How would we picture the gospel then? Could we even call it gospel—"good news"? Would we think of the God of Jesus Christ in positive terms? Would we think of salvation coming through Jesus Christ? In the rest of this chapter, I invite you to open up your imagination to think of God, humankind, sin, and salvation in light of the image of Christ as victor.

As we examine how we look at God, humanity, sin, and salvation through the image of Christ as victor, I want to suggest some possibilities and note some dangers and errors. Our discussion, of course, will not exhaust all the possible truth and error under this image. Moreover, as we consider this image of Christ as victor, I will be careful to restrict our "seeing" to this image. Each of the images we will consider in these chapters is important, and we need all of them to give a full and accurate portrait of the work of Christ. But it is also helpful to think of one image at a time. You may be tempted to add other more familiar images to the account given in this chapter, but I urge you to be patient, knowing that we will eventually bring the images together. What I hope to do in this chapter is to get you to start *seeing* things through the image of Christ as victor. Then as new challenges and situations come to you, you will be able to see them in the light of the kingdom of God.[13]

God as Warrior, Conqueror, and Liberator

If we look at the gospel of the kingdom in the teaching, life, death, and resurrection of Jesus Christ as a victory, then we can see God in particular ways. These ways of seeing give direction and substance to our knowledge of God. We do not "imagine" God; rather, we learn to see God through this image that has been given to us, not created by us. The image of Christ as victor that has been given to us by the gospel of the kingdom draws us into a particular field of meaning. Where do we talk about victory and triumph? In the context of battles and contests.

In that context, Christ as victor teaches us to see that God is *warrior.* Indeed, we may make this even more concrete by saying that God is *conqueror*. This image is prevalent throughout Scripture, but when we use it, we must be careful to connect this picture of God with Christ as victor. Making this connection teaches us that God fights and conquers as Christ fought and conquered. When Christ refused to fight with his enemies' weapons, he revealed to us how God conquers for our redemption.

There is great danger here. We may think of Christ as victor, picture God as a warrior, and go on deadly military or political crusades. But if Christ is fully God, then his story is the story of how God fights. God is victorious through the righteousness of forgiveness and love, not through sheer force. The theme of God as warrior is not "might makes right" but "righteousness is life."

Making the connection between God as warrior and Christ as victor also teaches us that the real enemy is not flesh and blood. The one that we think is the enemy (and all of us identify different enemies) is the one Christ calls us to love. Even on the cross, God in Christ "conquered" his enemies by forgiving them: "Father, forgive them, for they do not know what they are doing" (Luke 23:34). The true enemies are sin, death, and Satan. And they are not only "out there," they are also "in here"—within us, in our lives, and in our circle of friends and family.

Another description of God fits this image: God is also *liberator.* When God in Christ conquers sin, God sets us free from sin. This image of God as liberator draws on Christ's life as a ransom for us and as our freedom from the slavery of sin. Once again we must be careful to tie this image to the story of the kingdom. First, we must recognize that God does not liberate by freeing us from all boundaries so that "anything goes," so that "everything is possible." That is not liberation but destruction. God liberates by enabling us to live, not by the law of sin and death, but by the law of Spirit and life. Second, we must recognize that God liberates us to live with and for others. God's liberation is for a people, not mere individuals. Certainly, a people (nation, church, kingdom) is made up of individuals. But the point here is that God's liberation does not set us free *from* others; rather, it sets us free *for* others.

In this context of being set free for others, we must recognize that the story of Christ's victory does not end with the cross or the resurrection. It continues on through the work of the Holy Spirit in the life of the church.[14] Although we often marvel at the weaknesses and failings of the church, we should marvel even more at the continued existence and ministry of the church. No force has been able ultimately to triumph over the church. Here again, we may learn from the story of Christ's victory. The image of Christ as victor tells us how to understand the suffering of his life and his death. In the same way, without being complacent about the sin of the church, we should be rejoicing in God's faithfulness, God's victory, in the church through the Holy Spirit.

In all of these pictures of God seen through the image of Christ as victor, God comes to us as our champion, as the one who does not abandon us, as the one who fights on our behalf. God is for us. Who can be against us? (Rom. 8:31).

Humanity as Victims, Captives, and Hostages

If Christ is victor, then humankind, before Christ's victory, may be seen in several ways. These ways all answer the question, "If humankind needs a warrior and liberator, then who are we apart from that victory?"

If we think of Christ as victorious over sin, death, and Satan, then we can see that humans are the *victims* of these three. This picture illuminates the helplessness of humankind.[15] We have been overcome by enemies stronger than we are. Along these lines we may also picture humankind as *captives*. Thus, we are not living in sin because we have chosen to "immigrate" to that kingdom. Rather, we are living in sin because we have been captured by that kingdom. Or, even better, we are living in the kingdom of sin because our ancestors were captured by that kingdom and we, as their descendants, are born in that kingdom.

If this is our situation, then the kingdom of sin may seem very much like home: We were born here, this is all we have known, surely this is where we are supposed to live. This belief is one of the lies that Christ exposes through his victory. The world of sin is not our natural home, it is not our rightful inheritance.

In order to express this clearly, we may add one more picture of humankind under the image of Christ as victor: humankind as *hostages*. To see ourselves as hostages is to see humankind separated from our home and family by forces "beyond our control." Just as the news regularly reports a new "hostage crisis," so we may see the whole of the cosmos involved in a hostage crisis. An enemy invaded God's creation and took humankind hostage.

In these pictures of humankind, we see humankind as sinners—because we are born in that kingdom—but primarily we see humankind as sinned against. So we are challenged to look at others as the victims of sin, not as the perpetrators of sin. This gets tricky: Should we just excuse others' behavior because they cannot help it—the devil made them do it? Two responses may be made to this problem. First, we must remember that the three images—victor, sacrifice, and example—need each other. Each qualifies the others, so our account will not be complete until we reflect on the other images. Second, even if we see others as victims of sin, we cannot excuse their actions. To do so would be to abandon them to destruction. In Christ, we see that God does not abandon us to destruction. Therefore, we who follow Christ must not abandon the victims of sin. Rather, we must seek to expose the lies to which they are captive so that they leave the kingdom of sin and live in the kingdom of God.

For example, we may think of the poor as victims who need to be liberated. But we must also see that the rich person who oppresses the poor is victim to the lies of greed and also needs Christ's liberation in order to live. To the rich who oppress the poor, the gospel comes as good news that exposes the lie of greed so that they may enter the kingdom of life. To the poor who are oppressed, the gospel comes as good news of liberating justice so that they may know God is for them. And we may go one step further, to the rich who are oppressed by their greed and to the poor who are greedy for riches, the gospel comes as the truth that exposes their captivity and sets them free. Through Christ the victor, we who are victims, captives, and hostages are set free from the kingdom of death and brought into the kingdom of life.

Sin as Enemy and Prison

The pictures of sin that flow from the image of Christ as victor follow closely the pictures of humankind that we have just looked at. First, we may see sin as our *enemy,* our attacker. This is important because we humans often live exactly opposite to this. We look at actions and desires that are "natural" to us and think of them as good and positive. Then we discover that the Bible describes those actions and desires as "sin." We say, "How dare God (the Bible, the church, Christians) tell me not to do that! It's one of my favorite things, and it always makes me feel good. Everyone does it." And we go on our way as usual.

Of course, that kind of talk makes a certain sense if we recognize that we have been born in sin and it seems natural to us. But, as we saw above, we are victims and captives. Sin is not our friend, it is not our natural home, it is not true pleasure. If Christ is victor, sin is his enemy and our enemy. The evil that crucified him, and our greed, lust, envy, pride, and self-denigration are all part of the same kingdom of sin. Christ conquered sin by exposing it as the enemy of humankind. Therefore, one part of the Christian life is learning what our enemy—sin—looks like so that we cease to be victimized by it by looking on it as a good thing.

If Christ is victor and we are hostages, then we may also see sin as our *prison*. Apart from Christ we may be aware only that this world is not in very good shape, that there are many obstacles to life. Through Christ, we can see with increasing clarity that sin has chained and imprisoned us. In this picture, sin limits our possibilities, cripples our potential, and traps us in darkness. Human life, which is meant to be lived gloriously and joyfully, becomes dreary and dull through the chains and prison house of sin. In our attempts to escape that drab and dreary condition, we seek excitement and freedom only to enter more deeply sin's prison. Only through the light and liberation of Jesus Christ can we truly escape.

Salvation as Triumph, Liberation, and Homecoming

Some of the pictures of salvation that fit the image of Christ as victor have already crept into our study. Indeed, to begin with the image of victory is to color the whole discussion with an anticipation of the end of the story. Christ's victory reveals God, the human situation, and the character of sin, but it places all our pictures within the context of the redemption of the world, our salvation in Jesus Christ.

If Christ is victor, then salvation is *triumph*. Christ as victor teaches us that sin is our enemy, but it does not leave us at the mercy of the enemy or on our own before the enemy. As our champion, Christ wins the war:

> Did we in our own strength confide,
> our striving would be losing;
> were not the right man on our side,
> the man of God's own choosing.
> Dost ask who that may be?
> Christ Jesus, it is he!
> Lord Sabaoth, his name,
> from age to age the same;
> and he must win the battle.
>
> Martin Luther,
> "A Mighty Fortress Is Our God"

Therefore, the triumph that is our salvation is, as P. T. Forsyth said, "not the victory we win, but the victory we inherit."[16] As Jesus says, "In this world you will have trouble. But take heart! I have overcome the world" (John 16:33).

At this point, our picture of salvation seems to leave humankind passively inheriting the work of Christ. However, the New Testament carries the image one step further. In the letters from Jesus to the churches in Revelation 2–3, eternal life and authority are promised to those who overcome. Therefore, we must say that if we have truly inherited Christ's victory, then our own lives will be marked by our overcoming the world. Once again we must tie this picture back into the story of the kingdom and the image of Christ as victor. In the story of the kingdom, Christ is victor by obeying God's will and dying to the world, not by achieving great success in the world. Too often our pictures of triumphant Christianity owe more to worldly standards of success than to faithfulness to the story of Christ.

If Christ is victor, then salvation is also *liberation.* In this picture, salvation liberates us from the chains and prison house of sin. One of Charles Wesley's hymns powerfully pictures this:

> Long my imprisoned spirit lay,
> fast-bound in sin and nature's night;
> Thine eye diffused a quick'ning ray,
> I woke, the dungeon flamed with light;
> My chains fell off, my heart was free;
> I rose, went forth, and followed thee.

Once again we must be careful in how we work out this picture. What we think we need to be liberated from and what God actually liberates us from may be very different things. For example, in the 1960s and 1970s our culture went through a sexual revolution in the name of being liberated from outmoded ideas about marital fidelity. That kind of liberation is not God's salvation; it is another, heavier chain with which our enemy binds us.

Against this faulty notion of liberation, we must set the liberation achieved through Jesus Christ. We must recognize that God does not liberate us from all restraints so that now we feel free to do whatever we want. Rather, God liberates us from the kingdom of death so that we may live in the kingdom of life. Living in the kingdom of life is the freedom to be human. It is liberation that saves us.

Finally, if Christ is victor and we are hostages, then salvation is not just triumph over our enemy or liberation from captivity, it is also *homecoming.* This is a glorious and poignant picture of salvation. When hostages are released by their captors, the most memorable moments are not the pictures of those hostages freed and holding press conferences on their way home. The most memorable moments are when the hostages and their families are reunited and hold each other in their arms. For them salvation means not just freedom, it means homecoming.

In Christ, salvation is humankind's homecoming. After a long, torturous stay in the enemy's camp, after years in the darkness and dreariness of prison, we are delivered into the kingdom of light and life through Jesus Christ. Through Christ's victory, we discover our true home in God's kingdom. All our corrupt and distorted longings are judged and made pure and perfect. Then all that we long to be is fulfilled. We are, for the first time, fully human, fully alive.

Conclusion

In Christ as victor, we see God as our warrior, our conqueror, our liberator, who reveals our victimization and captivity, defeats our enemy, destroys our prison, and shatters our chains to free us and bring us home to live for eternity.

The great strength of this image of victory is that it teaches us that sin is something greater than any human power. Sin often becomes so much a part of the way we live and the way we look at things that it takes on a life of its own. Today, we may talk about systemic or structural evil. By this we mean sin that has imprisoned the way people live, the way we live. In such circumstances, Christ the victor is not content merely to "convert" the prisoners; he seeks to destroy the prison. As participants in the kingdom, we too must seek the destruction of the prison house of sin if we are to be faithful to Christ.

The great danger of this image is that we use the language of sin as "enemy" to talk of sinners as enemies. That kind of talk is not faithful to this image. (As we will see in the next chapter, when we talk about others as sinners we use the language of sacrifice.) For Christ, the enemy is not sinners but sin. The story of the gospel is good news because it is the story of God's triumph over sin in order to redeem sinners. Therefore, the image of Christ as victor does not allow us to identify another human being as enemy. Others may very well be in the enemy's camp, but they are there as captives and hostages. Christ's mission is not to destroy them but to liberate them. As his followers, liberation is also our mission.

If we look back to the roles of Christ in the kingdom of God, the most natural connection to Christ as victor is his role as king. When we look at the story of Christ's kingship, the image of Christ as victor comes into focus. Christ the King did not come as an arrogant, self-serving, harsh monarch to be served by his subjects. He came as a humble, self-giving, loving monarch to serve his subjects. "He subjected himself" is the description of his kingship. In that subjection, he triumphed; in his humility, he is victorious; in his love is his power. That is who Christ the victor is, and as that victor, he is worthy of our praise, our love, our obedience.

F I V E

CHRIST AS SACRIFICE

The image of Christ as sacrifice pervades the New Testament and gives us a crucial way of looking at the story of the kingdom of God in Jesus Christ. This image may seem to be the most natural way of reading the gospel story, partly because sacrifice plays such a prominent role in the Old Testament and partly because some interpretations of Christ's sacrifice have been so prevalent in the recent theology of the church. Indeed, one could argue that sacrifice is the basic image of Christ's work—that sacrifice is the key to his victory and the substance of his example.[1] But although there is a close connection among these images of sacrifice, victor, and example in the New Testament, they also shape our vision in different ways. Therefore, we will consider sacrifice as a separate image with many different facets. As we look at the biblical and historical material, we want to be sure that our image of Christ as sacrifice is shaped by the gospel of the kingdom and not by some other story or view of the world.

Biblical Basis

Since sacrifice shapes so much of the Old Testament, it is impossible to cover fully the biblical basis of this image.[2] Certainly, Jesus' own understanding of his life as sacrifice was shaped by the Old Testament teaching. But as we have seen in other instances, Jesus fulfills the Old Testament teaching on sacrifice through his own life and teaching.

In the Old Testament, the sacrificial system seems to stand at the center of Israel's relationship with God. The sacrifices that Israel brought to God served many different purposes. Some were offerings of thanksgiving for what God had done, some were an acknowledgment of God's supremacy, some were an expression of fellowship with God and other Israelites, and some fulfilled vows that had been taken to express commitment to God. But the sacrifices that provide the context for understanding Jesus' fulfillment are the sacrifices that dealt with guilt and sin.

The sacrifices that dealt with guilt and sin become the focal point of much that happens in the Old Testament. When we looked at the offices of prophet, priest, and king in the Old Testament, we saw the conflict that arose between them. Much of this conflict concerned their understanding of the role of sacrifice. It appears that Israel, poorly taught by their priests, corrupted by their kings, and misled by false prophets, had come to believe that how they lived did not matter as long as they were offering the right sacrifices.

God, through God's servants, confronts this situation, providing a clear picture of the purpose of sacrifice:

> But Samuel replied: "Does the LORD delight in burnt offerings and sacrifices as much as in obeying the voice of the LORD? To obey is better than sacrifice, and to heed is better than the fat of rams."
>
> 1 Samuel 15:22

> The LORD detests the sacrifice of the wicked,
> but the prayer of the upright pleases him.
> Proverbs 15:8

> For I desire mercy, not sacrifice
> and acknowledgment of God rather than burnt offerings.
> Hosea 6:6

These passages make clear God's purpose in the sacrificial system. Israel's sacrifices were not meant simply to allow holy God to live with unholy people. Certainly, this is a strong part of the Old Testament sacrificial system: Some of the sacrifices cover Israel's sins (Leviticus 16). But if the primary purpose of sacrifice was to cover Israel's sins, then God would have no complaint about Israel's sin as long as Israel was also sacrificing.

Rather, the point of the sacrificial system was to reveal and enact God's holiness so that Israel, in obedience to God, would seek holiness and live. In this case, God's call to Israel to obey, to practice mercy, and to acknowledge God makes sense, especially if Israel is faithful to the sacrificial system.

This view of the sacrificial system is reinforced by a recognition that God first chose Israel as God's people, then gave them the sacrificial system. In other words, God was present with Israel prior to their sacrifices. God did not say, "If you make these sacrifices, then you can be my people." Rather, God said, "Since I have made you my people, you must now live as these sacrifices indicate." Thus, the sacrifices are rooted in God's initiative and grace.

In the New Testament, Jesus is clearly seen as a sacrifice. John the Baptist uses imagery to identify Jesus Christ as sacrifice when he says, "Look, the

Lamb of God, who takes away the sin of the world!" (John 1:29). The Gospel of John follows up on this image by portraying Jesus as the Passover lamb. At the time when God delivered Israel from slavery in Egypt, Israel sacrificed their firstborn, unblemished lambs in order to mark their homes with blood so that God's angel would not kill their firstborn sons. In John's Gospel, Jesus is the Passover lamb whose blood now marks us as God's people and protects us from death. This same reference to Jesus as Passover sacrifice is made by Luke in the context of the Israelite meal that commemorated the first Passover. At the meal with his disciples, which we now celebrate as the Lord's Supper or Eucharist, Jesus takes one of the cups of wine that was drunk at that meal and says, "This cup is the new covenant in my blood, which is poured out for you" (Luke 22:20).

In the letters of Paul, one prominent theme is Christ as sacrifice. Paul's explanation of Christ as sacrifice raises many issues that we will consider when we examine the historical usage of this image. For now we may note that Paul emphasizes the image of sacrifice in relation to Jesus Christ:

> But now a righteousness from God, apart from law, has been made known, to which the Law and the Prophets testify. This righteousness from God comes through faith in Jesus Christ to all who believe. There is no difference, for all have sinned and fall short of the glory of God, and are justified freely by his grace through the redemption that came by Christ Jesus. God presented him as a sacrifice of atonement, through faith in his blood.
>
> Romans 3:21–25

> Get rid of the old yeast that you may be a new batch without yeast—as you really are. For Christ, our Passover lamb, has been sacrificed. Therefore let us keep the Festival, not with the old yeast, the yeast of malice and wickedness, but with bread without yeast, the bread of sincerity and truth.
>
> 1 Corinthians 5:7–8

In these two passages, Paul sees Christ as a sacrifice in keeping with the Old Testament's view of sacrifice. First, Paul connects the sacrifice of Christ with what God has done. The focus of sacrifice is on God's gracious initiative, not on humankind's manipulation of God through certain acts of sacrifice. Second, Paul connects sacrifice with a change in the way humans live. In Romans, a new righteousness is made available to Jew and Gentile through Christ's sacrifice. In Corinthians, Paul uses the image of unleavened bread at Passover to argue that we are to live holy lives as a result of the sacrifice of our Passover lamb, Jesus Christ.

Finally, the letter to the Hebrews largely concerns Christ as our priest and our sacrifice:

> And by that will [of the Father], we have been made holy through the sacrifice of the body of Jesus Christ once for all.

> Day after day every priest stands and performs his religious duties; again and again he offers the same sacrifices, which can never take away sins. But when this priest [Jesus Christ] had offered for all time one sacrifice for sins, he sat down at the right hand of God. Since that time he waits for his enemies to be made his footstool, because by one sacrifice he has made perfect forever those who are being made holy.
>
> 10:10–14

In this passage, the author repeats a theme we have seen many times: The purpose of the sacrifice of Christ was not just to cover our sins but to make us holy. The image of sacrifice teaches a way of life in relationship to God.

Two further points about Christ as sacrifice are important in Hebrews. First, as the above passage claims, Christ's sacrifice is superior to the Old Testament sacrifices and puts an end to those sacrifices. This truth is symbolized in the Gospels by the tearing in two of the temple curtain at the moment of Jesus' death. As Matthew tells it, "And when Jesus had cried out again in a loud voice, he gave up his spirit. At that moment the curtain of the temple was torn in two from top to bottom" (Matt. 27:50–51). This curtain separated the Holy of Holies, where the blood was sprinkled on the Day of Atonement, from the rest of the temple. The tearing in two of the curtain demonstrates the acceptance of Christ's sacrifice and the end of other sacrifices.

The second truth that Hebrews develops in relation to Christ as sacrifice is the importance of Christ's humanity. In Paul, it is clear that God is acting in the sacrifice of Christ. In Hebrews, it is clear that a human being, the one who suffered, who is like us in every way except sin, who sheds his blood, is also active in the sacrifice of Jesus Christ.

With these passages and their image of sacrifice in mind, we may look at the story of Jesus. Our most natural response is to connect Christ as sacrifice with his death. That is certainly the focus of the New Testament and the climactic act of his sacrifice. But before we look at Christ's death as sacrifice, we may see how his life is also a sacrifice.

In one of Paul's letters, the whole reality of Christ's life is seen as a sacrifice. He writes to the Philippians:

> Your attitude should be the same as that of Christ Jesus:
> Who, being in very nature God,
> did not consider equality with God something to be grasped,
> but made himself nothing,
> taking the very nature of a servant,
> being made in human likeness.
> And being found in appearance as a man,
> he humbled himself
> and became obedient to death—even death on a cross!
>
> 2:5–8

The passage continues by describing the exaltation of Christ. But it is the verses quoted above that give us the theme of sacrifice.

In these verses, which are almost certainly from an early Christian hymn that Paul is quoting, the image of sacrifice is clearly evident.[3] Two kinds of sacrifice are involved.[4] First, there is the sacrifice made by God the Son in becoming human. In him, God, rather than remaining aloof and untouched by human suffering and sorrow, participated in all the suffering and sorrow of humankind, even to the point of death. Second, there is the sacrifice made by Christ as human in his willingness to obey God even to the point of death. In Christ, a human being lived in obedience to God in an anti-God world, even to the point of death. In this dual sacrifice, as human and divine, Christ established and revealed the kingdom of God in this world. This image of sacrifice permeates all Christ's teaching and action so that we see the gospel story as the story of one long sacrifice of service to God and to humankind.

The climactic event of sacrifice in the gospel of the kingdom is the death of Christ. But to see the death of Christ as a sacrifice is something we have to achieve, for Christ's death is not obviously a sacrifice. He does not die on an altar; he is executed by a government. He does not die as part of a religious ritual; he dies as part of a political and legal ritual. He is not offered by the people to God; he is offered by the people to the political and religious authorities, or perhaps we could say that he is offered by the authorities to the people. This is the most obvious way to read the story of Christ's death: It is a "legal" execution.[5]

But Christians read the story in another way. For Christians, the death of Christ is a sacrifice. By seeing the particular death that Christ died as the climactic revelation and establishment of the kingdom of God, Christians change the way we think about God and humankind. Now we see that all of human life is turned against God. Even the very ways we seek to establish justice and goodness are corrupted. All that we are demands the blood of one who is innocent and righteous. Thus, in the death of Christ, who is innocent of the accusations that led to his execution, we can see the depth and horror of our corruption.

On the other side, Christians also see the death of Christ as God's act. As Paul says, "All this is from God, who reconciled us to himself through Christ and gave us the ministry of reconciliation: that God was reconciling the world to himself in Christ, not counting men's sins against them" (2 Cor. 5:18–19). We may also recall from Romans 3 that God presented Christ as a sacrifice of atonement. So the other side of Christ's death as a sacrifice is that God is the preeminent agent in the story. The story begins and ends with God's intentions and actions, not with those of humankind. How the sacrifice of Christ's death accomplishes God's intentions is a difficult question that we will consider in our historical investigations.

Finally, in a way that may seem unfamiliar, the resurrection of Christ may also be seen through the image of sacrifice. Here we must note that the resurrection of Jesus Christ is not just about his body coming alive again after death and being reunited with his spirit. The resurrection of Christ is also about his continuing presence in the world. The New Testament speaks of the continuing presence of Christ in connection with the sending of the Spirit. Even after the outpouring of the Spirit on Pentecost, the authors of the New Testament talk about the presence of Christ and of the Spirit in the same terms. So wherever the Spirit is present and at work, Christ is also present and at work. This is particularly true of the church, which is gathered and empowered and sanctified by the Holy Spirit but is also the "body of Christ."

Now we can see how sacrifice continues to mark Christ. As he is present in his body, the church, and as the church lives according to the sacrificial model of her Lord, Christ continues to sacrifice. Indeed, we may say that sacrifice is what it takes to be faithful in service and witness to the kingdom of God in this world. This is not the same as the perpetual crucifixion of Jesus Christ. But it does recognize that sacrifice is at the very heart of God, not in a way that overcomes God, but in a way that God overcomes our separation from God and reconciles us to himself.

The image of sacrifice is a pervasive biblical image that powerfully reveals to us the nature of God's love for the world in Jesus Christ. It draws on our best thinking, our deepest affections, our firm obedience in witness to what God has done and is doing. Over the centuries many teachers of the church have turned their gifts to developing the image of Christ as sacrifice.

Historical Development

In the history of the church, theologians have often taken the image of sacrifice and connected it to some particular reality in their social setting. By doing so, they made more particular, more specific, the image of sacrifice for their own times and places. Since this image has been the dominant one in the history of the church, the debates about it are nearly endless. Therefore, we cannot hope to cover all the issues here. Instead, our purpose will be to examine the major points so that we can develop a more mature and truthful understanding of Christ as sacrifice. Our examination will seek to discover the strengths and dangers of this image.

The person whose name is most closely associated with the image of sacrifice is Anselm of Canterbury, one of the church's greatest theologians. In his book *Cur Deus Homo (Why God Became Man)*, he gives his explanation by connecting the image of sacrifice with his social setting.[6]

Anselm lived in Europe circa 1033–1109. During this time, European life was feudal. Society was made up of various social levels. A person born into a particular level was thought of as "assigned" to that level. Lords and servants, princes and peasants—every level, every station in life had its duties and responsibilities. Relationships between people were built around the proper way in which they were to relate. For example, a lord related to a servant differently than he did to another lord. These ways of relating were understood and accepted by society. Maintaining proper relationships was essential to the health of society.

This social setting gave Anselm a way of understanding Christ's death as sacrifice, which restored our relationship with God. In Anselm's explanation, humans are God's servants who owe him obedience. Adam's sin is the rebellion of a servant that brings dishonor and rends the fabric of society. God's honor can be satisfied and society restored only by the obedience to God of one who owes God nothing and by the death of one who does not have to die. That is, the obedience of a mere human cannot restore God's honor, because we owe that to God anyway. And our death cannot satisfy God's honor, because as sinners we owe that death.

So God in mercy and love became a human, Jesus Christ. As the God-Man, Jesus Christ was perfectly righteous and obedient. But since he is God, and thus on the same social level as God, he does not owe God obedience. Therefore, his obedience to God is an extra that can become our obedience. Second, because he is God and a sinless human being, his death is not necessary. As the death of one who is fully human and fully divine, Christ's death is infinite in value and freely chosen. Therefore, his death can count as the death of all who believe in Christ.

Why did God become human? God became human to satisfy God's honor by paying the debt of obedience and death that humankind is incapable of paying. Apart from Christ's sacrifice, the universe is shattered and humankind is separated from God. Through Christ's sacrifice, God's honor is restored and humankind redeemed. Thus, Anselm's view and others like it are often called the satisfaction theory of atonement.

Over the years, Anselm has been criticized by many theologians.[7] Their major criticisms concern four aspects of Anselm's teaching. First, Anselm is accused of separating the humanity and divinity of Jesus Christ so much that no significance is given to Christ's humanity and the details of his life on earth. All that matters is God acting in a sinless human being. This criticism rightly points out that Anselm's account lacks any description of Jesus' life. As we have seen in earlier chapters, it is not just *that* Jesus lived or *that* he was sinless that is significant for his work. Of utmost importance is *how* he lived and *how* he was sinless. This first criticism of Anselm's account, then, is valid. However, his development of the image of sacrifice does not necessarily rule out an account of Jesus' way of life that is compatible with Anselm's teaching. In fact, the first section of this book is in part an attempt to show how Jesus' life and teaching redeem what sin destroys.

The second criticism of Anselm's work is that he too greatly separates the Father and the Son in the work of salvation. This criticism points to places where Anselm says that the death of Christ is paid to God and where the Father is said to owe the Son.[8] By using this language, Anselm seems to suggest that the Father is a reluctant, perhaps unwilling, participant in our salvation, forced to comply because of the Son's sacrifice. Here the danger is that God becomes divided against himself: The Father wills our condemnation; the Son wills our salvation. And by his work, the Son compels the Father to save humankind.

Not everyone agrees that Anselm should be understood in this way. Without getting into all the arguments, we may learn something from this criticism. If (and in so far as) Anselm teaches this separation of Father and Son, he is wrong. The passages of Scripture that we have already looked at make it clear that the Father is as loving and active in our salvation as is the Son and the Spirit. So one clear rule to follow in developing the image of Christ as sacrifice is to avoid separating the Father, the Son, and the Spirit.

A third criticism directed at Anselm's account is that he views the salvation of humankind as an impersonal, legal transaction. According to this criticism, Anselm describes the working out of our salvation through Christ's death as something God does just to keep the books balanced, the universe tidy.

This criticism, like the others, seems to point out a weakness in Anselm's account that does not destroy his general approach. Anselm's picture of God as "feudal Lord" is positive. God is not an arbitrary, dictatorial, domineering Lord. Rather, God is the Lord who is responsible for maintaining the order of the universe. When that order is disrupted, the Lord must act to restore order. So Anselm's use of feudal imagery yields a positive picture of God. Nevertheless, the emphasis in his account falls very much on the side of God's justice and righteousness. God's love and mercy become secondary elements that are not integral to Anselm's account in the way they are integral to the New Testament.

Finally, Anselm's account is criticized because it seems to develop an account of the salvation of humankind that focuses simply on our redemption and gives no further direction for the life of the redeemed. This, too, seems to point to an omission in Anselm's view that is tied to his failure to attend to Jesus' way of life. God does not "simply forgive" us in Jesus Christ. Rather, God redeems us for a whole new way of life. God does not just want to forgive us continually for our sin; God forgives us so that we may be restored to the life we are intended to live. As we have seen, the New Testament passages that speak of Christ's sacrifice continually talk about the new life made possible by that sacrifice.

Another development of the image of Christ as sacrifice may be found in John Calvin and many who follow his theology. In Calvin's time (1509–1564), Europe had changed from a feudal society to a society based more on legal relationships. Calvin, therefore, used concepts from law and order to develop the image of Christ as sacrifice. His development has come to be known as penal substitution.[9]

In viewing Christ's death as penal substitution, Calvin drew on several biblical passages:

> Since we have now been justified by his blood, how much more shall we be saved from God's wrath through him!
>
> Romans 5:9

> All who rely on observing the law are under a curse, for it is written: "Cursed is everyone who does not continue to do everything written in the Book of the Law." Clearly no one is justified before God by the law, because, "The righteous will live by faith." The law is not based on faith; on the contrary, "The man who does these things will live by them." Christ redeemed us from the curse of the law by becoming a curse for us, for it is written: "Cursed is everyone who is hung on a tree."
>
> Galatians 3:10–13

These passages, and passages from Isaiah 53 and Hebrews, teach us that humankind, apart from Christ, is subject to God's wrath and vengeance. According to Calvin, these passages teach that we are delivered from God's wrath by Christ taking upon himself the penalty for sin that we deserve: Christ becomes our penal substitute.[10]

Through the centuries, many have criticized and defended various forms of this notion of penal substitution.[11] Since Calvin and others who follow him tie their view of Christ as penal substitute into other aspects of their theology, it is difficult and sometimes misleading to deal with this doctrine alone. However, if we keep in mind that we are exploring this image and not their theology, then Calvin and his followers may be of some help to us.

Many of the criticisms of penal substitution are similar to those directed at Anselm. And like those criticisms, they point to weaknesses and omissions in some accounts and dangers to which this image of sacrifice is susceptible. So in our criticism of this view we want to discern the good and the bad.

We can identify one of the controversies surrounding this development of the image of sacrifice by comparing the italicized words in the following passages:

> For there is no difference: for all have sinned, and come short of the glory of God; being justified freely by his grace through the redemption that is in Christ Jesus: whom God hath set forth to be a *propitiation* through faith in his blood.
>
> Romans 3:22–25 KJV

> For there is no distinction; since all have sinned and fall short of the glory of God, they are justified by his grace as a gift, through the redemption which is in Christ Jesus, whom God put forward as an *expiation* by his blood, to be received by faith.
>
> Romans 3:22–25 RSV

> There is no difference, for all have sinned and fall short of the glory of God, and are justified freely by his grace through the redemption that came by Christ Jesus. God presented him as a *sacrifice of atonement,* through faith in his blood.
>
> Romans 3:22–25

These three versions of the Bible translate the same Greek word *(hilasterion)* in three different ways that reflect decisions about the meaning of Christ's death as sacrifice.

The Greek word refers to the place on the Ark of the Covenant where the blood was sprinkled on Israel's Day of Atonement. The King James Version uses "propitiation" to translate the Greek because the translators believed that Christ died to appease God's wrath. The Revised Standard Version uses "expiation" because those translators believed that Christ died to expunge human guilt. Much argument has centered on the question raised by these translations: Does Christ's death change something in God (propitiation) or something in humankind (expiation)? The NIV (and now the New Revised Standard Version) uses "sacrifice of atonement" in order to avoid the dilemma in their translations.

The criticism leveled against "propitiation" is right to point out the problems in talking about God's wrath against sinners. If God is angry at sinners and wants to punish them, then what motive does God have for sending Christ to save sinners?[12] How can we speak of God's wrath against sinners when Paul says that "God demonstrates his own love for us in this: While we were still sinners, Christ died for us." And further, "For if, when we were God's enemies, we were reconciled to him through the death of his Son . . ." (Rom. 5:8, 10). How do we make sense of John 3:16: "For God so loved the world . . ."?

Yet, the criticism leveled against "expiation" is also telling. The New Testament continually ties Christ's death and our predicament to language about human guilt, but also about God's wrath: "The wrath of God is being revealed. . . ." And, "Since we have now been justified by his blood, how much more shall we be saved from God's wrath through him!" (Rom. 1:18; 5:9).

So we must find a way to talk about God's wrath and love, and human guilt. The best way to do this, I think, is to understand that the ultimate object of God's wrath is sin, not sinners. God hates sin. Sin destroys God's creation. God would not be worthy of praise if God did not hate that which destroys what God has made good. The situation is complicated by the fact that sin is a personal, moral notion. Sin does not exist apart from personal, moral beings who act sinfully: Humans are guilty. But God loves humankind.

In order to redeem that which God loves, God must find a way to overcome sin without destroying sinners. In this understanding, God accomplishes redemption by becoming the God-Man and by pouring out on God in Christ God's wrath against sin, not against sinners. In so doing, God makes it possible for sinners to be freed from the penalty of sin. Out of love, God becomes sin for us so that we might be redeemed, not destroyed by either sin or God's wrath against sin.

In order to fill out this account, we must add two more things. First, we must note that some of humankind so loves sin that they refuse to be separated from their sin. Thus, they become subject to God's wrath against sin and suffer condemnation. Second, we must note that God's redemption is not meant merely to forgive us our sin but even more to free us from sin for a new life. Sin is overcome, we are forgiven, now we no longer live in sin.

The other controversy surrounding penal substitution as a development of the image of sacrifice is similar to one of the criticisms of Anselm and concerns the roles of the Father, Son, and Spirit. In some popular accounts of this view, the Father is pictured as wrathful and vengeful, an angry, violent God anxious to destroy sinners, and the Son is portrayed as loving and merciful, a sacrificial, patient God anxious to forgive sinners. In this account, the only thing standing between humankind and the Father's destroying wrath is the loving sacrifice of the Son.

This is a terrible portrayal of the Triune God. To believe that God is three-in-one is to believe that the Father, Son, and Spirit are not divided against one another. The Father, Son, and Spirit all look at sin and sinners the same way. Father, Son, and Spirit are all equally wrathful toward sin and merciful and forgiving toward sinners. We must not divide God against himself. The love of the Father, Son, and Spirit accomplishes our salvation through Christ.

In our consideration of the historical development of the image of Christ as sacrifice, we have covered many complex and controversial issues. Our purpose has not been to understand all the controversies but to use the controversies to deepen our understanding of the image of sacrifice. Although there are many theological dangers in developing this image, it is solidly rooted in Scripture. As we reflect on the image, we will seek to avoid the pitfalls we have identified and develop the insights we have acquired.

Systematic Reflection

As we reflect on the image of Christ as sacrifice, we want to consider the biblical basis of this image and reflect on the story of the kingdom in Jesus Christ while also keeping in mind the lessons learned from the historical investigation. In particular, we want to remember that sacrifice is characteristic of the life of Christ as well as his death; that sacrifice is the work of Christ as fully human, fully divine; that sacrifice is the work of the Trinity, not just of the Son; and that humankind participates in this sacrifice. Since this image of sacrifice has been developed in several different contexts historically, we will see that it teaches us to see the gospel in several different ways.

God as Judge and Judged

The great danger with the image of sacrifice is the tendency to divide God. As we talk about God in this section, therefore, we must keep in mind that although the three eternal, personal distinctions of God are active in different ways, the nature, the character, the disposition of God is the same for Father, Son, and Holy Spirit.

If we see the story of the kingdom as the story of sacrifice, then one of the ways in which we must see God is as *judge*. Whether we connect the image of sacrifice with the Old Testament, with Anselm's feudal setting, or with Calvin's courtroom, according to this image, God has made a judgment. Human actions have been judged wrong, guilt has been established, punishment has been declared and enacted.

Again, although it is most natural for us today to connect the language of judgment with the legal-penal system, the image of sacrifice is more flexible than that. We may think of many settings in which judgments are made: the classroom (when grades are assigned), business (when contracts are signed), and the marketplace (when goods are purchased). What is clear from the biblical material is that God's judgment is set within a world of moral, personal relationships. God's judgment is not merely that there is a deficiency or fault in humankind but that the deficiency is moral in nature. God's judgment is not that human action violates some law but that human action violates God's character. Whatever contemporary setting we connect with the image of sacrifice, therefore, we must guard the moral, personal dimensions of the story of the kingdom as the story of sacrifice.

If we apply our rule that the Trinity is always involved at every point in the story of the kingdom, we must recognize that Father, Son, and Spirit are equally our judge. But if the Son is incarnate in Christ, then we must also say that under the image of sacrifice we see that God is "the judge judged in our place."[13] In Jesus Christ, God, who judges humankind, takes that judgment upon himself. In Old Testament terms, God offers up God's Son as the sacrifice; in Anselm's terms, God satisfies the demands of God's honor; in Calvin's terms, God suffers our punishment for us.

Here we see the love of God working together with God's justice to establish the kingdom. God cannot overlook or ignore sin. For God to do so would be like a surgeon telling you that you have a cancerous tumor, but "we are just going to pretend that it is not there." In the sacrifice of Christ, God displays God's judgment of sin and sinners. By taking that judgment on himself, God can forgive sin, rather than ignore or overlook it. Thus, as the judge judged in our place, God makes possible the forgiveness of humankind and the redemption of creation without compromising who God is or who humankind is.

Only through the sacrifice of the Father, who did not spare his Son, through the sacrifice of the Son, who gave up his life for us, and through the sacrifice of the Spirit, who incorporates us into the kingdom, lives within us, and patiently nurtures us can we enter the kingdom. Through the image of sacrifice, we see that our salvation costs God. The greatness of God, then, is not God's distance from suffering but God's ability and willingness to redeem us through sacrifice.

Humanity as Perpetrators, Rebels, Collaborators, and Criminals

In the previous image—Christ as victor—we saw that humankind is mainly seen as victims and captives who bear little, if any, responsibility for our predicament. The image of sacrifice adds another angle to our understanding of humankind. After we explore the image of sacrifice in relation to humankind, we will consider the different pictures given by the images of victory and sacrifice.

If the human predicament is such that God must sacrifice the Son's life for us and our sins, then humankind must be seen as responsible participants in and agents of sin. Here, then, we are not primarily sin's victims; rather, we are sin's *perpetrators*. We are not ones to whom sin happens; we are the ones who make sin happen. Under the image of sacrifice, we learn that humans help perpetuate sin in our world by human action. Here we are not the victims of an invading army or the hostages of an alien force; we are the *rebels* who resist the rightful ruler and the *collaborators* who empower alien rule. We are not victims; we are *criminals*.

This picture of humankind qualifies the picture that the image of Christ as victor gave us. There, humans were victims, not responsible for sin. Here, humans are perpetrators, responsible for sin. Since both of these pictures are true and rooted in Scripture, we must resist the desire to find some higher concept that reconciles the pictures.

The images of Scripture give us perceptions of reality from many different angles. We cannot see all of the truth at once. In some situations, the image of victory may give us a more truthful view of humankind. In other situations, the image of sacrifice may be more truthful. The great mistake would be to reject altogether one or another of these images. Wisdom is the ability to know which image to apply in particular circumstances. For example, if a person goes to his or her pastor and tells a story of being an abused child, is it truthful to tell that person that he or she is responsible for sin? In some churches, an exclusive emphasis on humans as perpetrators has forced victims of sin to see themselves as responsible for their own suffering. In this situation, Christ as victor and sin as enemy is the theological approach that a wise counselor will take.

On the other hand, if someone comes to confess that he (or she) is a child abuser but excuses it on the grounds that he was a victim of abuse, then the truth is a bit different. Certainly, most child abusers are victims themselves. But to overcome that evil, they must not only acknowledge their victimization, they must also acknowledge their collaboration with evil and their perpetuation of it in their own practice of abuse. Here the wise counselor will draw on the image of Christ as sacrifice in order to lead the person to see that he or she is not merely a victim but also a perpetrator. The abused abuser not only needs to be freed from victimization but must also ask for forgiveness from his or her victims.

Sin as Rebellion

If we follow up the picture of humankind we have just developed, then under the image of sacrifice we can see that sin is *rebellion*. In this picture, humankind is actively resisting the rule of God in the world. No longer do we see sin as the enemy (as with the image of victory). Now we see that we are the enemy through our sin. Why is the kingdom of God resisted? Not because of an invasion from outside God's creation, but because of rebellion from within creation.

According to this account, sin is not an external condition that threatens to destroy from outside. Here, sin is an internal condition that threatens to destroy from inside. In this case, we must speak not so much of the destruction of sin as an external enemy as of the healing of creation from its internal sickness and rebellion. We might say that the struggle is to kill the disease without losing the patient.

This image of sacrifice, then, challenges the illusion that humans are not responsible for sin. Certainly, we are sinned against. But we are all also sinners. The pictures of God, humankind, and sin that the image of sacrifice creates force us to acknowledge that we are part of the problem.

In some theologies that rely exclusively on the image of Christ as victor, salvation or the kingdom of God is seen as a result of simply changing our circumstances. If sin is entirely external to humankind, that makes some sense. But if we add to our theology the biblical image of Christ as sacrifice, then we can see that it is not enough merely to change our circumstances for us to enter the kingdom of God. Humankind must also be changed; the work of salvation is internal as well as external. The image of sacrifice does not tell us in detailed, conceptual language how God accomplishes this change, but it does give us some images of salvation that are appropriate to Christ as sacrifice.

Salvation as Forgiveness, Pardon, Innocence, Righteousness, and Peace

Our earlier discussions have unavoidably foreshadowed the understanding of salvation taught by the image of Christ as sacrifice. The biblical and historical studies have particularly shown the importance of salvation as something involving personal relationships and our participation.

With these lessons in mind, we see first that salvation is *forgiveness*. Under the image of Christ as sacrifice, salvation as forgiveness carries two aspects. First, forgiveness must be seen in the context of a personal, moral relationship. Although we may speak of forgiveness apart from personal relationships, such as "forgiving a loan," seeing forgiveness through the image of Christ as sacrifice makes sense only in the context of personal, moral relationships. Second, the forgiveness of Christ as sacrifice implies a situation that involves blameworthiness on the part of one party. Here the sinner is not the victim needing rescuing but the perpetrator needing forgiveness.

Forgiveness, then, draws out the personal-moral world of the biblical story of Christ's sacrifice.[14] When we connect the notion of forgiveness with that story, our understanding is deepened. We are led beyond our typical view of forgiveness as an event and enabled to see that forgiveness describes the continuing character of our relationship with God and others. In other words, forgiveness is not something we do now and then; forgiveness is the very way we live in the kingdom. Forgiveness is one way to characterize God's life and our life in the kingdom.[15]

Forgiveness is life in the kingdom of God. This is why Jesus can say that unless we forgive those who sin against us we cannot be forgiven (Matt. 6:14–15). It is not that our forgiveness of others is a prerequisite for our own forgiveness. It is, rather, that forgiveness is the very life of the kingdom. If we are not forgiving, we are not living in the kingdom, which is the forgiveness of our sin.

A second way to look at salvation through the image of sacrifice is to see it as *pardon*. This image may bring to mind the picture of a governor pardoning a convicted criminal or, for those old enough to remember, the presidential pardon of Richard Nixon by Gerald Ford—without Nixon ever being convicted of anything. This latter example, by its exceptional nature, points us to the natural understanding of pardon: It is a declaration that no more punishment is necessary for the crime that was committed.

We must be careful of two things at this point. First, in the biblical image of sacrifice, the offense of which we are guilty is not a legal, impersonal offense. It is a moral, personal offense. We are not pardoned for breaking a law; we are pardoned for offending the character of God. Second, the Bible extends the effect of Christ's sacrifice beyond pardon to a declaration of our innocence. We are not merely pardoned; we are "cleansed" of our sin:

> If we confess our sins, he is faithful and just and will forgive us our sins and purify us from all unrighteousness.
>
> 1 John 1:9

> For if you possess these qualities in increasing measure, they will keep you from being ineffective and unproductive in your knowledge of our Lord Jesus Christ. But if anyone does not have them, he is nearsighted and blind, and has forgotten that he has been cleansed from his past sins.
>
> 2 Peter 1:8–9

These two passages tie together forgiveness, cleansing (not pardon), and the Christian life. Somehow, in a way not described but imaged, the sacrifice of Christ makes us righteous.

Along with this notion of cleansing, then, is the image of salvation as *righteousness*. We are not merely forgiven, we are not merely cleansed; we are also made righteous. The sacrifice of Christ accomplishes something positive and creative in our lives: It makes us righteous.

The theological tradition has often talked about two kinds of righteousness: justification and sanctification. Justification is an immediate, once-for-all change in my status. When I come to Christ in faith, I am made absolutely righteous. Sanctification is an ongoing process of change in my character. As I live in Christ, I become more righteous.

These two go together; you cannot have one without the other. Perhaps the best way to think of these two concepts is to think of them as descriptions of life in the kingdom of God. Justification identifies the reality that through Christ we are in the kingdom of God. Sanctification identifies the reality that through Christ we are maturing as citizens of the kingdom.

Finally, as we think about salvation as life in the kingdom and connect it to the sacrifice that Christ made so that sin could be the object of God's wrath and we could be forgiven, we may think of salvation as *peace*. Here peace is not merely the absence of conflict; it is the restoration of wholeness.

In the Old Testament, the Hebrew word *shalom* conveys this larger, more profound understanding of peace. Shalom is not set over against war and conflict; it is set over against sin and evil. Anselm came very close to this concept when he viewed sin as rending the fabric of society. Although Anselm does not develop it, on that account, salvation may be seen as mending the tear, restoring the wholeness, of society.

In the Old and New Testaments, the sacrifice of Christ effects an even greater shalom. There the sacrifice of Christ is a cosmic event that is restoring the entire creation to shalom: "For God was pleased to have all his fullness dwell in him, and through him to reconcile to himself all things, whether things on earth or things in heaven, by making peace through his blood, shed on the cross" (Col. 1:19–20). This passage reminds us that although the sacrifice of Christ is set within the world of the personal and moral, the person with whom we are concerned is the one who created the world good. So the story of the kingdom as the sacrifice of Christ leads us to see that humankind is redeemed within the context of the redemption of all creation. In Jesus Christ as sacrifice, God in love redeems the cosmos.

In the kingdom of peace, we are given life within the world that is made whole, where, as Christ declared, creation and our longings are perfected. Through the sacrifice of Christ, that kingdom of peace is revealed and established. As we live in that kingdom here and now, we too will live sacrificially. But that life will be sacrificial only by the standards of a world that is at war with God. The resurrection reveals that the life of "sacrifice" is really the life of the eternal kingdom of God:

> And he said, "The Son of Man must suffer many things and be rejected by the elders, chief priests and teachers of the law, and he must be killed and on the third day be raised to life."
>
> Then he said to them all: "If anyone would come after me, he must deny himself and take up his cross daily and follow me. For whoever wants to save his life will lose it, but whoever loses his life for me will save it."
>
> Luke 9:22–24

In this passage, Jesus connects his own sacrifice with the resurrection and calls all who would follow him into the kingdom to live that same life of sacrifice. "Losing my life" means losing that life of rebellion and the perpetuation of sin. "Saving my life" means living by forgiveness, living righteously, living at peace. In a world marked by conflict, unrighteousness, and rebellion, the call to kingdom living is the call to sacrifice. But since it is a call to life in the kingdom, it is also a call to salvation, to eternal life.

Conclusion

In Christ as sacrifice, God our judge is judged in our place, reveals our perpetration of and collaboration with sin, ends our rebellion, forgives our guilt, cleanses us, makes us righteous, and establishes us in the kingdom of peace.

The great strength of this image is its revelation that God has done something about our responsibility for sin. Sin cannot be eradicated simply by dismantling the sinful systems and structures of the world. Sin has found a home in the human heart, so wherever humans go, sin will be there. The only way to eradicate sin is to destroy sinful systems and structures *and* destroy humankind—or change the human heart. Without telling us how, the image of Christ as sacrifice teaches us that the sin in us has been forgiven.

The image of Christ as sacrifice runs two dangers. First, we may make the mistake of simply attaching meaning and salvation to any sacrifice. It is not any sacrifice that saves; it is Christ's sacrifice as fully human, fully divine that redeems humankind.[16] Second, we may become pathological in our way of life and think that being a victim is the same as following Christ as sacrifice. But as we have seen, the language of victim is appropriate to the image of Christ as victor, not to Christ as sacrifice. When we are victims, God does not delight in our sacrifice; being victimized is not the same as making a sacrifice.[17] When we are victims, God rages against the sin that is our enemy and through Christ triumphs over that sin.

To follow Christ as sacrifice involves our active obedience in living according to the kingdom in a world at war with the kingdom.[18] Sacrifice is the act of mature, "powerful" citizens of the kingdom, not of weak, powerless victims. In relation to others who are sinners (that's all of us), our calling is not to triumph over them but to sacrifice for them in such a way that the kingdom is made manifest and Christ is represented to them. Therefore, to act as sacrifice requires the greatest wisdom and perseverance if we are not to be victims or bitter manipulators. In this light, we can see that faithful sacrifice requires the maturity of community and not of mere individuals.

If we think back to the roles of Christ in the kingdom, the most natural connection to Christ as sacrifice is the role of priest. In the story of the kingdom, Christ the priest offers himself as sacrifice in order to reconcile humankind to God. As priest, Christ does not assuage our guilt, cover up our disobedience, or offer false comfort. Instead, he exposes the truth of our sin so that it might be forgiven. We no longer have to lie in order to live with ourselves, with one another, and with God. The truth is that we have been rebels against all that is good and true and beautiful, but through Christ the truth also is that we may be perfectly good and true and beautiful.

SIX

CHRIST AS EXAMPLE

The image of Christ as example has a strong hold on the popular imagination. Even those who do not consider themselves Christians may nevertheless view Christ as an example of how one should live. In the church, too, there is often an emphasis on following Jesus' example.

As we look at the biblical and historical expressions of Christ as example, we will see that this image raises many questions. For instance, is it reasonable to consider Jesus an example of how to live but not accept his claims about himself and his relation to God? In what ways may Jesus be our example? He was never married, had no home, knew nothing of many difficult contemporary problems such as nuclear weapons, toxic waste, and global warming—so how can we follow him?

Although we will not just be looking for answers to these questions, we will keep them in mind as we investigate the biblical and historical material for insight into Jesus Christ as example. Even more importantly, I hope that our investigation will lead you to new questions and a new understanding of Christ as example. If the story of Jesus Christ is the story of one who is both fully human and fully divine, then our understanding of his example must reflect that story. Too often, we have fallen into the error of locating Christ's example only in his story as human, to the neglect of his story as divine.

Biblical Basis

The image of example that the New Testament authors develop in relation to Christ has its roots in the Old Testament. This connection between the Old Testament and New Testament image of example is an important corrective to our habit of setting the testaments in opposition to one another, especially concerning their doctrine of God. We may not often think of God in the Old Testament as an example for us, but that is where the New Testament authors rooted their image of Jesus Christ as example.

In the Old Testament, the clearest call to live like God is found in the imperative, "I am the LORD who brought you up out of Egypt to be your God; therefore be holy, because I am holy" (Lev. 11:45). This call to holiness is worked out in the Old Testament in every area of life—in worship, in diet, in legal, political, and moral relationships (though these "categories" are not clearly recognized in Israel's organization of corporate life). The details of this outworking are complex and problematic, but what is undeniable is that Israel is called to a particular way of life because it is the way of life lived by Yahweh: Israel is to follow God's example.

This call in the Old Testament to live like God has four important characteristics. First, it is rooted in God's prior action: "I am the LORD who brought you out of Egypt." This characteristic identifies the God-Israel relationship as one of grace. Following or imitating God depends first on God's activity, not human activity. Second, this following, which is made possible by God's activity, is then the human activity of a people, not of individuals. The object of God's action is Israel. Although today we may not be able to avoid thinking of Israel as made up of individuals, the Old Testament clearly sees Israel as a people. Living like God, therefore, is intended for a community, not for isolated individuals. Third, following God cannot be restricted to one aspect of life. As the complex outworking of holiness shows in the Old Testament, the call to be like God concerns all of life. Finally, we should note that as the Old Testament works out this calling, it preserves the distinction between God and humankind: Israel is called to be *like* God, not to *be* God.

In the New Testament, this call is immediately repeated by Jesus: "Be perfect, therefore, as your heavenly Father is perfect" (Matt. 5:48). In the New Testament, this call to be like God becomes a call to follow Jesus. In the context of his last time with the disciples before his crucifixion, Jesus washes their feet:

> "Do you understand what I have done for you?" he asked them. "You call me 'Teacher' and 'Lord,' and rightly so, for that is what I am. Now that I, your Lord and Teacher, have washed your feet, you also should wash one another's feet. I have set you an example that you should do as I have done for you. I tell you the truth, no servant is greater than his master, nor is a messenger greater than the one who sent him. Now that you know these things, you will be blessed if you do them."
>
> John 13:12–17

This call to discipleship, to following Jesus, is the New Testament form of the call to be like God. Of course, this new form of the call makes perfect sense if Christ establishes the kingdom of God and is fully divine. In short, to follow God now means following Jesus.

In the New Testament, following Jesus takes on some very specific directions:

> My command is this: Love each other as I have loved you. Greater love has no one than this, that he lay down his life for his friends. You are my friends if you do what I command.
>
> John 15:12–14

> Dear friends, let us love one another, for love comes from God. . . . Whoever does not love does not know God, because God is love. This is how God showed his love among us: He sent his one and only Son into the world that we might live through him. This is love: not that we loved God, but that he loved us and sent his Son as an atoning sacrifice for our sins. Dear friends, since God so loved us, we also ought to love one another.
>
> 1 John 4:7–11

As these passages develop the image of Christ as example, they teach us many important truths about both God and humankind.

In the first place, this image of Christ as an example for humankind is tied to his way of life, particularly his sacrificial way of life. Of course, this sacrificial way of life is most clearly seen in his death, but sacrifice, laying down his life, also involves Jesus' whole way of living. In his foot washing, Jesus is servant. That is our model. Following Jesus cannot be reduced to a willingness to die for another if the occasion should arise, while ignoring opportunities for service now. John makes this clear:

> This is how we know what love is: Jesus Christ laid down his life for us. And we ought to lay down our lives for our brothers. If anyone has material possessions and sees his brother in need but has no pity on him, how can the love of God be in him? Dear children, let us not love with words or tongue but with actions and in truth.
>
> 1 John 3:16–18

Here the example of Christ is not just a willingness to die but a daily laying down of one's life.

This way of working out the image of Christ as example threatens to become a prescription for victimization. That is, if not set in the proper context, the example of Christ could simply make Christians into professional victims and losers. Such a role must be rejected not because it is distasteful or repugnant (this was one of Friedrich Nietzsche's attacks on Christianity) but because it misunderstands or overlooks the context for Jesus' example and our following.[1]

In the New Testament, Jesus' example and our following make sense only within the context of the coming of the kingdom of God. "Laying down one's life" and "losing one's life" do not have meaning and value in and of themselves. In the Christian understanding, they have meaning and value only as they are expressions of our following of Christ in living out the life of the kingdom. In order to be faithful to Christ's example, then, we must know the story of the kingdom.

When we talk about "knowing the story of the kingdom," we are returning to the notion that following God is rooted in God's prior activity. Thus, the image of Christ as example in the New Testament is an example of divine life. We have already quoted the passages in which John describes this. In Romans, Paul also describes Christ as an example of God's activity:

> You see, at just the right time, when we were still powerless, Christ died for the ungodly. Very rarely will anyone die for a righteous man, though for a good man someone might possibly dare to die. But God demonstrates his own love for us in this: While we were still sinners, Christ died for us.
>
> 5:6–8

Together, Paul and John regard the story of the kingdom in Christ as an example of God's activity, even more, of God's active love for humankind. This aspect of Christ as example will be very important in our examination of historical developments of the image.

Finally, in this biblical use of the image of example, we must observe the corporate setting for the image. As a demonstration of God's love, Christ dies for a people and calls into existence a people. The work of Christ is the fulfillment of God's work in Israel, a people. And it is the establishment of God's kingdom—an image of a particular kind of community.

As an example of humankind, Christ also portrays this corporate dimension. In Jesus' call for his disciples to follow him, he calls them by ones and by twos, but he calls them into a fellowship, a community. The substance of their following of Jesus' example is love for one another. Rather obviously, this cannot be practiced alone.

We can see this corporate living out of Christ's example in Paul's letters. Although Paul does not retell the story of Christ in his letters (because he assumes his readers' knowledge of the gospel story), his writing makes sense only if he is reflecting on Christ as example. In a passage we examined in an earlier chapter, Paul calls on the Philippians to guide their communal life by "having the same mind that was in Christ Jesus" (cf. Phil. 2:5). And in Ephesians, Paul calls that community to Christ's example:

> Be kind and compassionate to one another, forgiving each other, just as in Christ God forgave you. Be imitators of God, therefore, as dearly loved children and live a life of love, just as Christ loved us and gave himself up for us as a fragrant offering and sacrifice to God.
>
> 4:32–5:2

For Paul, as well as for John and the other authors of the New Testament, Christ's example is meant to be realized by humankind in community.

In our examination of the biblical image of Christ as example, we are taught to see the story of the kingdom come in Jesus Christ as an example of God's activity and of human activity. This twofoldness has already found expression in chapter 3, where we saw how the church came to acknowledge that Jesus was fully human, fully divine. We may bring these two ways of looking at Jesus together: As the story of one who is fully divine, the story of Christ is an example of God's activity; as the story of one who is fully human, the story of Christ is an example of human activity. But just as fully human, fully divine describes one person and his one story, so Christ as example images one reality. That one reality is the life of the kingdom that God in Christ establishes and in which humankind in Christ lives. Story and image mutually illuminate one another.

So, on the one hand, the story of the kingdom in Jesus Christ determines how Christ is example. For instance, Christ is not an example of sheer self-sacrifice; he is an example of sacrificing the life of this world for life in the kingdom. Nor is Christ an example of sheer self-fulfillment; he is an example of the perfection and fulfillment of what God intended for us.

On the other hand, the image of Christ as example determines how we are to read the story. The story of the kingdom is not something done merely for us. Nor is the story something we merely do for ourselves. Rather, the story of the kingdom is the story of God and humankind participating together in a reality established and revealed by God in Jesus Christ. That is to say, the activity of human life and divine life is changed by the kingdom. The kingdom is a new reality of relationship between God and creation in which humankind now lives. Jesus Christ is the exemplification of that new reality.

Historical Development

In the history of the church, this image of Christ as example has been developed in many different directions. To some people, the historical development of this image represents a turning from biblical teaching and a denigration of the Christian tradition. In other words, for some this image represents a liberal, modernist Christianity that whittles away Christian convictions so that Christianity is trimmed to fit modern belief or, perhaps better, "unbelief."

However, we have already seen the clear biblical roots of this image. Moreover, every development of this image differs from other developments of it. As we examine these developments, therefore, we want to discern the differences between them and keep in mind three biblical concerns: First, Christ as example concerns the activity of God and humankind; second, the development of the image accords with the biblical concern for the priority of God's activity and for human participation in that activity; third, the image is shaped by the biblical story.

In the twelfth century, the image of Christ as example was developed by a theologian named Peter Abelard (also spelled Abailard). Abelard, who is also known for his tragic relationship with Heloise, which gives us some classic medieval love letters, was a student of Anselm, the great theologian of the image of sacrifice. Abelard has often been seen as a medieval liberal or rationalist theologian. As we will see, however, this characterization is not entirely fair to Abelard.

In his *Exposition of the Epistle to the Romans,* Abelard develops his image of Christ as example.[2] In his discussion, Abelard clears the ground for his own view by criticizing the classical "ransom" theory and Anselm's theory.[3] His criticisms are ones we have already noted and taken into account in developing the images of victor and sacrifice. Abelard, however, advances his criticisms not to correct other views but to reject them.

In rejecting other views of Christ's death as our redemption, Abelard clears the way for his own view of how Christ saves us:

> Now it seems to us that we have been justified by the blood of Christ and reconciled to God in this way: through this unique act of grace manifested to us—in that his Son has taken upon himself our nature and preserved therein in teaching us by word and example even unto death—he has more fully bound us to himself by love; with the result that our hearts should be enkindled by such a gift of divine grace, and true charity should not shrink from enduring anything for him.[4]

This quote clearly expresses three characteristics of Abelard's teaching. First, the central theme of his theology is the love of God. Second, that love is shown most clearly in Jesus Christ. Third, the redemption of humankind through Jesus Christ is to be found more in what humankind does in response to God's act than in what God does for humankind.

As general statements, the first two characteristics of Abelard's theology are difficult to quarrel with. They simply seem to express the teaching of John 3:16: "For God so loved the world that he gave his one and only Son." However, as the details of the general position are developed, there may indeed be difficulties. In what way is Christ an expression of God's love for us? If Abelard rejects the ransom and satisfaction theories, then how can we give substance to the love of God?

Abelard develops his understanding of the love of God in Christ in the third characteristic of his theology. In Christ, God shows us God's love for humankind. That demonstration of God's love generates in humans a love that involves turning from sin and from fear. In other words, as an example of God's love, Christ's life and death teach us how we should live and motivate us to live as we have been taught. Again, this emphasis in Abelard seems to develop many of the themes we discovered in the biblical basis of the image of example.

So in relation to the biblical emphases that we are looking for in any development of this image of example, we may note that Abelard keeps together the activities of God and humankind. Moreover, God's activity has clear priority: Jesus is "this unique act of grace." Nevertheless, at this point Abelard is less than clear about God's activity in generating our response of love. Rather than a conjoining of God and humankind in our response of love, there seems to be a gap between the two. God's activity is confined to "setting up" a demonstration of love that we are to imitate. The change that this demonstration generates in humankind seems to have no organic connection to God's activity.

In relation to the third biblical emphasis, the integration of Christ as example with the story of the kingdom, we may question Abelard's position, not so much concerning what he says as concerning what he does not say. If Abelard rejects the images of victor and sacrifice and the notions of sin that go with them, then why did Jesus have to die to show God's love? Abelard does speak of Christ's death as "for our sins," but he leaves that notion undeveloped. We are left with no guidance as to what sin is or how the human predicament involves sin. We just know that sin is something that did awful things to someone who loves us. Therefore, we do not want to sin. But by leaving undeveloped the notion of sin and neglecting the story of the kingdom in Christ, Abelard leaves us with a truncated picture of the human predicament and of sin.

Nevertheless, Abelard's focus on the love of God yields some important criticisms of other developments that we have earlier taken into account. And his development of the image of example highlights a biblical emphasis that other theologians have often ignored. While we will never arrive at perfection, we must continue the development of the image of Christ as example, even as Abelard did, in order to be faithful to Scripture.[5]

In a way very different from Abelard, the image of Christ as example was developed in the nineteenth century by a theologian named Friedrich Schleiermacher. Schleiermacher is often regarded as the father of liberal theology. Such labels are not entirely helpful—how is Schleiermacher a liberal? Is being a liberal bad? The label does not answer these kinds of questions. After I have exposited Schleiermacher's position, we will consider its strengths and weaknesses. At that time we will also consider whether it is appropriate to place Abelard and Schleiermacher together, as is often done.

Schleiermacher based his interpretation of the atonement on the central concept in his theology, "God-consciousness." The concept of God-consciousness was developed by Schleiermacher in response to criticisms of

Christian beliefs. Schleiermacher lived at a time when Christianity was increasingly rejected by those who were under the influence of the rise of modern science. According to this mind-set, science was showing that religious belief was based in superstition and claims that could not be verified by science. Schleiermacher addressed this rejection of religion in his first book, *On Religion: Speeches to Its Cultured Despisers*.[6] In this book, he sought to interpret religion as being concerned with one's inner disposition toward life. Faith is about an inner attitude, a deep awareness of "the quiet uniform course of the Whole."[7] According to this understanding, religion is removed from the realm of science and history to this inner state. Later, Schleiermacher develops his position further, arguing that the inner disposition that marks the religious person, especially the Christian, is an inner disposition of "God-consciousness."[8] For Schleiermacher, this God-consciousness is something that marks all humankind to a greater or lesser degree. We can identify and describe this God-consciousness simply by observing and reflecting on humankind's religious activity.

On this account, religion does not compete with science; it complements science and rounds out what it means to be human. Such an approach protects religion from the criticism of science, but at the same time relegates Christian faith to a part of human life, rather than the whole of life.

In the context of Schleiermacher's theology, Christ is seen entirely as an example. Like Abelard, Schleiermacher has no use for other images of Christ. However, unlike Abelard, Schleiermacher ties Christ as example to a notion of God-consciousness: Christ saves us because he is the one human being in history who exemplified perfect, complete God-consciousness.[9] The God-consciousness that Christ exemplified is present in all humankind, but because of sin, we are not perfectly God-conscious. Christ's perfect God-consciousness becomes ours as we are united with him.

This union with Christ is a "mystical" union. By "mystical" Schleiermacher means to avoid two approaches that he views as erroneous. First, he wants to indicate that the relationship between Christ and a Christian is more than a relationship between a teacher and pupil. The latter relationship is purely external, while the relationship between Christ and a Christian is much closer. Second, Schleiermacher wants to avoid the opposite extreme: the view that salvation is a transaction between Christ and God that is then applied to the believer without the believer playing any role. Here, the salvation of humankind is a magical act: Like the magician waving his wand and changing the bunny into a pigeon, God waves Christ over humankind and we are transformed from sinners to saints. In contrast to these views, Schleiermacher seeks a middle way, emphasizing the close relationship between Christ and the believer without turning it into magic.

This last emphasis in Schleiermacher is a particularly helpful reminder of the strength and danger of the image of Christ as example. The strength of the image is its avoidance of any magical view of salvation. This results from the importance placed on Christ as an example for humans to follow. The danger of the image of example is that the relationship between Christ and the believer may be seen as a purely external relationship: Christ points the way, demonstrates the life; humankind is left on our own to follow the way, live the life. Schleiermacher's description of the Christ-Christian relationship helps us to see clearly this strength and weakness.

On other points, Schleiermacher falls far short of the biblical teaching as he develops the image of Christ as example. Many of Schleiermacher's errors derive from the way he develops the notion of God-consciousness. Schleiermacher develops the notion apart from Christianity, then he trims Christian belief to fit his notion of God-consciousness. Therefore, his theology can seem very biblical, using the familiar language of the kingdom of God, the forgiveness of sin, the divine nature of Jesus Christ. However, all this language is reinterpreted so that it fits Schleiermacher's prior notion of God-consciousness.

Thus, for Schleiermacher the kingdom of God is not identified by Jesus' teaching, life, and work; it is identified by the extent to which Jesus conforms to Schleiermacher's conception of God-consciousness. There might be a way to say that Jesus is supremely "God-conscious," but it would have to be a way in which Jesus defines what God-consciousness is. In Schleiermacher's approach, rather than defining the notion, Jesus is defined by it. The kingdom of God, then, is not established and revealed by Jesus; it is established and revealed by religion and exemplified by Jesus Christ.

At this point, we can identify Schleiermacher's great error: He did not see the example of Christ as the example of God and God's loving activity in the world. For Scripture, Jesus Christ is first an example of God's love active in the world to redeem humankind. On the basis of this prior love of God, we can then say that Christ as fully human is also an example of how we are to live. For Schleiermacher, Christ is the example of human God-consciousness; the "divine nature" of Christ is merely his achievement of this perfect God-consciousness. Thus, for Schleiermacher the story of Jesus Christ is the story of one who is fully human and like a divine being, but not fully divine.

In this examination of Abelard and Schleiermacher on the image of example, we have discovered that any development of the image runs two dangers. First, it is difficult to hold together the full divinity and full humanity of Christ as example. Abelard accomplishes this more faithfully than Schleiermacher, but even his account falls short. The second danger in the image may be seen in the failure of Abelard's account to do full justice to the image of example and in Schleiermacher's great error. This danger is the tendency to disconnect the image of example from the story of the kingdom and simply attach it to principles or concepts that have no organic relationship to the good news of the kingdom come in Jesus Christ.

For instance, if we think of Jesus as an example of triumphing against all odds, we can think of ourselves as following Jesus' example in all sorts of circumstances: beating our archrivals at football, winning the contract, making the sale, getting the grade. We say, "Thank you, Lord, for giving me the victory and helping me to defeat the foe." But the foe in all of these cases may be just as righteous, perhaps more righteous than we. The other team may have more "Christians" than we have. Perhaps our tactics have not been entirely fair, legal, or ethical, but because we won, we see ourselves as exemplifying Christ. Disconnecting the image from the story of Jesus enables us to tell all of these lies about our "example."

The image of Christ as example does not teach us to interpret how we live as the kingdom of God. Rather, it teaches us to see the story of the kingdom come in Jesus Christ as the way to live. The image of Christ as example teaches us to read the story of the kingdom as more than just "another story," as more than just an inspiration for our own dreams and ambitions, as more than the embodiment of human motivation, as more than the impact made by a committed individual. The image of Christ as example teaches us to read the story of the kingdom come in Jesus Christ as the story of God's activity in the world in which humans participate by following Christ, by being "in him."

Systematic Reflection

When seen as example, Christ teaches us many things about God, humankind, sin, and salvation. As we take each of these topics and explore what the image of Christ as example teaches us, we will see the image gradually develop. That is, not everything that must be said about Christ as example can be said all at once. Nevertheless, by the time this account is complete, I hope to have presented Christ as example in a way that is faithful to the gospel. To the extent that my account is faithful, it will also enable us to see the kingdom of God more clearly and participate in it more fully.

God as Teacher, Enabler, and Lover

If Christ is fully divine, then according to the image of example, Christ shows us God and God's activity in the world. Although we must later supplement this description, we may begin by seeing God as *teacher*. Certainly, Jesus spent a major part of his ministry teaching. He was called "Rabbi," the common term for a teacher of religion. In his training of the Twelve, Jesus displayed himself as teacher.[10]

When we see Jesus as the example of God as teacher, we also discover a response to those who say that Jesus' teaching was confined to a particular place and time: His agrarian, peasant teaching and his itinerant lifestyle make the specifics of his teaching irrelevant today; at most we may discern a few principles to apply or discover a basic attitude toward life to adopt. But if Jesus is God as teacher, then his teaching must have a more permanent claim on us. And it does, as his teaching in word and deed reveals and establishes the kingdom of God.

Jesus did not come to teach calculus, nuclear physics, music composition, or literary criticism. In so far as he came to teach, he came to teach the kingdom of God. Since he teaches that the kingdom of God is an everlastingly actual reality, his teaching remains for eternity. Since he teaches that the kingdom of God perfects all creation and all human aspiration, his teaching also encompasses physics, composition, and criticism.

However, "teacher" does not exhaust Jesus' exemplification of God. In Christ as example, we also see God as *enabler.* In Christ, God did not remain apart from humankind, shouting instructions to us as we try desperately to follow his teaching. By becoming human in Christ, God enables humankind to follow God's teaching. God in Christ does not merely reveal and establish the kingdom of God, God also incorporates humankind into the kingdom.

Here we may think encouragingly about God's righteousness. If we restrict thought about God's righteousness to the other images of Christ, we might end up seeing righteousness as God's unattainable ideal that keeps humans in our place and allows God to control humankind and maintain God's privilege. If we think of God's righteousness in the context of God as enabler, then righteousness becomes God's promise of how we can and will live. Here, too, God's judgment becomes that which enables us to see our sin and be free of it. Of course, if we do not see Christ as example, then God's righteousness and judgment are our condemnation.

Finally, Christ's example teaches us that God is our *lover.* Of course, this is very strong language, which we often reserve for those whose relationship involves sexual intercourse. Properly understood, however, the language is entirely appropriate for describing God. As the example of God, Christ does not merely show us God's love, he shows us God as our lover. In Christ, God is closer to us than we are to ourselves. The intimacy that God the Holy Spirit then establishes with us is greater than any other we can know. Thus, when Paul writes about the horror of a Christian uniting with a prostitute, he can talk about the intimacy of the Spirit: "Do you not know that your body is a temple of the Holy Spirit?" (1 Cor. 6:19).

As the example of God, then, Jesus Christ shows us God as teacher, enabler, and lover. Together, these three pictures of God portray God with us, for us, and in us. God does not redeem humankind at arm's length or through an intermediary. In Christ, God becomes human and comes to us with understanding to teach us, with presence to enable us, and with intimacy to love us.

Humanity as Ignorant, Feeble, and Alienated

If Christ exemplifies God as teacher, enabler, and lover, then we can see humankind outside of Christ in three corresponding ways. If Christ is God as teacher, then we must confess that humankind is *ignorant*. We must acknowledge that in our sin we have not only refused to do the truth, we do not even know what the truth is. In particular, the story of Christ teaches us that we are ignorant about the very nature of reality until we learn the kingdom of God come in Jesus Christ.

This conviction has been deeply offensive to modern Western civilization. Most of us have been shaped to believe that humankind knows what we need to know and that we simply need the time, energy, and technology to actualize that which we know. If we are ignorant, it is an ignorance that time and human effort can dispel. To claim with Christ that humankind is ignorant at the most fundamental level and can only know the truth through God's activity in Christ is to challenge the conviction that has shaped the past three hundred years of Western culture. For disciples of Jesus Christ, we do not measure the gospel by what we know elsewhere; rather, we measure what we know elsewhere by the truth of the gospel. Of course, this is no neat formula to be quickly applied, but it is a reversal of the way our culture has taught us to think. If Christ is example, then he is where our thinking must begin.[11]

Christ's example compounds the offense: If God is enabler, then humankind is *feeble*. Again, the culture that has shaped us views the human will and power as Promethean. In Greek mythology, Prometheus is the Titan who stole fire from the gods and gave it to humankind, thus making humankind independent of the gods. In our own culture, the Promethean viewpoint believes that humankind is its own and can solve its own problems. In the face of horrendous wars, technological disasters, and human evil, we have clung to the belief that our knowledge and technological abilities can save us from the tragedies that our knowledge and technology have caused or made possible.[12]

In Christ, the kingdom reveals that humankind is not only ignorant of the truth but that when we are shown the truth we are also unable to do it apart from God's enabling. As Paul says, we are unable to please God because of the weakness of our sinful nature (Rom. 8:3).

Finally, if Christ comes to exemplify God as our lover, then humankind apart from Christ must be seen as *alienated* from our lover. Interestingly, alienation is one of the powerful themes in our culture. Unfortunately, the source of alienation is seldom traced to its root; the portrayal of alienation is never "radical" enough. For some existentialists, the source of human alienation is alienation from self. So I am always trying to find myself, discover my true self, accept myself. For some Marxists, alienation is alienation from the means of producing capital. So I am constantly seeking to establish my economic control by purchasing goods, by organizing against management, by becoming a part of the establishment.

None of these analyses of alienation acknowledges what Jesus Christ reveals to us: The human predicament is alienation from the God who is our lover. At this point, the alienation is entirely on our side of the relationship. God has always been our lover. In Jesus Christ, God reveals the depth and intimacy of that love. The root of all our alienation can be traced to this alienation from God.

In Christ as example, humankind is revealed as ignorant, feeble, and alienated. This predicament is not one that can be ameliorated by some teaching, mild exercise, and a little therapy. In the story of the kingdom in Christ, we see the example of what is necessary to redeem the human predicament. Although the image of example has often been seen as the source of a more positive picture of humankind, a faithful exposition of it reveals that outside of Christ there is no more hope for humankind in this image than there is in the images of victory and sacrifice.

Sin as Ignorance, Weakness, and Separation

In describing the human predicament under the image of Christ as example, we have already anticipated much of our discussion of sin. In this section, we will seek to develop further the previous discussion of the human predicament.

If we pursue our understanding of humankind as ignorant, then we can see that sin is a kind of *ignorance*. However, as we develop this notion of sin as ignorance, we must do so in connection with the story of the kingdom. In that regard, we can see that sin is a particular kind of ignorance. In our culture, ignorance has taken on the connotation of being ignorant of facts and information. As we move into a culture in which "knowledge is power," we must be careful to say what we mean by "sin is ignorance." Do we agree that society is moving toward salvation by regarding knowledge as power?

When we see sin as ignorance in relation to the story of the kingdom, we see that the ignorance of sin cannot simply be equated with knowledge as facts and information. In the story of the kingdom, ignorance does not have to do with simple intelligence or education or control of information. Ignorance means not knowing how to live in this world as God's kingdom. The ignorance of sin is not redeemed by facts but by wisdom. In his ministry, Jesus clearly regarded the poor and marginalized as closer to the kingdom, closer to losing their ignorance, than the educated, powerful establishment. This is true because the establishment was captive to the lie that they were not ignorant and so could not easily hear Christ's exemplification of God as teacher and sin as ignorance. One can have as much difficulty entering the kingdom due to perceived intellectual riches as due to perceived economic wealth.

Under the image of Christ as example, sin may also be seen as *weakness*. There will be moments in our lives when we understand sin better if we view it not as a prison (Christ as victor) or as rebellion (Christ as sacrifice) but as weakness. In particular, some who have been nurtured in Christian homes may have difficulty seeing any need for Christ's act on their behalf if they do not see captivity or rebellion in their lives. The place to begin then is with the recognition that only Christ can incorporate us into the life of the kingdom so that we can please God. In this instance, although sin as weakness may be the place to start, it is not the place to end. For all of us, sin must be seen to some degree under all three images.

Finally, sin is *separation* from God. Although this image may seem rather mild at first, further thought teaches us its power. If God is the source of all goodness, all life, all love, then separation from God is to dwell in the kingdom of evil, death, and hate. Separation from God is hell. In a way, then, we may sharpen the image by saying that apart from the active presence of God's kingdom in our world, we are already living in hell.

Salvation as Knowledge, Power, and Love

The good news of the kingdom has once again been anticipated in our reflections. In the kingdom of God come in Jesus Christ, God transforms our ignorance, our weakness, and our alienation.

In place of our ignorance, God grants us *knowledge*. To be saved is to know Christ and all his benefits. This knowledge is not the work of Christ alone but also of the Holy Spirit, who guides us into all truth (John 14–16 passim). If we take this passage as a cue, we may say that salvation is not only knowledge, it is *truth*. Here we get closer to our desire to show that salvation is not facts or information. Truth is not "mere" knowledge. It is a way of life—it is *wisdom*.[13]

Truth is for living and it is known in a way of living. In other words, salvation is not simply gaining some knowledge or understanding some ideas. Nor is it getting the knowledge and then deciding whether to live by it. Rather, salvation is knowing Christ as we live like him and in him. That is, we do not know Christ apart from our life in Christ. The knowledge that is salvation is the knowledge of the kingdom of God. That knowledge is available only in Christ. He is the wisdom of God for our salvation; as we know him, we enter into wisdom.

To say that the knowledge of the kingdom is available only in Christ leads us to the truth that through Christ as example, we also see salvation as *power*.

If humankind apart from Christ is feeble, then Christ's gift to us is power. However, this power is not the power to accomplish whatever we have dreamed of; it is not power at large, ready for any task. Rather, salvation as power is the ability to live in the kingdom of God.

The story of the kingdom in Christ shows us what this power enables in us: It enables us to follow the example of Christ. The life that Christ lived is not some dreamed-of ideal; it is not the divine life beyond the reach of humankind; it is not an out-of-date Galilean peasant life. The life that Christ exemplified and empowers us for is life in the kingdom. Since that kingdom is an everlastingly actual reality, and since the ruler of that kingdom empowers us, we are called to live in that kingdom today. Since the kingdom is truth and life and peace, that call is good news for us today. There is no waiting list; we can enter the kingdom now.

As we enter that kingdom, we enter into a salvation that is also the way of *love*. Love is a terribly debased term today, almost beyond rescue as a description of the good news of the kingdom come in Jesus Christ. However, the New Testament is full of the language of love, particularly as Christ exemplifies God's love and enables that same love in us. Therefore, we must work to recover an understanding and practice of love.[14]

The best way to begin to recover love is to reflect once again on the story of the kingdom as the image of love. The characteristics of the kingdom, Christ's enactment of the kingdom, his death and resurrection are the story of the kingdom of love. In this kingdom, love is the continual acting of God. This love originates in God, in the life that God shares as Father, Son, and Holy Spirit. So to enter the kingdom of God is to enter into the life of God, eternal life, which is love. As we enter into that life, we lose our imperfect, sinful selves and this evil world, only to find our perfect, righteous selves and a new creation. Love does not judge in order to destroy; love judges in order to redeem. The perfection of humankind and creation in this kingdom of love marks out its value. Love is good when it is not promise or ideal or manipulation but act. The kingdom of God is God's act of love for humankind. Such love in this world is not only good, it is costly. We see what love cost God: "He gave his one and only Son." If the kingdom of love cost God the life of his Son, then the kingdom will cost humankind no less. Finally, we can see in this kingdom the openness of love. In Christ, God's love is prodigal, lavish, indiscriminate. But it is prodigal, lavish, and indiscriminate not in overlooking sin but in overcoming sin. This is a tough love that recognizes sin for what it is but refuses to turn away from any sinner. The rule of love's openness is this: "Where sin increased, grace increased all the more, so that, just as sin reigned in death, so also grace might reign through righteousness to bring eternal life through Jesus Christ our Lord" (Rom. 5:20–21). Love is not overcome by evil; evil is overcome by the love of God. Salvation is living in the way of love.

Conclusion

In Christ as example, God our teacher, enabler, and lover dispels our ignorance, strengthens our weakness, and heals our alienation so that we might live in the truth, power, and love of the kingdom of God, which has come in Jesus Christ.

The great strength of the image of Christ as example is the closeness it establishes between God and humankind. Late in his career, Karl Barth began to speak of the humanity of God.[15] That is what we have focused for us in Christ as example: the humanity of God. In Christ, we do not have an alien creature whose way of life we would be foolish to follow. Rather, in Christ, we have one who is fully human in his way of life. He does not call us to quit eating or to leap off tall buildings. He calls us to live in the kingdom of God. And his call is accompanied by the presence of his full divinity, which teaches, enables, and loves us into the life of the kingdom.

The great danger of Christ as example is that disconnected from the story of the gospel and from the conviction that the story is about one who is fully human, fully divine, the image may be distorted into the claim that the kingdom is within the grasp of human achievement. In our desire to downplay our victimization and powerlessness, our rebellion and alienation, we may discard the other images of Christ for the image of example alone. When this is done, we tell ourselves that our situation is not so desperate, we do not need outside help, we just have to overcome our ignorance and be stronger. But if we ignore our captivity and rebellion, then our attempts to overcome ignorance and weakness merely plunge us deeper into sin.

If we think back to the roles of Christ in the kingdom, then the natural connection for Christ as example is to the role of prophet. The prophet is the one who identified with the people and taught them God's truth. In Christ as example, God identifies with humankind and teaches us truth. As example, Christ the prophet goes beyond any other prophet. His words come to us not merely as words that tell us truth about our situation; they come to us as words that change our situation. Christ the prophet does not merely proclaim the kingdom of God, he establishes the kingdom of God through his own person. As prophet, Christ does not point us to the kingdom of God, which is separate from his own life. Rather, he calls us to the kingdom of God, which he embodies. When Christ the prophet points to the kingdom of God, he points to himself. Therefore, to follow Christ as example is to be incorporated into Christ. In Christ we are able to live according to the words of Christ the prophet.

CONCLUSION

In the previous three chapters, we looked *at* three images of Christ from the New Testament and Christian history. We also looked *with* these images at our world in order to understand the reality of the good news of God's love in Jesus Christ. These images are not inventions of human fantasy or projections of our unfulfilled wishes. These images of Christ are the work of the Holy Spirit guiding humanity into an understanding of the story of the gospel.

As the Spirit has guided, human insight and creativity have been redeemed and put in service of the gospel. We cannot say how the Spirit redeems and guides humanity any more than we can say how Jesus is fully human, fully divine. But we can and must say that the Spirit is at work in these images. This work of the Spirit finds expression in the Bible and in the community of faith as we gather around the Bible to hear God's Word today.

However, since images are flexible and susceptible to distortion and misinterpretation, we need some ways to judge whether images of Christ are being faithfully interpreted in our words and lives. Since these images are the continuation of the story of the gospel in the everlasting actuality of the kingdom, we find a criterion for evaluating the truth of an image in its relationship to the gospel of the kingdom.

In the story of Jesus Christ, the kingdom of God as an everlasting actuality is established and revealed.[1] Since the Bible is the original witness to the kingdom that is come in Jesus Christ and since the Spirit guided the community as it told the story and developed the images, our interpretations must not violate biblical teaching. But that does not mean that all we can do is repeat the words of the Bible. Since the kingdom is a present reality, we must find words and images in the present in order to witness to that reality. At the same time, we must also remember that the present reality of the kingdom is a continuation of the story of the gospel in Jesus Christ.

So the first question regarding images of Christ asks whether those images fit the biblical teaching. Throughout the past three chapters, we were concerned with the congruence of image and biblical story. We noted dangers and failures in the development of the images of Christ. In our own development of these images, we sought to learn from past mistakes in order to be faithful to the gospel.

In addition to their congruence with biblical teaching, images may also be evaluated by a second criterion: their revelatory power. By this I mean that images shape the way we look at reality and the way we live in relation to our perception of reality. Therefore, when we contemplate these images of Christ, we must ask ourselves whether they reveal our situation to us. Do we see more clearly who we are? Who we are created to be? Who we are redeemed to be? Do we see God more clearly? Do we see God's work of redemption and creation? Have we learned more profoundly what sin is, and do we see more clearly its presence in our lives? Are we enabled to live in peace with God and our neighbors? These and countless other questions call us to ponder the images of Christ as we participate in the kingdom that is God's love and our salvation.

These two criteria must be located within community. None of us can make the judgments required on our own. We need each other to help us judge our faithfulness to the gospel and the revelatory power of our work. Moreover, this judgment is not merely the judgment of other scholars. Theologians and biblical scholars must not simply talk to one another; judgments about theological work must take place within the whole disciple community. At the present time, we do not have a Christian community that can do this well. Today, many Christian scholars have separated themselves from the church and attached themselves to the academy; they answer only to other scholars in their fields. At the same time, many in the church have decided that most scholarship is irrelevant to the church. This is a dangerous situation that I hope this work and others like it will overcome. In the end, this work needs to take its place within the community of disciples and be judged by that community.

At the same time, this account of God's love for the world in Jesus Christ may also shape and guide the gospel proclamation of the disciple community. In this work, the question is whether those who do not know God's love in Christ are getting the message. Because these images of the work of Christ reveal the human situation, it is imperative that we ask whether the world is getting the message. But as Julian Hartt notes, this question "may quickly and anxiously be supplemented with another: 'Do you *like* the message?' And this with yet another: 'Will you go on loving me even if you don't like my message?'"[2] If we believe that Jesus Christ reveals the truth about the human situation, then in faithfulness to that good news, we must always seek to proclaim it with clarity and truth to our present age. And in the end, we must acknowledge that such clarity and truth are also the work of the Spirit, who since Pentecost has empowered the witness of the church.[3]

In the church today, one of the most radical challenges to these images of Christ has come from some feminist theologians. This challenge is directed not merely at the images or some accounts of them but at the very idea of atonement itself. Not all feminist theologians agree with those who have voiced these criticisms, but the criticisms are serious enough that we must give some attention to them. If the criticisms are valid, then these last three chapters rest on a faulty foundation and simply need to be expunged from any responsible work of theology.

According to Joanne Carlson Brown, one critic of traditional Christian doctrine:

> Christianity is an abusive theology that glorifies suffering. If Christianity is to be liberating for the oppressed, it must itself be liberated from this theology. We must do away with the atonement, this idea of a blood sin upon the whole human race which can be washed away only by the blood of the lamb. This blood-thirsty God is the God of patriarchy who at the moment controls the whole Christian tradition. We do not need to be saved by Jesus' death from some original sin. We need to be liberated from this abusive patriarchy.[4]

The author goes on to assert a commitment to justice and liberation and a rejection of many Christian doctrines. Her argument is so sweeping in its assertions and rejections that we may be tempted to ignore it, but we must not do so. Our ability to respond to such critiques is in part a measure of our understanding. In the end, Brown's argument leads to the removal of the heart of the gospel and indeed to the replacement of the good news of Jesus Christ with another message. Our ability to show this on the basis of my foregoing account is essential to its truth and power.

Brown is right to say that our doctrine of the atonement has sometimes led us to glorify suffering. But as I have argued in the previous chapters, we need to be circumspect in our application of the images of Christ to instances of suffering. At times we need to seek Christ as victor and God as our warrior, conquering the evil and injustice around us. At other times, we need to recognize the root of evil and injustice in our own hearts and the hearts of others, drawing on Christ as sacrifice to find healing for our own sin. When Brown throws out the atonement, she leaves the human race with no adequate response to suffering and injustice.

Brown also asserts that "Jesus was not an acceptable sacrifice for the sins of the whole world, because God demands not sacrifice but justice. No one was saved by the death of Jesus."[5] In response to this, we may simply ask how God is to establish justice if there is no forgiveness of sins. In other words, where does God put the sins of injustice when God establishes justice? The Christian answer is that God in Christ takes the sins of the world upon himself in order to be just in forgiving sinners. By dispensing with the atonement, Brown has no persuasive account of God's justice.

Brown may see no need for such an account because she seems to deny that we are all sinners. In her rejection of "original sin" and her separation of the human race into oppressors and oppressed, she implies (but does not directly assert) that the good news of Jesus Christ is not for all (since we are not all sinners) but only for some (the oppressed). The only work needed in this world is the liberation of the oppressed and the destruction of their oppressors. Thus, only some of the human race are sinners—the oppressors—and what they receive from God is not freedom, forgiveness, and transformation but destruction. Others of the human race—the oppressed—are the victims of sin and receive from God justice and liberation. Here Brown has severed her accounts of liberation and justice from the story of the kingdom in Jesus Christ and the images of the New Testament. She uses some of the words but removes them from the power of the everlasting actuality of the kingdom of God.

Brown is right to point out the abusive uses of the atonement in the church, but she is wrong to think that we can correct those abuses by jettisoning the doctrine of the atonement. As she asserts, her view means that "suffering cannot be redeemed."[6] In the end, her view leaves us hopeless and powerless in the midst of the undeniable suffering of our world. In the work of Jesus Christ and a wise understanding of the images of his work, his disciples offer our suffering world the one source of victory, change, and hope.

Jesus Christ is victor, sacrifice, and example, and as such, he has established and revealed the everlasting actuality of God's love for the world. As the gift of God's love for the world, Jesus Christ redeems humankind from sin and death, bringing humankind into the kingdom of righteousness, peace, and joy. Through the Holy Spirit, Christ's work continues today as a present reality. By the power of the Spirit, his disciples participate in and bear witness to the kingdom established by Christ's victory, sacrifice, and example. The message with which we are entrusted is that Jesus Christ came not to condemn the world but to save it. Thus, the reality of God's love for the world is not exhausted by the story and images of the kingdom established and revealed by Jesus Christ. That reality continues in the world today through the practices that are the presence of Christ.[7]

PRACTICES

PART THREE

INTRODUCTION

Christology does not typically include the category of "practices." Christology is about doctrine—what we believe, what we assent to. Christology may have implications for our lives, but the identification of those implications is the work of ethicists or writers of devotional works on the Christian life. However, I am one of a number of contemporary theologians who believe that theology is a "church practice" and that doctrines are also practices.[1] In the following chapters, therefore, I develop an account of the practices of Christology.[2]

My commitment to the practices of Christology is rooted in the conviction that Jesus Christ is alive and present today. This conviction is rooted, in turn, in the belief that Jesus Christ is risen from the dead. This belief is not an opinion, a fantasy, or a hope; rather, it is sure knowledge that comes by faith.[3] Since Jesus is risen, there is a "Christology" that continues the story and the images of the New Testament today.

This Christology of the resurrected one is not a new Christology; it is not the story of a Christ different from the one we have been considering. The risen Christ is the one who proclaimed the kingdom, fulfilled the messianic roles, and is fully human, fully divine. He is the one who was and is victor, sacrifice, and example. At the same time, with his resurrection comes a new part of the story.

The resurrection is seldom presented in this way. Typically, in conservative Christianity, the resurrection is a focus of historical and philosophical argument intended to establish the credibility of the resurrection. These arguments have an important place in the development of belief in Christ for many people. But we seldom go beyond establishing that the resurrection occurred to consider its significance for Christian doctrine.[4]

When we do consider the significance of the resurrection for Christology, we are led to the continuation of the story of Jesus Christ through the work of the Holy Sprit. To solidify this continuity, we need to observe several aspects of the New Testament story. We must consider the promise of the Holy Spirit that Jesus announces in John 14–16. There he clearly describes the continuity between his mission and the work of the Spirit. In John 14:15–19, Jesus connects the coming of the Spirit with his continued presence with the disciples and with his resurrection. In John 14:25–26, he connects the Spirit with his own teaching and with the disciples' progress in the truth. In John 15:26 and 16:7–15, Jesus promises that the Spirit will testify to him and bring him glory. We may also remember that the Book of Acts is the second of a two-volume work by Luke. The theme of the two volumes is the history of Jesus Christ—so much so that several commentators have suggested that the Book of Acts should be properly titled, "The Book of the Acts of the Risen Lord through the Apostles by the Power of the Holy Spirit."

We are right, then, to think of the practices of Christology as a continuation of the story of the risen Jesus Christ through the presence and power of the Holy Spirit. But we would be wrong to think that this story only begins with the resurrection or the day of Pentecost. Rather, we must recognize that the gospel itself may be told as the story of the Holy Spirit.[5] We must take care here, for, as I have already noted, in John 14–16, the Spirit teaches the truth of Jesus Christ and directs all glory to him. Moreover, Luke's two-part story is the story of Jesus Christ, and it is Jesus Christ whom we are to proclaim. So the story of the Spirit is not to replace the story of Jesus Christ.

At the same time, if our faith is trinitarian, then all of the story must be told of the Father, Son, and Spirit. If we direct our attention to the Spirit, then we discover that Jesus is conceived by the Holy Spirit, led by the Spirit, empowered by the Spirit, and raised by the Spirit. And we discover that our life in Christ is also "conceived" (or born) by the Spirit, led by the Spirit, empowered by the Spirit, and "if the Spirit of him who raised Jesus from the dead is living in you, he who raised Christ from the dead will also give life to your mortal bodies through his Spirit, who lives in you" (Rom. 8:11).

Therefore, as we explore the practices of Christology in the following chapters, we are simply continuing the story and the vision that I developed in the previous chapters. Indeed, as I develop an account of these practices, I will regularly draw on the previous chapters. At times, these connections may seem overly schematic to you; I include them to show that we have already been engaged in reflection on the practices of Christology and to show that how we live is integral to the gospel we believe and to which we are called as witnesses and servants.

SEVEN

THE KINGDOM

When the church proclaims the gospel today, we usually proclaim Jesus Christ as the good news. That is right and good for us to do. Indeed, the earlier chapters of this book were concerned with the good news of God's love for the world in Jesus Christ. But often lost in the preaching of the church is the message that Jesus himself proclaimed—the message of the kingdom of God. In this chapter, I seek to recover not merely what Jesus proclaimed about the kingdom—as I did in chapter 1—but what that proclamation means for our practices of the kingdom today.

There are several reasons for the church's neglect of the good news of the kingdom. One reason is that the kingdom seems to be important in the Gospels but not in the other books of the New Testament. This has led some to conclude that the preaching of the church should proclaim Jesus rather than the kingdom of God. But this conclusion rests on two faulty distinctions. One error separates Jesus from the kingdom of God. The kingdom of God is not something that Jesus merely proclaimed; it is also something he enacted and embodied. So to proclaim Jesus is to proclaim the kingdom. The second error separates the Gospels and the church's proclamation. The Gospels are the church's proclamation. What we have in the letters of the apostles are not the proclamation of the early church but letters that follow up that proclamation. Certainly, the letters give us some indications of the preaching of the church. But the preaching of the church is to be found primarily in the Gospels, where the kingdom of God is central.

The absence of the kingdom in the church's proclamation also results from two faulty theological conclusions about the kingdom today. In some theological traditions, the kingdom is simply absorbed into the world. In these traditions, the presence of the kingdom is given its identity and shape by the world. The kingdom is thus cut off from the biblical narrative and simply becomes part of the world's narrative. In other theological traditions, the kingdom is an entirely future event or state for which we wait in hope. We may look forward to the kingdom that will be established when Christ returns, but in the meantime, the kingdom is absent.

Over against this, my account seeks signs of the kingdom already present but not yet fully present today. If we come to the biblical teaching without the above preconceptions, we discover that Scripture does indeed identify the kingdom present among us today. As I noted in chapter 1, the kingdom that Jesus proclaimed is an everlasting actuality. Therefore, it is present today in the continuing activity of God, which matches Jesus' own proclamation of the kingdom. As we will see in later chapters, God is also active in specific ways in the church and the world. What we seek to understand here is the present activity of the kingdom of God.

Although Paul's letters contain few specific mentions of the kingdom, Luke's account of his ministry in the Book of Acts demonstrates that the kingdom is not absent from Paul's thinking. In his account of Paul's ministry in Ephesus, Luke tells us that "Paul entered the synagogue and spoke boldly there for three months, arguing persuasively about the kingdom of God" (Acts 19:8). And as he concludes his narrative, Luke tells us that "boldly and without hindrance [Paul] preached the kingdom of God and taught about the Lord Jesus Christ" (Acts 28:31). Clearly, then, the kingdom of God was central to Paul's preaching.

If we look to one of Paul's letters, we will find the structure for my account of the practices of the kingdom of God. In Paul's letter to the Romans, he reminds them that "the kingdom of God is not a matter of eating and drinking, but of righteousness, peace and joy in the Holy Spirit" (Rom. 14:17). Here I take Paul's use of "is" to be not merely a definition of something that is yet to come but an identification of something that is already here. This understanding is reinforced by the connection of the kingdom to the Holy Spirit. Since the Holy Spirit has come, the kingdom is present in righteousness, joy, and peace.

But this righteousness, joy, and peace is not just any righteousness, joy, and peace. It is the kingdom form of those characteristics; it is God's activity of righteousness, joy, and peace. To learn the kingdom forms of those activities, we need to turn to the New Testament, specifically to Paul's writings. We will learn what righteousness, peace, and joy mean *in the Holy Spirit* by apprenticing ourselves to the apostle Paul. In three of Paul's letters, we find these three themes receiving prominent treatment: righteousness in Galatians, peace in Ephesians, and joy in Philippians. Each of these letters is about other things as well, so I am not attempting to summarize the entire teaching of each of these letters. Rather, we seek to learn from Paul what it means to practice kingdom righteousness, peace, and joy in the Holy Spirit.

In order to further guide this account by Scripture, I also connect each of these practices to a characteristic of the kingdom in Jesus' proclamation. Thus, the righteousness of the kingdom will be tied to Jesus' proclamation of the perfection of the kingdom, peace to the openness of the kingdom, and joy to the value of the kingdom. We will see that without stretching a point, Paul's identification of the righteousness, peace, and joy of the kingdom continues the story of the kingdom that Jesus proclaimed.

Of course, that leaves one other characteristic of the kingdom that Jesus proclaimed—its reality. We have already noted the presence and actuality of the kingdom in Paul's use of "is" and in his reference to the Holy Spirit. What I will observe here is that wherever righteousness, peace, and joy in the Holy Spirit are present, the kingdom is a reality. After learning more about these practices of the kingdom, we will return to this claim to see how the reality of the kingdom is present today through the Holy Spirit.

In what follows, I invite you to become a "naturalist of the kingdom of God." Have you ever been for a walk with a naturalist—someone who knows the plants and animals of a particular area? I well remember my first summer at Boy Scout camp. Six times in the first two days I walked through a field on my way to the dining room. The third day I walked with my scoutmaster, and as we walked he pointed out to me plants that I had not seen before. Oh, I had seen them, but I had not known what I was looking at. Or have you ever been out in the woods with an expert on birds—someone who could identify birds by their calls? I hear bird calls all the time, but I have no idea which species of bird I am hearing. It takes someone with eyes to see and ears to hear what is around us all the time.

The kingdom of God is present today in the power of the risen Lord through the Holy Spirit. As we study the righteousness, peace, and joy of the kingdom, the Holy Spirit invites us to develop eyes that see and ears that hear so that we may become "naturalists of the kingdom."

Before we consider the practices of righteousness, peace, and joy, I must make two general comments. First, it is important to clarify the use of "practices" in relation to the kingdom. Because the kingdom is God's activity, the practices in which we engage are first of all God's action in us. By that action we are made participants in the kingdom and engage in its practices. Therefore, the practices are not our way of bringing the kingdom but our way of embodying the kingdom that God enacts by the power of the Holy Spirit. Second, my account of these practices is not the only account that could be given. Nor are the connections that I make between these practices and Jesus' proclamation of the kingdom the only connections that may be made. My account here is not an exhaustive account of kingdom practices; it is illustrative of the kind of thinking and living that we are called to as disciples of the Risen One.

Righteousness: The Perfection of the Kingdom

Righteousness is an important theme in Paul's writings,[1] most evident in his letter to the Romans. Here, however, we will explore his shorter letter to the Galatians, which contains many of the same arguments and themes as Romans. One of the obvious concerns of Galatians is the freedom that we have in Christ. But foundational to Paul's talk about freedom is an ultimate concern for the righteousness of the kingdom. What is righteousness? What is the righteousness of the kingdom? It is absolutely crucial to recognize that righteousness isn't simply one aspect or characteristic of a person's life. Righteousness is not something we add to a personality. Kingdom righteousness isn't some peculiar kind of piety that we may live or exhibit; rather, that righteousness is the very life of the kingdom. That righteousness is the very way we live in Jesus Christ. Righteousness is the whole of life. It's not just a particular way of living; it is life. We cannot choose to live righteously or unrighteously. We either live or we die. If we live, then we live righteously.

To live righteously is to live the way God intended us to live. "Righteousness" may sometimes have negative connotations. It may connote judgmentalism or superiority. But if we understand it properly, it is a wonderful, life-giving word. In order to begin to rehabilitate the practice of righteousness, I will consider an ordinary illustration.

In many of our churches today, we sing with overhead transparencies. If that is not part of your experience, then imagine a classroom in which the professor projects an outline of her lecture on an overhead transparency. Now imagine that the transparency has been placed crookedly on the projector. A part of the song or the lecture outline is not visible. You find yourself tilting your head to line up the transparency. The worship leader or lecturer does not notice the crookedness. You try to worship or pay attention, but your distress increases. Finally, someone notices and straightens out the transparency. You breathe a sigh of relief; now things are the way they should be.

Righteousness is the cosmic and life-giving process of lining up the world the way it should be. Whenever we confront the reality that something is wrong with this world, that life in this age is not the way it is supposed to be, we are discovering a longing for the righteousness of the kingdom. In Jesus' proclamation, this is the perfection of the kingdom. The perfection of creation lines up the world the way God intended it to be. The perfection of human longings directs our desires and affections toward their God-intended goal. Far from being dull and dead, righteous living is—simply—life.

In Galatians, Paul describes this righteousness by alluding to three stories. He does not tell these stories in full because he has already preached them to the Galatians. His purpose in this letter is simply to remind them of these stories and call them to the righteousness identified in these stories.

Each of these stories finds its center in Jesus Christ. Thus, the practice of the righteousness of the kingdom is christological.

The first story is God's action to free humanity from living under the law. Paul says this over and over again. "Did you receive the Spirit by observing the law, or by believing what you heard?" (Gal. 3:2). And again, "Christ redeemed us from the curse of the law by becoming a curse for us" (Gal. 3:13). The first story of the gospel is the story of God's desire to free us from the curse of the law. The curse of the law is simply death. Does that make the law bad? Paul goes on to say in effect, "No, the law is good" (see 3:21).[2] The law identifies righteousness. The law identifies the way we are meant to live.

Why then is the law a curse? Perhaps the best way to understand how the law becomes a curse for us is through a medical analogy. Someone you know may be allergic to a particular food—perhaps corn or peanuts or fish. The person who is allergic to that food may become very ill, may even be threatened with death if he or she happens inadvertently to eat that food. Does that mean the food is bad? No. It means there is something wrong, something missing in the person that makes that particular food dangerous to him. The story of the law is that the law describes God's way of life, describes righteousness, identifies righteousness for us, but we who are sinners cannot live by the law. Thus, the law also identifies the curse under which we live in sin and the death that is not life.

The story of the gospel is the story of God's activity to bring us out from under the burden and the curse of the law. That activity, that freedom, is established in Jesus Christ. It is vital for us to note that by setting aside the law, God does not set aside righteousness. We may sometimes equate keeping the law with righteousness and conclude that when God freed us from the law, God freed us from the claims of righteousness. But Paul's argument here is that what the law could not do, God has done for us in Jesus Christ (Rom. 8:1–3). What Paul describes here is the means by which God makes us righteous—not by the law but by faith in Jesus Christ.

The second story of kingdom righteousness is the story of God's desire to make us members of his family. In the Greek, this is the story of our being adopted as sons. Paul here is not contrasting sons to daughters. He has already (in Gal. 3:28) erased all the social distinctions (Jew and Greek, slave and free, male and female); the story of becoming adopted as God's "sons" is the story of everyone who is in Christ. Here "sons" refers to the status of one who has reached the age of maturity and has full rights as a member of God's family. When life is lined up the way God intended, we live as members of God's family. Once again the obstacle that God faces in adopting us as members of the family is our sin. The same thing that places us under the curse of the law also makes us slaves, not "sons," not responsible members of God's family. That sin is carried away by Jesus Christ, so that when we come to faith in him, we are made responsible members of God's family. This is kingdom righteousness.

The third story Paul alludes to in Galatians 3 is God's desire to fulfill the promise to Abraham, that even the Gentiles are to be brought into God's family.[3] In Genesis, God promised Abraham that all the nations of the earth would be blessed through Abraham. That word *nations* is actually the word that is used later on to refer to the Gentiles. The Jews are not the nations of the earth—they are the people of God. Everybody else belongs to "the nations." God's love for the world in Jesus Christ brings the Gentiles into that blessing, into life. Thus, in the kingdom established and revealed by Jesus Christ, the people of God are now made up of all the people of the earth.

The story of the Risen One is that God desires to free us from the curse of the law so that we may be righteous, to bring us into his family so that we may be mature, responsible members, and to incorporate all the nations of the earth into God's people so that all may receive God's blessing. There is a deep appeal in these three stories. They render an account of righteousness—life aligned as God intends it.[4]

We participate in these stories in many different ways. We could gather them all together by repeating Paul's statement that "the kingdom of God is . . . righteousness . . . in the Holy Spirit" (Rom. 14:17). It is the Spirit who accomplishes in us what the law could not—make us righteous; it is the Spirit who bears us into God's family and gifts us for responsibility; it is the Spirit who draws together the nations of the earth by being poured out on young and old, men and women, slave and free, Jew and Gentile.

If we pursue more specifically the practice of the righteousness of the kingdom, Paul leads us to the fruit of the Spirit[5] (Galatians 5). His account of this fruit follows immediately upon his recounting of these three stories of righteousness. He begins by reasserting that in Christ we are free, then immediately warns us, "But do not use your freedom to indulge the sinful nature; rather, serve one another in love" (Gal. 5:13). The connection to the story of the righteousness of the kingdom is evident when Paul then asserts that the law is summed up in the command to love (Gal. 5:14). In freeing us from the curse of the law, God does not set aside righteousness. Rather, in the Spirit, God makes available to us the righteousness that we could not achieve ourselves.

Born by the Spirit into God's family, we are assured of God's acceptance and approval. We are guaranteed inheritance of the kingdom of God and called to live in that kingdom now as we bear the fruit of the Spirit. Assured of God's acceptance and approval, we need no longer build walls between ourselves and our neighbors. We no longer have to protect ourselves and our puny attempts to achieve righteousness. God's righteousness is present with us in the Holy Spirit. The fears that bind us and constrict our love are healed by the knowledge that the Spirit incorporates us into the life of the risen Christ.

But this love is not whatever we make it; rather, this love is what the Spirit makes in us. It is the same love that God displayed for the world in Jesus

Christ. To love the world as God loves the world, we are to bear the fruit of the Spirit. That fruit is cultivated by many practices that enable us to participate in the continuing life of Christ. We participate in that life by putting to death the acts of the sinful nature (Gal. 5:19–21). These acts display a misaligned life, an unrighteousness that is death. We put these acts to death by first identifying them. In this work, we need perceptive guides that discern the misalignment of the world—the culture that opposes the kingdom.[6] The world in which we live sows many seeds in our lives. These seeds produce the weeds that choke out the fruit of the Spirit. We need "naturalists of the kingdom" who can distinguish weeds from fruit. We eradicate these weeds by confessing them as sin and receiving God's forgiveness that frees us from habitual sin.

As we eradicate the weeds in our lives, we also need to cultivate the fruit of the Spirit. This fruit is the work of the Spirit, not our work, but we can do much to make fruitfulness possible. We make fruit bearing possible as we engage in a variety of Christian disciplines.[7] Although I cannot give an account of these disciplines here, we should note that these disciplines are simply our present participation in the life of Christ. We do not follow the disciplines to become better, happier, or more successful people. We follow the disciplines because they form Christ in us.

The perfection of the kingdom proclaimed by the words and deeds of Jesus Christ is the life God intended for us. That life is not merely a distant hope; it is the present reality of the power of the risen Christ at work in us through the Holy Spirit. "Righteousness" is another description of that present reality. The fruit of the Spirit describes the character of Jesus Christ and gives specificity to the perfection of the kingdom. As we engage in the practices that make possible the fruit of the Spirit in our lives, we proclaim the righteousness, the perfection, of the kingdom. In so doing, we practice the Christology of the Risen One.

Peace: The Openness of the Kingdom

The peace of the kingdom is not what we typically mean by peace today. In our world, "peace" is the absence of war. Or in North America particularly, "peace" is "peace of mind." These concepts are not alien to the peace of the kingdom, but they do not display the deepest meaning of that peace. Peace is not merely the absence of war; it is not merely psychological health. The deepest understanding of the peace of the kingdom comes when we ask how that peace is related to or simply *is* our participation in the continuing presence of the risen Lord by the power of the Holy Spirit.

The peace of the kingdom is central to Paul's letter to the Ephesians. The letter begins with an extended doxology praising the cosmic work of God in Christ. That cosmic vision is simply a reiteration of God's love for the world in Jesus Christ. But it is a reiteration that has very specific content. In Ephesians, the cosmic love of God is manifest in the peace of the kingdom. And the peace of the kingdom is displayed in the uniting of Jew and Gentile.

In the Gospels, Jesus speaks enigmatically about peace. In John 14:27, Jesus says, "Peace I leave with you; my peace I give you. I do not give to you as the world gives. Do not let your hearts be troubled and do not be afraid." Two chapters later he tells his disciples, "I have told you these things, so that in me you may have peace. In this world you will have trouble. But take heart! I have overcome the world" (John 16:33). In these two statements, Jesus presents himself to us as our peace. But hoping for this peace in the kind of world in which we live may often seem like trying to keep a candle lit in the midst of a windstorm. And so we often reduce peace merely to the absence of war or the presence of inner calm.

We may recognize the absence of peace in our discontent or acquisitiveness. And so we may seek peace in the reduction of our desires. Such peace, however, is far from active participation in the peace of the kingdom. The peace of the kingdom that Paul describes in Ephesians is the cosmic reconciliation that God accomplishes in Jesus Christ. It is the peace that continues the story of the kingdom by the work of the Spirit through the power of Christ's resurrection. As we understand and practice that peace, we extend Christology into our world today.

Although the entire vision of Ephesians is cosmic, Paul begins his exposition on a human scale. In Ephesians 2, Paul identifies the peace of Christ and points out the fundamental conflict that keeps us from peace. Peace does not begin in our hearts and in our psyche. Peace does not begin in our worldly relationships. Peace begins in our relationship with God. The fundamental conflict that peace resolves is the conflict between God and humankind. The establishment of peace between God and humankind becomes the foundation for the revelation of the cosmic peace of God's kingdom.[8]

Paul's exposition of the cosmic peace of the kingdom centers on its manifestation in the story of the reconciliation of Jew and Gentile. He reminds us that before Christ, Gentiles

> were separate from Christ, excluded from citizenship in Israel and foreigners to the covenants of the promise, without hope and without God in the world. But now in Christ Jesus you who once were far away have been brought near through the blood of Christ.
>
> Ephesians 2:12–13

That this is a continuation of the story of Jesus Christ is made clear by the fact that Gentiles are "in Christ." That this is the story of the peace of the kingdom is made clear by Paul's assertion that "[Christ] himself is our peace, who has made the two one and has destroyed the barrier, the dividing wall of hostility" (Eph. 2:14).

The imagery here is rich. I live in the midst of a community of walled estates. The walls that we build literally and figuratively demonstrate our fear and the hostility of the world in which we live. We build walls to protect ourselves from enemies and thieves. But in the kingdom of God, our lives are guaranteed by Christ's resurrection. We have no more need of walls if we truly understand the peace of the kingdom. In the words and deeds of Jesus, God "vandalizes" our walls and opens the kingdom to all.

The peace of the kingdom that has come in Jesus Christ is made manifest to the world by the joining together of all humanity—Jew and Gentile:

> His purpose was to create in himself one new man out of the two, thus making peace, and in this one body to reconcile both of them to God through the cross, by which he put to death their hostility. He came and preached peace to you who were far away and peace to those who were near.
>
> Ephesians 2:15–17

This peace begins on a human scale, but it displays the peace of the kingdom that is cosmic in scope.

As Richard Hays argues, the joining together of Jew and Gentile as followers of Jesus Christ is the revelation of God's intention for all creation. Ephesians

> represents a theologically noteworthy development of Paul's view that the church, being transformed into the image of Christ, reflects the glory of God (2 Cor. 3:18). In Ephesians, the church is not only the recipient of revelation (1:9), but also the singular medium of revelation to the whole creation, including the cosmic powers that still oppose God's purposes (3:10, 6:10–20).[9]

This cosmic revelation of the peace of the kingdom in the church is the revelation of God's "manifold wisdom" and of the "mystery" of God's eternal plan for all creation (Eph. 3:1–12).

When we consider how to practice this kingdom-peace, we may be immediately drawn to discussions of peace-making and to long-standing differences in the church over "pacifism" and "just war."[10] These are important topics that are much debated. However, rather than engage in this tangled debate, I will follow Paul's exposition in Ephesians to uncover one of the practices of kingdom-peace to which Christ calls his disciples.

After his celebration of God's work in Christ making us one people, Paul urges the Ephesian disciples to "make every effort to keep the unity of the Spirit through the bond of peace" (Eph. 4:3). Paul reinforces this call through a series of "oneness" statements: one body, one Spirit, one hope, one Lord, one faith, one baptism, one God and Father of all (Eph. 4:4–5). But Paul follows these verses with a recognition of the diversity of the church.

In Paul's account of this diversity, we find one of the practices of peace: the practice of the gifts of the Spirit. Paul recognizes that unity does not erase all differences. When we are made "one" in the body of Christ, we are not made identical in every respect. The practice of peace begins at this very basic, ordinary level: learning to recognize our differences in the body of Christ as God's gifts to us.

In Ephesians and other New Testament passages, many diverse gifts are acknowledged and encouraged (Rom. 12:6–8; 1 Corinthians 12; 1 Peter 4:10–11). These diverse gifts do not separate us from one another in the kingdom of God; rather, they bring us together. But they do this only when we recognize that others' "differences" are their gifts to us—more correctly, the Spirit's gifts for us through the other. This is not the celebration of difference for the sake of being different, nor is it a celebration of difference without boundaries. Instead, it is a difference guided by the Holy Spirit.

This is where the practice of peace begins. We must see that our differences are not walls that divide us but gifts that bring us together. Our gifts are not precious possessions to be guarded by the building of walls or hoarded by depositing them in safes; they are to be shared with others, given away lavishly because we know that the source of those gifts is the lavish and inexhaustible God.[11] When we use our differences to protect ourselves from others and when we use others' differences as a reason for rejecting them, we deny the peace of the kingdom that brings unity without erasing difference.

Wealth, intelligence, prophetic insight, and rhetorical power are obvious examples of differences among Christians, but behind these differences lie differences in race, social status, sex, and culture that shape these other differences. What if Christians began to see these differences not as marks of privilege or superiority but as gifts for others? What if Christians began to ask themselves how others' differences gift them for service to the kingdom? The peace of the kingdom is realized by disciples of Jesus Christ when we subsume "worldly" differences under spiritual giftedness and see that giftedness as the place of our unity. In that unity, we practice the openness of the kingdom and witness to the mystery of God's eternal purpose and manifold wisdom.

In Paul's writings, one foundation of the peace of the kingdom is the recognition of spiritual gifts among individual believers. We may also begin to practice kingdom-peace by extending that practice to various traditions within the one church. Today, one of the obstacles to the embodiment of kingdom-peace is the variety within the Christian community. To those outside Christ and to many in Christ, the existence of Orthodox, Catholic, and Protestant communions is a scandal. This is further complicated by the existence of Lutheran, Reformed, Baptist, Charismatic, and other traditions. One step toward overcoming this scandal would be for the church to recognize in this diversity the diversity of gifts. What if we recognized, among Orthodox, Catholic, and Protestant, the different contributions that each makes to the riches of the one church? What if we affirmed, among the traditions, the contributions that others make to our understanding of the gospel? These practices would not be merely toleration but would witness to the openness of the kingdom—a peace grounded in our common identity and diversity in Christ.

In Jesus' proclamation of the openness of the kingdom, he welcomed all. He did this because he knew God's purpose and wisdom. He knew that by the power of the Holy Spirit all of his disciples would be gifted for ministry. Paul's call to the church, to maintain the unity of the Spirit in the bond of peace by the practice of our diverse gifts, is the proclamation of the kingdom's openness in the power of Christ's resurrection through the coming of the Holy Spirit. This practice of kingdom-peace is a continuation of the story of Jesus Christ and of the Christology of the resurrection.

Joy: The Value of the Kingdom

Paul's letter to the Philippians is filled with joy. I find this surprising, because Paul is writing this letter from prison. Imagine the circumstances. The churches Paul has established and whom he views as his children are being preyed upon by false teachers. And he is in chains. He can't visit those churches to protect them and keep them in the truth of the gospel. And yet he writes about joy. Paul, who has had such incredible power and spiritual authority in preaching the gospel to those who have never heard, who has this missionary gift, is in chains, unable to share that gift broadly, unable to travel further. And yet he writes about joy. Paul who has such close relations with others in the work of the gospel, who has developed such deep, abiding friendships, is unable to see most of his friends and spend time with them enjoying memories and their common purpose. And yet he writes about joy. How is it that in those circumstances he can write so happily about such joy? How is it that he can say, "Rejoice!" Where does this joy of the kingdom come from?

Before we look at the foundation of Paul's joy, let's identify one source from which it does not come. Paul's joy does not come from a naturally optimistic, sunny temperament. He is not one of those people who seems oblivious to life's difficulties. Paul is sometimes perplexed and downcast (2 Cor.

4:7–12). He describes his labor for the church in terms of the pain of childbirth (Gal. 4:19). Rather than deny suffering and weakness, he sees them as marks of faithfulness to Christ. Paul's gospel is not one of health and prosperity. What then is the source of his joy?

The first foundation on which Paul's joy is built is fellowship with others. This entire letter is in a sense his sharing of his life with others. Obviously, the Philippians had a special place in his heart. He writes, "I thank my God every time I remember you. In all my prayers for all of you, I always pray with joy" (Phil. 1:3–4). One source of Paul's joy was his fellowship with other believers—the life and the ministry that he shared with them. His chains did not affect this joy, because he knew that his fellowship with them was grounded in the kingdom of God, which cannot be overcome. He knew that his fellowship with them was grounded in eternity.

Second, Paul's kingdom-joy rests on the foundation of his larger vision. Paul is in chains, but he sees beyond his chains to what is happening with the gospel:

> I want you to know, brothers, that what has happened to me has really served to advance the gospel. As a result, it has become clear throughout the whole palace guard and to everyone else that I am in chains for Christ. Because of my chains, most of the brothers in the Lord have been encouraged to speak the word of God more courageously and fearlessly.
>
> Philippians 1:12–14

Even when people preach to provoke Paul and make him jealous, he still rejoices, because what is important is not his reputation nor his chains but the gospel: "The important thing is that in every way, whether from false motives or true, Christ is preached. And because of this I rejoice" (Phil. 1:18).

Paul's joy depends not on his circumstances but on the freedom of the gospel. As Christ is proclaimed, the kingdom is revealed. Paul may be in chains, but the kingdom can never be chained. And so Paul finds kingdom-joy in all circumstances.

As Jesus proclaimed the value of the kingdom, he called his followers to give up their own (dying) lives in order to receive the life of the kingdom. Paul here participates in that call as he sees beyond the circumstances of his own life to the reality of the kingdom. His life is not about his own success and fulfillment but about the spread of the kingdom through the preaching of the gospel. His joy is grounded then in the value of the kingdom proclaimed by Jesus Christ.

Although Paul clearly draws joy from his fellowship with the Philippians and the spread of the gospel, we reach the heart of his joy and the value of the kingdom when we turn to the third pillar on which Paul's joy rests: his participation in Christ. According to Paul, we are to rejoice *in the Lord* (Phil.

4:4). Paul's joy is kingdom-joy. It is not rooted in a sunny disposition or an optimistic view of life. Paul's joy has a very specific source—Jesus Christ. Paul draws joy from his fellowship with the Philippians because he knows that it is an unending fellowship grounded in the kingdom. He draws joy from the spread of the gospel because he knows that the gospel of the kingdom has the highest value for all creation. As Paul rests his joy in knowing Jesus Christ, however, his joy takes a specific shape. For Paul, the joy of the kingdom is shaped by Christ himself. In one of the most studied and memorable passages in Philippians, Paul calls Christ's disciples at Philippi and elsewhere to follow Christ's example:

> Who, being in very nature God,
>   did not consider equality with God something to be grasped,
> but made himself nothing,
>   taking the very nature of a servant,
>   being made in human likeness.
> And being found in appearance as a man,
>   he humbled himself
>   and became obedient to death—
>   even death on a cross!
> Therefore, God exalted him to the highest place
>   and gave him the name that is above every name,
> that at the name of Jesus every knee should bow,
>   in heaven and on earth and under the earth,
> and every tongue confess that Jesus Christ is Lord,
>   to the glory of God the Father.
>
> 2:6–11

This lengthy hymn expresses precisely the value of the kingdom, for it cost God the life of the Son. It is this story, this reality that grounds Paul's kingdom-joy.[12]

Because Paul knows what the kingdom cost God, Paul knows that his own circumstances, his own suffering for the cause of Christ, is his participation in that same kingdom. For Paul, "to live is Christ and to die is gain" (Phil. 1:21). That certain knowledge is grounded in Paul's life in Christ. Before coming to know Christ, Paul had many reasons for confidence: "circumcised on the eighth day, of the people of Israel, of the tribe of Benjamin, a Hebrew of Hebrews; in regard to the law, a Pharisee; as for zeal, persecuting the church; as for legalistic righteousness, faultless" (Phil. 3:5–6). But Paul gave all of that up for Christ: "I consider everything a loss compared to the surpassing greatness of knowing Christ Jesus my Lord, for whose sake I have lost all things. I consider them rubbish, that I may gain Christ" (Phil. 3:8).

This confession by Paul is simply a redescription of the value of the kingdom, which costs us everything, so that we might gain Christ and his kingdom.

Moreover, Paul ties this confession to a Christology of the resurrection: "I want to know Christ and the power of his resurrection and the fellowship of sharing in his sufferings, becoming like him in his death, and so, somehow, to attain to the resurrection from the dead" (Phil. 3:10). For Paul, his suffering has meaning and even joy when it is participation in Christ's sufferings. Paul's life in the kingdom is his participation with Christ in dying to the fallen world and rising with Christ to the kingdom of God.

Paul's joy, then, is kingdom-joy. It is a continuation of the story of the value of the kingdom through life in the crucified and risen Christ by the power of the Holy Spirit. Because we still live in a fallen, not-yet-fully-redeemed world, this joy comes to us as the activity of the kingdom. It is not yet our full possession. But there are practices that we can engage in so that we may know this joy. These practices can be gathered together under the rubric of "living by the Spirit."

If we live by the Spirit, then we die to self. Just as Paul could have listed all his "religious" claims (Phil. 3:5–6), we too may be tempted to make such a list. But that is to continue living in the old reality; it is not life in the kingdom. If we locate life in the kingdom, then our "spiritual resumes" will look very different. When Paul wanted to establish his apostolic credentials, he listed his suffering for the sake of Christ (2 Cor. 11:16–12:10). If we find life in the kingdom, then we too will suffer in this fallen world. That is what it means to live by a new reality in the midst of the old reality. That is what it means to die to self.

If we live by the Spirit and die to self, then we also live in Christ. This is the new reality, the kingdom whose value is beyond measure. When we live for others, as Paul lived for his fellowship with the Philippians and other believers, we live the life of the kingdom established and revealed by Jesus Christ. When we live for the spread of the gospel of Christ as Paul did, we live the life of the kingdom. Living for others and for the gospel is simply life in Christ. These are the practices of the resurrection as we celebrate the fact that death cannot separate us from Christ, cannot separate us from the fellowship we have in Christ, and cannot defeat the gospel of the risen Lord. As we know the power of Christ's resurrection and live with joy in the midst of a world opposed to the kingdom, we participate in that kingdom and proclaim its value for a world that is dying in sin.

Conclusion

The story of God's love for the world in Jesus Christ is the story of the coming of the kingdom of God. The Old Testament looks forward to that coming and prepares us for it. In Jesus Christ, the kingdom is established and revealed. It has come and yet it continues to come into the world. The kingdom is here, but it is not yet fully here. It comes not in its own power but in the power of God present in Jesus Christ. It continues to come today through the power of the risen Christ in the presence of the Holy Spirit.

The kingdom of God is not an ideal toward which we are to strive through human power. We do not bring the kingdom; rather, the kingdom comes as God is active in the world. The kingdom is a reality that presses down upon us.[13] Outside that kingdom is death—as Paul has it, we are dead in our "transgressions and sins" (Eph. 2:1). In the kingdom of God is life—as John says, "God so loved the world that he gave his one and only Son, that whoever believes him shall not perish but have eternal life" (John 3:16).

Eternal life is simply the life of the kingdom that is unending because it is established by the crucified and resurrected Messiah, Jesus of Nazareth. Today, that kingdom is present through the sending of the Holy Spirit. The Spirit makes us citizens of the kingdom and members of God's family, as we cry out by the Spirit, "Abba, Father" (Gal. 4:6). Our lives in the kingdom and in God's family are marked by righteousness, peace, and joy. These markers are a continuation of the kingdom proclaimed by Jesus Christ in words and deeds.

Those words and deeds—the kingdom's righteousness-perfection, peace-openness, and joy-value—are first of all God's actions in the world empowered by the Christology of the Risen One. By the work of God—Father, Son, and Holy Spirit—that kingdom is now open to us. Today, we do not look merely to the past or the future for the kingdom; we do not have to conjure it out of the past or wait in its absence. The kingdom is the reality that began in the past, sweeps us up in the present, and carries us into the future of God's final redemption.

As we enter that kingdom, God's activity becomes our practice. The kingdom is not our possession; rather, in the kingdom, we become God's possessions. As God's possessions, we are transformed. We now "suffer divine things" and live by the "truth of things."[14] The righteousness, peace, and joy of the kingdom is reality lived in the midst of a world of unreality. That reality irrupts into this world as we engage in the practices that make possible the perfection of the fruit of the Spirit, the openness of the gifts of the Spirit, and the value of the life of the Spirit.

The kingdom of God is present today for our redemption. Yet we know that our participation in that redemption is broken. Disciples of Jesus Christ live as not-yet-fully redeemed people in a not-yet-fully redeemed world. Therefore, our practice of the Christology of the Risen One is not exhausted by the practices of the kingdom. We learn to see and live in the kingdom as we live in this world. So we must not only become "naturalists of the kingdom," we must also become "naturalists of the world." To that quest we now turn.

EIGHT

THE WORLD

When Christians confess that Jesus Christ is Lord, we confess that he is Lord of all creation, that "there is not an inch in the whole area of human existence of which Christ the sovereign of all does not cry, 'It is mine.'"[1] But Jesus does not rule over every part of creation in the same way. As we will begin to discover in this chapter, his rule is expressed differently in the kingdom, the world, and the church, but we have not always recognized this truth. Because God's rule is expressed perfectly in the kingdom, we tend to fall into one of two traps—either thinking that whatever is happening in the world is the kingdom of God or thinking that God's kingdom is absent from the world. In the previous chapter, we sought to learn how to discern and participate in God's kingdom. That kingdom is present today in the righteousness, peace, and joy of the Holy Spirit. But the kingdom is not the only place that God is active today. God is also active in the "world," and God's "worldly" activity is different from God's kingdom activity.

In this chapter, we will seek first to understand the specific meaning of the "world"[2] theologically. Then we will explore the world in christological categories. Here I will show how the world is a rebellion against and a corruption of the rule of Jesus as the Messiah. The world we create in rebellion against God is an attempt on our part to usurp, to overthrow, Jesus Christ as king, priest, and prophet. Next, I will display how the risen Lord, through the presence of the Holy Spirit, reveals and judges the world's rebellion. Finally, I will identify the practices to which disciples of Jesus Christ are called as we live in this world.

Describing the World Theologically

The New Testament exemplifies an apparent ambivalence concerning the world. The world is both that which God loves in Jesus Christ and that which Christ's disciples are not to love (John 3:16; 1 John 2:15). Jesus is the one who overcomes the world and is the Savior of the world (John 16:33; 1 John 4:14). This apparent ambivalence is resolved if we recognize that the world is all that is opposed to God. To overcome that opposition is its redemption. God opposes the world to save it: "Jesus Christ's victory is not simply a victory *over* the world; it is a victory *for the sake of* the world.[3] Although I want to distinguish the mode of God's action in the world from the mode of God's action in the kingdom, Julian Hartt's description of God's kingdom in the world is apt:

> The kingdom of God is in the world for the reproof, chastisement, and condemnation of the world. But he who judges the world is God, whose ways are not our ways and whose thoughts are not our thoughts. He condemns and chastises for the redemption of the world, because his purposes in all things is a creative one. The pressure of the kingdom of God upon and in the world is the pressure of infinite solicitude. The relentlessness of the kingdom of God is the relentlessness of the divine love, which will not relinquish the world to a condign fate.[4]

The Christian understanding of the world is grounded in four realities. The first reality is that God is creator and that God remains creator even of the fallen world. The fallen world has no life independent of God. Even in its rebellion it is dependent on God. The second reality is that in Jesus Christ, God redeems creation. That redemption is not salvation *from* the world but the salvation *of* the world through repentance and faith in Jesus Christ. The third reality is that Jesus Christ is in a real sense absent.[5] As a result of his ascension, Jesus is no longer present in the way he once was or as he will be. The fourth reality is that the risen Christ is in a real sense present through the work of the Holy Spirit. Today is the day of salvation as the Spirit bears witness to Christ and makes possible our entry into the kingdom of everlasting life.

These four realities will implicitly guide our attempt to perceive God's action in the world. As I invited you in the previous chapter to become "naturalists of the kingdom," I now invite you to become "naturalists of the world." One of the tasks of discipleship to Jesus Christ is to grow in our ability to identify the world as all that we live in and that lives in us as opposed to God. To live increasingly in the kingdom, we must also discern what is not the kingdom. In that task, we are enabled by the presence and power of God the Holy Spirit.

The bulk of this chapter is devoted to an account of the world in its rebellion against Jesus as the Messiah of God. But before we turn to that account,

I will give a briefer description of the world in rebellion against the kingdom proclaimed by Jesus Christ. In our study of Jesus' proclamation of the kingdom, I identified four aspects: reality, perfection, value, and openness. In its rebellion against the reality of the kingdom, the world falls into cynicism. This cynicism often masquerades as sophistication: "This is how the world is. You better learn the rules so you can protect yourself and succeed." Having denied the reality of the kingdom, the world then opens the door to other death-dealing ways of life. In place of the perfection of the kingdom, the world affirms dualism. The physical and the spiritual are torn asunder and set in conflict with one another. In this conflict, the world often sets before us ways of healing the conflict. But having turned from the Creator of matter and spirit, the world provides no hope of redemption. In place of the value of the kingdom, the world pursues narcissism. The world's way of salvation is not in giving up our selves but in pursuit of self. In place of the openness of the kingdom, the world falls into chauvinism, the war of one group against another. Salvation is not found in the reconciliation of all people in Christ but in the assertion of our rights and the protection of "our kind of people." And so we live in a world marked by a new tribalism. The fact that the life of Jesus' disciples is often characterized by these worldly ways rather than the life of the kingdom is the measure of our need for Jesus as the Messiah who establishes God's kingdom in our midst.

Understanding the World Christologically

In this book, we are seeking to understand and make sense of the claim that "God so loved the world that he gave his one and only Son. . . . For God did not send his Son into the world to condemn the world, but to save the world through him" (John 3:16–17). Although other Christian accounts of the world are possible, here I will give a christological account of the world by tying that account to the story of Jesus as Messiah.

As Messiah, Jesus is king, priest, and prophet. In faithfully fulfilling these roles, Jesus overcame the world and made possible its redemption. But Jesus is Messiah in the face of opposition so intense that it led to his death. That death is the final judgment on our rebellion against God. For that reason, the world appears as a threat to God's activity in the world and to our faithfulness. The world is under the rule of an alien power—the "prince of this world" (John 12:31). But in that very death, the world is judged and the prince of this world is driven out.

Therefore, the world is also possibility. Even in its fallen state, alienated from God, the world as creation remains under God's care. God "will not relinquish the world to a condign fate."[6] As we live in the world as disciples of Jesus the Messiah, we are called to discern the world. Too often, followers of Jesus Christ accept uncritically the world into which we are born. It seems like our natural home. But if we have been born again into a new home as members of God's family, then we can no longer live passively in the world.

Instead, we must live actively in the world. As I will argue in the next section, the world is embodied by specific cultures. One of the ways that we live actively as God's people in the world is by understanding and criticizing culture:

> Theology of culture is interpretation of a system of values, creations, and attitudes in the light of and on the basis of the revelation of being and good in Jesus Christ. The aim of such interpretation is very much more than to discover how far and in what ways a culture falls short of "Christian standards." The aim is to enable the church to discharge more adequately their responsibilities in the present moment. To "save the present age"; this is the aim.[7]

As followers of Jesus Christ, we are situated in the world to be witnesses to the good news that in Jesus Christ God loves and saves the world. In what follows, I am not concerned so much with the theological interpretation of specific cultures as with an account of the world that makes the good news of Jesus Christ more evident.[8] That goal lays the foundation and gives directions for the practice of a Christology of the risen Lord.

Before turning to the specifics of a christological account of the world, I will give a brief overview. Beginning with our rebellion against Jesus as king, I will argue that we usurp Christ's kingship by creating our own worlds. These worlds are attempts to give an account of the creation and sustenance of life apart from God. When we usurp Christ as priest, we have no source of comfort and assurance of life outside life itself. Thus, our priestly rebellion leads us into false comfort. But because we are creatures not creator, our own royal and priestly worlds are doomed to failure. When this happens, we intensify our priestly efforts and we take on the mantle of pseudo-prophecy. At this point, we usurp Christ as prophet. We tell ourselves "truth" that does not rise above our own creation and prophesy deliverance that comes from within the systems we have created. In all of this, God is active in the world through Christ judging and overcoming our rebellion in order to redeem us. As we perceive that activity and as the Spirit enables us, we are called to practice the proper creaturely roles of king, priest, and prophet.

The King and the World

In his royal role as king, Jesus the Messiah rightfully claims rule over a creation that was created "by him and for him" (Col. 1:16). This rule was given to humankind as stewards responsible to God. In the perfect righteousness of the kingdom, our rule is a positive, life-giving force. But in the rebellion of this world, that rule becomes death.

When we rebel against God, we cut ourselves off from the source and sustainer of life. In this situation, there are only three alternatives: There is no creation, we are our own creators, or creation is its own creator. Our rebellion is typically a mixture of these three alternatives as we seek to sustain life cut off from its source. As we seek to come to terms with the circumstances of our rebellion, we create cultures. We have been given gifts of creativity by our Creator that are appropriate to our status as creatures. In righteousness, those gifts serve God; those gifts remain in our rebellion, though in broken form, as a mixture of good and evil, truth and lie.

The cultures we create in our rebellion against Christ as king are our attempts to make sense of a creation without God. We live first in the natural world, a world of time and matter that in our rebellion is marked by decay and death. We seek to overcome this reality by our own efforts, whether the magic of earlier ages or the technology of today.[9] Ironically, in its efforts to overcome death and decay, the world fails to see that death and decay result from our rebellion against God. In its efforts to defeat the natural world, the world simply deepens its rebellion and plunges more deeply into death and decay.

In the blindness of its rebellion, the world creates systems and beliefs that seek to render an account of the world without God. Our attempts to overcome the natural world become enshrined in a second creation of rebellious humankind, the everyday world in which we live. This everyday world is simply the culture that is the air we breathe. We do not recognize its failures and its rebellions because it is the world into which we are born. It is the "natural" world for those who have turned away from the rightful rule of Christ the King.

This everyday world takes many different forms. It is a mixture of cultural fragments left over from the past and cobbled together from the many cultures in which we live today. It is simply "the way things are." It teaches us how to see our lives and place ourselves in the world. This world, created by those who are not creator, lies to us about the real world, created by God to sustain life.

In C. S. Lewis's wonderful Chronicles of Narnia, he gives this rebellion concrete form. In *The Silver Chair*, the children who have traveled to Narnia and their friend, the Marsh-wiggle Puddleglum, are assigned a task by Aslan, the Christ-figure.[10] In the process of carrying out their assignment, they arrive in "the underland," ruled by "the Lady of the Green Kirtle, the Queen of the Underland."[11] The children have been sent there by Aslan to rescue a Prince who has been kept under an evil spell. After breaking the spell, they are discovered by the Queen, who then begins to weave her spell once again. The children and the freed Prince ask to leave for Narnia, the land ruled by Aslan and their proper home. In response, the Queen lulls them with sweet smells and soft music. Is there really a Narnia or have you just imagined it? she asks. Is there any other world but this one? Under her spell, one of the children finds herself saying:

> "No, I suppose the other world must be all a dream."
> "Yes, it is all a dream," said the Witch, always thrumming.
> "Yes, all a dream," said Jill.
> "There never was such a world," said the Witch.
> "No," said Jill and Scrubb, "never was such a world."
> "There never was any world but mine," said the Witch.
> "There never was any world but yours," said they.[12]

This is the illusion, the enchantment under which the world lives—"This, the world we have created, is the only world there ever was or ever will be. So get used to it and learn to live with it."[13]

Jesus Christ comes into this rebellious world as the messianic king to expose our lies and break the spell of our everyday world. Because he comes as the embodiment of God's love for creation, his ultimate purpose is not to deepen our despair or consign us to death; his ultimate purpose is to be the Savior of the world.

To save the world, Jesus refuses the world's construction of kingship. In fulfilling the criteria for Israel's king, he turns the world right side up. He did not fight by the world's standards to protect his life; he depended on God, the source of life. He did not use his power to command service; he came not "to be served, but to serve" (Mark 10:45). He did not use his life for himself but for others.

In Jesus' fulfillment of his role as messianic king, we see two activities of God in the world. The first is his exposure of our lies and illusions. Jesus comes to disillusion the world. We typically think of disillusionment as a bad thing, but if we think carefully about it, we can see that it is a good thing. Disillusionment removes the illusions by which we live. In rebellion against God, the world lives under the illusion that its creation is the only world there ever was or ever will be. We live under the illusion that we are our own creators and that we are charged with overcoming death and ruling the world without God. If that illusion is not exposed, we face eternal death, separation forever from the source of life and goodness.

Jesus exposes that lie by accepting the verdict that our everyday world imposed upon him—crucifixion. He comes to his own, the world he gave life, and it kills him. He is the source of life, and the world turns away from him, preferring its own rule of death. Today, the world seeks frantically to extend life through diet, exercise, and medical technology, when eternal life is in its midst through faith in Jesus Christ.

The second activity of God that we see in Jesus as king is the creation of another reality, the kingdom of God. Jesus reveals this reality through his miracles of healing and rule over creation. These establish another world, the world of creation in which human beings rule as God intended them to. We also see this other reality through the parables of Jesus. In his parables, he takes the language, the concepts, the stories of the everyday world and bends them to reveal another world. In this world, the despised Samaritan displays God's love for his neighbor, the wayward son is welcomed home by the prodigious grace of the Father, and the one who sees beyond his own supposed righteousness is forgiven (Luke 10:30–35; 15:11–32; 18:10–14).

But ultimately, the lies we have created and the other reality given by God is revealed in the resurrection of Jesus Christ. In Christ's resurrection, the verdict of the everyday world is revealed as false and powerless. Death cannot hold him, because he lives in another world—the world of life. Jesus Christ comes not to destroy life but to give it. That is his rule as messianic king.

Since Jesus Christ comes to give life not destroy it, he also comes to give us back the natural world. In him, we see beyond death to life. He also gives us back the everyday world. The creativity with which humans create culture and everyday worlds is not a bad thing when exercised in obedience to God. For example, the very things I earlier identified as expressions of our rebellion may become expressions of faithfulness to God. For this to be so, however, we must have our illusions and rebellions exposed and enter into the new reality established by Jesus Christ.

As we have been noting, the activity of the risen Christ continues in his absence through the presence of the Holy Spirit. In John, Jesus teaches his disciples that when the Holy Spirit comes,

> he will convict the world of guilt in regard to sin and righteousness and judgment: in regard to sin, because men do not believe in me; in regard to righteousness, because I am going to the Father, where you can see me no longer; and in regard to judgment, because the prince of this world now stands condemned.
>
> John 16:8–11

This work of the Holy Spirit is simply a continuation of Jesus' work as messianic king, exposing the illusions of the world. Sin leads to death because it is the refusal of the author of life. Righteousness is living as God intended us to live. In the death and resurrection of Jesus Christ, the world and its ruler are judged.

As those who have received the Holy Spirit, Christ's disciples today are called to practices that participate in Christ's kingship. These practices are the embodiment today of the life of Christ as king. Earlier in John, Jesus warns his disciples,

> If the world hates you, keep in mind that it hated me first. If you belonged to the world, it would love you as its own. As it is, you do not belong to the world, but I have chosen you out of the world. Remember the words I spoke to you: "No servant is greater than his master." If they persecuted me, they will persecute you also. If they obeyed my teaching, they will obey yours also.
>
> John 15:18–20

In this passage, Jesus calls his disciples to "rule" the world as he ruled the world. That kingdom-rule expresses God's love for the world by exposing its lies, its injustice, and its unrighteousness. Christ's disciples overcome the world by refusing to live by its standards, the everyday world created in rebellion against God.

In the rebellious world, that way of life has one outcome—suffering and persecution. The final New Testament vision of Christ's disciples as those who overcome the world takes place in John's Revelation. In the letters to the seven churches, Christians are repeatedly admonished to overcome (Revelation 2–3). Along with this admonishment comes many promises. We see these promises fulfilled in later chapters. There, the saints cast their crowns before the throne; they are celebrated as those who have overcome by the blood of the Lamb; they are made to be a kingdom; and they inherit the new creation, the fulfillment of the reality guaranteed by Christ's resurrection (Rev. 4:10; 6:10; 7:14–17; 12:10–12; 21:7).

Empowered by this vision, Christ's disciples live in this world by another reality. They use power to serve others; they give away privilege so that others may live. The opportunities their lives bring are not opportunities for self-aggrandizement, for building their own kingdoms, but for serving God's kingdom. When we do these things, the world hates us just as the world hated our Master. But in that very act, the world's lies and illusions are once again exposed.

One of the concrete practices by which the church turns from the kingdom of this world to the kingdom of God is worship.[14] In worship, Christ's disciples turn from the pursuit of this world and its power to the celebration of Christ's rule. In so doing, we are also caught up into Christ's resurrection, the power that enables us to overcome the world. Worship, by the standards of the rebellious world, is the most useless thing that we can do; it is a "royal waste of time."[15] As John Howard Yoder argues, when the church of Revelation gathered for worship,

> their primordial role within the geopolitics of the *Pax Romana* was neither to usurp the throne of Nero or Vespasian, Domitian or Trajan, but to persevere in celebrating the Lamb's Lordship and in building the community shaped by that celebration. They were participating in God's rule over the cosmos, whatever else they were or were not allowed to do by the civil powers. That it was not given to them to exercise those other more blatantly "powerful" roles—whether

> assassinating Trajan or becoming his chaplain—was not for them either a renunciation or a deprivation. They considered themselves to be participating in ruling the world primordially in the human practices of doxological celebration—perhaps in Ephesus?—of which John's vision of the Heavenly Throne Hall is the projection.[16]

When the church lives by the standards of the world rather than by the standards of the messianic King, the world continues in blissful illusion toward death. The world only knows it is the world—in rebellion against the giver of life—when its lies and illusions are exposed and the reality of the kingdom is revealed. Through the Holy Spirit, the risen King calls to himself a people whose practices are to be the disillusionment of the world for the salvation of the world.

The Priest and the World

In his role as messianic priest, Jesus comes to reveal to us and teach us God's way of life. Israel's priests, when they were faithful, foreshadowed this priestly work. They were charged with teaching the Torah and calling Israel to covenant relationship with God by the offering of sacrifices. In this way, God's people returned to the creator and source of life.

In its rebellion against God, the world cuts itself off from this priestly guidance. But such guidance is an essential part of our humanity. We must always have those who reflect to us the way of life—the everyday world—that we have created in rebellion against God. Having constructed a world of its own, the world now has to maintain that world.

In our culture, that world is maintained by a new priesthood, represented by "the manager."[17] The "manager" is one of the stock characters identified by Alasdair MacIntyre who provides the world "with a cultural and moral ideal" that "morally legitimates a mode of social existence."[18] In other cultures, the priesthood may be filled by other characters—the "engineer" in Victorian England, the "social democrat" in Wilhelmine Germany.[19]

Today, the manager serves the world as priest by appearing to have control over the world. Social science becomes the discipline by which managers assure us that we have control over the world. Their bureaucratic expertise keeps the world that we have created running smoothly. Managerial power is rooted in the mastery of techniques that obscure the brokenness, decay, and death that marks the modern world. The continuing success and prosperity of this priesthood depend on the continuing fiction that we can create the world in which we live. For this reason, MacIntyre argues that "the most effective manager is the best actor."[20] Having created a world that is rooted in the illusion that we are the creators and sustainers of life, we honor a priesthood that maintains that illusion "by acting it out convincingly."[21]

But at some point, the illusion fails. We are not the creators and sustainers of life. Apart from Christ, we do not know how to live. And so the worlds we create begin to fall apart. At this point anxiety sets in.[22] Our managers begin to lose their claim to the priesthood. When this happens, the world turns to another priesthood, the priesthood of the "therapist."

In the midst of our anxiety, therapists assure us that everything is really okay. All we need is to heal the inner brokenness that creates our anxiety. Therapists enable us to adjust to the world we have created. In this task, they become a new priesthood, teaching us a way of life that enables us to live happily in the world.

In the manager and the therapist, the world simply creates characters that fit the world we have created. Management and therapy are not bad when they are expressions of faithful priesthood to the world God has created. But their success in the world depends on their belief in the world. For this reason, the manager and the therapist, by their worldly success, obscure the salvation that comes in Jesus Christ. Moreover, because their success depends on their collusion with the world we have created, their work appears to us to be just what we need.

The church, in disobedience to God's calling, often colludes with the world in maintaining this illusion. That is, the church may become a false priesthood, just as some of Israel's priests colluded with the world to become false priests. In these instances, the priests and the church assure the world of God's blessing on its way of life. In place of the covenant in which we are called to God's way of life, false priests intone a contract in which God blesses our way of life as long as we maintain the sacrificial system to which God calls us. God is obligated to us as long as we meet the obligations that God has placed upon us. What this false priesthood obscures is that God calls us out of an illusory world of decay and death into the real world of creation and life.

When Jesus comes as the priestly Messiah, he comes into a world in rebellion, a world that creates and maintains its own fiction of life apart from God. In his priestly role, Jesus calls us not to an improved morality but to the perfect righteousness of the kingdom. He comes not to maintain the world but to judge it. He comes not to adjust the world and our lives but to proclaim a new world and a new life established by God's power in him. As messianic priest, Jesus continually violates the everyday world and its way of life in order to teach us God's way of life. In his Sermon on the Mount, he continually announces, "You have heard it said . . . , but I say to you" (Matthew 5–7). He violates the Sabbath of the everyday world to teach us the Sabbath of the kingdom of God. He challenges the way the temple simply reflects the social division of the world and calls his followers to make it a "house of prayer for all nations" (Mark 11:17). In the end, his challenge to the priesthood of the world is one of the factors that leads to his death, the ultimate sacrifice of the messianic priest.

As the priestly Messiah, Jesus refuses to adjust our lives to the everyday world. At that time, many in Israel had sought to adjust their righteousness to the everyday world. But Jesus says, "Unless your righteousness surpasses that of the Pharisees and the teachers of the law, you will certainly not enter the kingdom of heaven" (Matt. 5:20). He commands his disciples not to accept the righteousness that the world allows but to seek God's righteousness. This righteousness does not fit us for life in the world; it fits us for life in the kingdom. In that sense, then, Christ's followers are misfits. But that is a blessing, because to be fit for the world is to be fit for death. The world does not have the power of life in it; it has only the power of death. Jesus' call to righteousness beyond the everyday calls us out of death and into life. Jesus, the messianic priest, acts in the world to call his followers to be "blessed misfits."[23]

As the true priest of God, Jesus sets before the world the covenant-life to which God has called us. The depth of the world's rebellion against God and its captivity to an illusory world are fully revealed in its rejection of Jesus as messianic priest. The world refuses God's call to life, and in so doing displays its imprisonment in death—the world crucifies Jesus. Just before his death, Jesus raises the cup of wine and says, "This cup is the new covenant in my blood, which is poured out for you" (Luke 22:20). As messianic priest, Jesus not only teaches and maintains the covenant between God and humankind, he establishes a new covenant. This new covenant is the life of the kingdom that Jesus Christ establishes and reveals as Messiah.

The story of Jesus as messianic priest does not end with his death. Because Jesus as Messiah lives faithfully according to God's covenant and because he is God, death cannot hold him. His resurrection reveals for all time that the way of life he teaches and the covenant he establishes are eternal: "But when this priest [Jesus Christ] had offered for all time one sacrifice for sins, he sat down at the right hand of God" (Heb. 10:12).[24] From that position of authority, Jesus Christ continues his work as priest in the world today through the power of the Holy Spirit.

By the Spirit, disciples of Jesus Christ, "like living stones, are being built into a spiritual house to be a holy priesthood, offering spiritual sacrifices to God through Jesus Christ" (1 Peter 2:5). Peter makes clear that this work is first of all God's work. We are not "building ourselves"; we are "being built." Our sacrifices are not acceptable in themselves; they are acceptable "through Jesus Christ." Nevertheless, as the church is being built and her sacrifices made acceptable, her life takes a concrete form.

The concrete life of the priestly community takes shape as the life of a people who do not live according to the world. That life is first of all priesthood before God. We do not offer our sacrifices to the world, we offer them to God. Therefore, we do not measure our sacrifices by the world's response but by their faithfulness to God. Sacrifice is not another way of effectively managing the world; sacrifice is the way we live in God's reality and witness to it. Because we are born into the everyday world created by rebellious humankind and because it is our first home, we who have been born again into the kingdom of God are often drawn by the world.

The second way we live is as priests to one another. In the faithful church, the gift of administration replaces the world's manager (1 Cor. 12:28). The administrator is one who "knows the ropes" but who uses that expertise to guide the church in the life of the kingdom. Faithful priestly administrators ensure that everyone's voice is included so that the church can hear the Spirit's guidance through a multitude of gifts. Furthermore, these faithful priests ensure that the church does not sustain its life by adopting the techniques of the world.[25] When we live as priests to one another, we also displace the world's therapist. We do this by admonishing and disciplining one another not to adjust to the expectations of the everyday world but to live in faithfulness to the kingdom. Faithful priesthood does not comfort us in our sin; it comforts us by calling us out of our sin by the power of the Holy Spirit.

Finally, we embody God's spiritual priesthood by being priests to the world. The church, as a kingdom of priests, exemplifies the life of the kingdom before a watching world. In this task we are not called to manage the world by God's standards but to witness to another way of life that calls people out of the world and into the kingdom. For this reason, Stanley Hauerwas reminds us that "the church does not have a social ethic; the church is a social ethic."[26] If the church merely *had* a social ethic, then we would simply have a better program for managing the world. But Jesus came as the messianic Priest not to manage the world more effectively but to save it. His disciples continue that activity in the world only when we embody and celebrate in our common life the new covenant that God has established through the blood of Jesus Christ.

In C. S. Lewis's Narnia tale *The Silver Chair,* the spell of the witch is broken when Puddle-glum, the Marsh-wiggle, makes a sacrifice. He does not give up his life, but he does stomp on the witch's fire with his bare foot.[27] This act exposes the witch's world as illusory. Today, we do not often think of suffering as an essential mark of the true church, but if we are to be faithful priests of the Messiah, who gave his life for the sake of the world, then we must recover this reality. We must stomp on the fire that holds the world in the grip of a way of life that leads to death. The church that lives by the kingdom in a rebellious world will suffer, just as her Lord suffered and was rejected. Knowing the risen Lord, we must not fear such sacrifice as the end of the church's life but as the very life of his disciples in the kingdom that has no end.

The Prophet and the World

As messianic prophet, Jesus came to proclaim to the world the truth about itself. When the prophets of Israel were faithful to Yahweh, they declared to Israel the truth about itself. This truth is never simply truth about the world or Israel; it is always the truth about the world and Israel *in relation to God.* Since God is truth and since true words are God's words, messianic prophecy is the source of truth for us.

When the world in rebellion turns away from God, it turns away from truth. The counterfeit "creation" that is constructed by the world may be maintained for a period of time. The kings and priests of the world sustain the illusion of life. But eventually that counterfeit world begins to fail, because it is counterfeit and thus no real world. It has no life within it, only death. When this happens, the world in its continuing rebellion usurps the role of Jesus as messianic priest and produces its own "prophets."

These false prophets may be the philosophers, cultural critics, social engineers, and futurists of our time. They reassure us that the ideal world toward which we strive is still available to us. Yes, the social fabric we have constructed is unraveling, but if we will simply adopt this philosophy, correct that cultural trend, implement this social program, the future may be ours.

These proposals may for a time stave off social disintegration. They may lead to new forms of civilization that promise the fulfillment of the old dreams. For Christians, these may be signs of God's providential love for a world in rebellion, the patience of God that gives the world time to turn from rebellion in repentance. But for the world that does not recognize the care of its Creator, these prophecies are simply the continuation of the illusion that we are our own creators.

Into this rebellion, Jesus Christ comes as prophet to declare God's truth: "'The time has come,' he said. 'The kingdom of God is near. Repent and believe the good news'" (Mark 1:15). We enter the kingdom not by denying our participation in the world but by acknowledging it in repentance. This prophetic call is a profound affront to those who deny their need of God for life and to those who believe that their own righteousness is the source of life.

As the messianic prophet, Jesus strips away our illusions and confronts us with the truth:

> The demands of truth are built into our bones, they are of God. We can lie and cheat, and we can build a house, a world, of lies. But since we cannot lie to God we must be lying to ourselves, each to himself, each to his fellows. Thus, God puts us in a very awkward spot: we lie and we know that we lie, we make counterfeit and we know that it is counterfeit. We are not the creatures and victims of a lying civilization, we are its creators. But we are absent-minded creators.[28]

Jesus Christ comes to bring us to our right minds. He declares to us that even the life and creativity we use to rebel against God are rooted in the gift of God. He declares to us not the unrecognized and unrealized possibilities of our "natural abilities"; rather, he declares to us the decay and death that are the consequence of our "natural inabilities."[29] He does not point us to a new way to dominate and conquer creation; he proclaims that life is possible only in complete dependence on God. And he declares that God in mercy stands ready and willing to receive us and to make our lives true.

Christ's disciples are called to this prophetic ministry. Our task is to proclaim to the world today the truth of Jesus Christ in word and deed. Yet the pressure of the world upon us is so great that we are often unfaithful to this calling. When the prophetic church falls prey to the world, we proclaim a false gospel. One way we do this is by portraying the gospel as providing the piety that every civilization needs.[30] Everyday life needs a certain amount of piety and religion; the church becomes the source of that need rather than the herald of the truth about the world. Or the church becomes the guardian of morals and turns the gospel into a morality that the world needs to adopt.[31] Everyday life needs morality; the church provides it. In these roles, the church colludes with the world to extend the house of lies and to create a "Christian" civilization instead of witnessing to the reality of the kingdom that has come in Jesus Christ, the messianic prophet.

When Jesus' disciples are faithful to him as messianic prophet, then "the revealed righteousness of God is the platform and criterion of the criticism of culture."[32] The prophetic preaching of the church does not bless the aspirations of the world, however lofty and noble they may be. The prophetic church does not call the world to self-transcendence. Nor does messianic prophecy simply announce a new social program for the betterment of humankind. Messianic prophecy announces the righteousness of God available to all who turn from the world to God, who give up their dreams of self-transcendence in self-surrender. The good news of the messianic prophet and the faithful church is that a new society—the kingdom of God—has broken into the world. That society is just and righteous because it is formed by people who have been made new, transformed in their inner-being by the power of God.

When the church faithfully discharges this prophetic calling, it learns more fully the identity of Jesus as the messianic prophet. True prophecy is enabled by the presence of the Holy Spirit in the power of the risen Lord. At Pentecost, the Holy Spirit came from the ascended Christ to empower the church's preaching. That same Spirit remains with the church today to disclose in its prophetic proclamation the demands of the kingdom. It is by the power of the Holy Spirit that we repent of the world and are born into the kingdom of God.

This truth is hard to bear and even harder to hear in a rebellious world. In its rejection of the truth proclaimed by the messianic prophet, the world shut its ears and then sought to shut up the messenger by killing him. The church must expect the same from the world. But the church must also know that the words of the true prophet come to pass. Jesus, the messianic prophet, was put to death by the world. But his prophecy also came true: "Destroy this temple, and I will raise it again in three days" (John 2:19). Only later, did the disciples realize that he was speaking of his resurrection. Today, we who are his disciples know him as the true prophet of God through his resurrection from the dead. And in that power we continue the story of God's love for the world in Jesus Christ, the messianic prophet.

Conclusion

Disciples of Jesus the Messiah live today "between the times"—the time of Christ's first coming to establish and reveal the kingdom and the time of his second coming to consummate that kingdom. We live in Christ, but we also live in the world. We live in the world today to bear continuing witness to God's love for the world in Jesus Christ, the "Savior of the world." By the Spirit, we are enabled to live that story and to deepen our participation in Christ.

But we still live in the world and the world still lives in us. Thus, even Christ's disciples bear in this time between the times, the revelation of God's judgment on the world: "It is time for judgment to begin with the family of God" (1 Peter 4:17). Since that judgment is God's judgment, it is for our salvation to eradicate all in us that is not obedient to God. That judgment is fearsome for the world that does not repent: "And if [judgment] begins with us, what will the outcome be for those who do not obey the gospel of God?" (1 Peter 4:17).

Today is the day of salvation. That truth is described by Julian Hartt in words so powerful that they deserve to be quoted at length:

> God is our judge and redeemer. The unreality systems created by man threaten to throttle man's created possibility, or at least disfigure it. When therefore God speaks as present with us in Christ, our essential being stirs in drugged sleep and begins the struggle to welcome its true Lord. In this sense the essence of man is struggle, conflict, tension; man is an *agon*, a momentous contention with God. The end of that contention is disclosed in Jesus Christ: that we might become, in the whole circuit of our life, and in the vital center, what we are in the creative seeing of God. "Be transformed" is the imperative of the righteous God communicated in Jesus Christ. The essential work is to free "the original plan of creation," the created possibility, from the dead weight of character and institution produced to block or dis-

> tort the full realization of creative spirit. Victory in this struggle is impossible without the power of God. The name of Jesus Christ is also Immanuel: God with us.[33]

May the continuing presence of Jesus the messianic king, priest, and prophet make his disciples faithful witnesses of this good news by the power of the Holy Spirit.

NINE

THE CHURCH

In the previous two chapters, we explored the christological significance of the kingdom and the world. Between those realities and in their midst stands the church.[1] Of course, the church has never been entirely absent from my account. When we speak of the kingdom and the world, the church too is present, and we have already begun indirectly to explore the christological significance of the church.

In this chapter, I bring into focus the church and seek to deepen our understanding of the good news of Jesus Christ by exploring the relationships the church has to the kingdom and the world and by describing three christological practices to which it is called. Ecclesiological issues are many and complex. In my account, I do not intend to address every issue or give a full doctrine of the church.[2] My purpose, rather, is to further develop an understanding of Jesus Christ by reflecting on his continuing work in the church by the power of the Holy Spirit.

The Church and the Kingdom

In order to understand the continuing work of Christ in the church, we must be clear about the relationship between the church and the kingdom. Christ, by the one Spirit, is at work in the kingdom and in the church. But that does not mean that the church and the kingdom are identical. Yes, they (along with the world, as we will see in the next section) have their identity in Christ's work by the Spirit, but that work takes a different form in the church and the kingdom. For this reason, I must identify improper ways of relating the church and the kingdom before I identify proper ways of construing that relationship.

First, the church is not the kingdom. If we assert that the church is the kingdom, then when we are confronted with the imperfections of the church, we have to acknowledge that the kingdom is not the perfect fellowship of God and creation. To avoid this clear mistake, we may then distinguish between the visible church and the invisible church. The invisible church, we say, is the kingdom. Seldom, if ever, do we explicitly acknowledge that this is the implicit claim we are making when we divide the church visible and invisible, but that is the practical effect. This division, however, makes the kingdom invisible. It is better biblically and theologically to recognize the difference between the church and the kingdom. This recognition, as I show below, yields a faithful account of both the kingdom and the church.

Second, the church is not the precursor to the kingdom. It is not the present, imperfect form of the kingdom. This construction of the relationship between the church and the kingdom again capitulates to the imperfections of the church at the expense of a faithful account of the kingdom. We may think that because the kingdom is not yet fully present, it is appropriate then to say that it is imperfectly present. But to say that the kingdom is not yet fully present is not the same as saying that the kingdom is imperfectly present. When the kingdom is present, it is present in perfection. Therefore, the church is neither the presence of the invisible kingdom nor is it the presence of the imperfect kingdom.

When Christ is present in his kingdom, that event, that activity, that reality displays the perfections of God and life as God intended it. To witness and serve that reality, God calls into existence the church of Jesus Christ. Whenever and wherever Jesus Christ is witnessed and served, he is active in the church. This does not mean that the church must be perfect to witness to Jesus Christ; it means that the church must learn how to witness to and serve Jesus Christ in its imperfections. To do this, the church must learn what the world does not know, that in obedience and disobedience, it owes its life to the grace of God active in Jesus Christ.

The church is witness to the kingdom. By the power of the Holy Spirit, the church has come to know Christ and his kingdom. This knowledge places upon the church the responsibility for witnessing to the presence of the kingdom. That kingdom is larger than the church, but it is the church that is given the ability to perceive its presence. Earlier, I invited you to become "naturalists of the kingdom." That is an apt description of the church as witness to the kingdom. By the presence and power of the Holy Spirit, Jesus Christ continues to sustain his kingdom today. The world is either blind to that presence or misconstrues it; the church is the community called and equipped by God to tell the world what is going on when the kingdom is present.

The church is also servant of the kingdom. This means the church does not merely speak for the kingdom, it lives for the kingdom. The church is not the kingdom, but the kingdom is most clearly present in the church. The church is the community that listens to God's commands and seeks to do them. In this life, the church is servant of the kingdom. Because the church has been given eyes to see the kingdom and ears to hear God's commands, the church is called to serve that kingdom wherever it perceives its presence and its demand. These moments and movements of the kingdom may occur outside the church. When that happens, the church is obligated to be present. But as I further clarify in the next section, it is to be present as the servant of the kingdom not the servant of the world.

When the church is faithful to its calling, it displays the marks of the Spirit's presence—it is one, holy, catholic, and apostolic. However, these are never predicates of the church; rather, they are descriptions of God's work in the church: "'The holiness of the church' is purely and simply a way of speaking of the presence of God the Spirit come to infuse the community with the powers of the spiritual life of Christ."[3] Although these descriptions do not match perfectly the characteristics of the kingdom that Jesus proclaimed, we can see many similarities. The kingdom is made real in the church when the church displays the perfection of the kingdom in holiness, the openness of the kingdom in its oneness and catholicity, and when the value of the kingdom is proclaimed in its apostolic message.

But the church is not always faithful. Even in its unfaithfulness, however, the church still bears witness to the kingdom and serves it. Because the church knows what the kingdom looks like, when it is unfaithful it knows it. When it denies that unfaithfulness, the church ceases to be the church and becomes the world. In this case, the "church" falls under the judgment of God. When it acknowledges its unfaithfulness, the church bears witness to the kingdom by confessing its sin and asking for God's forgiveness. The church is the human community that knows the reality, perfection, value, and openness of the kingdom. With that knowledge comes the mission to bear witness to and serve the kingdom.

The Church and the World

Since the church is called to witness to and serve the kingdom of God that is present as an everlasting actuality in the world, God places upon the church the demand that it be present in the world. Confident that Jesus Christ came into a world of human rebellion and yet proclaimed and embodied the kingdom of God, the church also enters fully into the world, confident also that the kingdom it is given to proclaim triumphs over the principalities and powers that rule the world. To serve and witness to this kingdom, the church must also be in the world, not because that condition is unavoidable but because it is impelled by Christ, the Savior of the world.[4]

To carry out this mission in the world, the church must speak a language that the world understands. This demand must not be mistaken as an imposition of the world upon the church. Instead, this demand is placed upon the church by the very gospel we proclaim.[5] To faithfully proclaim the kingdom, the church must know how the kingdom is present in a particular time and place. And it must proclaim that kingdom in an idiom appropriate to that time and place.[6]

But the church that is in the world for the sake of the kingdom is also not of the world. The world is in rebellion against God. The church is the human community that has heard the gospel and responded in the obedience of faith. By faith in Christ, the church has overcome the world. It is in the world in faithfulness to the kingdom; therefore, it is also not of the world.

This means that when the church faithfully proclaims the presence of the kingdom in the language of the world, it does not trim the gospel of the kingdom to fit the world's expectations. To preach the gospel of the kingdom so that it may be understood is not the same as preaching the gospel so that we may be liked. The church in the world faces continually the temptation to be liked by the world. But because it is not of the world, the church is continually recalled to the knowledge that we are already loved unconditionally by God in Jesus Christ.

In this call to be in the world but not of the world, the church in Western culture faces particular challenges because the life of the church has been so intertwined with that culture.[7] To be in the world means that we have to live with and discern our history in the world. In the West, the church lives with a world that it has helped shape. Our history is replete with visible church support for unjust practices such as slavery. We have affirmed the unjust rule of dictators and presidents. We live with a legacy of institutionalized racism and anti-Semitism. The church has often identified with the world rather than with the kingdom.

Moreover, as we proclaim the kingdom in our culture, we find there many apparently "Christian" words, concepts, and practices that are left over from the church's impact on culture. These words, concepts, and practices may seem to convey the gospel, but in the end they betray the gospel because they no longer bear witness to the kingdom.[8] To bear witness to and serve the kingdom, the church must be in the world. But because the church's presence in the world is a demand of the kingdom,

> the church can only learn from the Gospel of Jesus Christ what to preach. The church can learn only from the most diligent scrutiny of contemporary life how this word is to be mounted, in what idiom it will be intelligible. The living church

> preaches to living persons, not to the people of the past or the people of the future. In the Gospel the church has something infinitely precious to communicate. It must therefore exercise the utmost sagacity and shrewdness in determining the idiom in which to cradle this Gospel of Jesus Christ: God for man and man for God.[9]

In this mission, the church is sustained in faithfulness by the presence of the risen Messiah through the power of the Holy Spirit.

At the same time that the church learns the ways in which it has shaped the world, it must also learn the ways in which it has been shaped by the world. In Western culture, the church in the world has, among other effects, become democratized.[10] Too often the church measures its faithfulness by opinion polls and popularity contests rather than by faithfulness to its Lord.

To recover its mission in the world but not of the world, the church must return to participation in the life of Jesus Christ in the world. The church is to be in the world but not of the world just as Jesus the Messiah is in the world but not of the world. As messianic king, Jesus creates in the world a new reality. In that new reality, power is not the means to dominate others but the means to serve them. Here we must remember that Jesus, and his disciples, do not serve the world by giving it what it wants. We serve the world by witnessing to the Messiah in whom is life everlasting. As messianic priest, Jesus brings to the world the comfort of a new way of life. That comfort is not the news that the world is really okay. It is the news that God's judgment on the world has come as the salvation of the world. Here we must remember that this "new" way of life is a recovery of life as God intended it. As messianic prophet, Jesus proclaims good news to the world. That news is not that the world is truly life-giving. It is the news that the world is a fabric of lies and illusions that lead to death. It is also the news that God's kingdom has irrupted in this world as the place of truth and life. Here we must remember that this news is not something the world knows as the world. It is known by the world only as the faithful church witnesses to and serves the kingdom that has come in Christ. As the church continually returns to life in Christ, it sacrifices its life in the world, only to discover that it has been raised by the power of God the Spirit into life in the kingdom. By this work of God, the church is enabled to witness to and serve that kingdom in the world.

The Church and the Messiah

As I have been delineating the relationship between the church and the kingdom and the church and the world, I have also been delineating implicitly the relationship between the church and Jesus Christ. As the one who brings the kingdom in his preaching, work, and person, Jesus Christ is the kingdom to which the church is called as witness and servant. As the Messiah who is Savior of the world, Jesus is the shape and power of the church's faithful presence in the world but not of the world.

As I bring into focus the relationship between the church and Jesus Christ, I follow the continuing story of Jesus Christ. In his resurrection from the dead, the kingdom is planted in this age, never to be dislodged, worn down, or overcome. In his ascension, the world is given time and space, within the patience and providence of God, to come to know God's love in repentance and faith. In Pentecost, the risen Christ continues to act, but another arena of God's activity comes into view: the church (Acts 2).

Because the continuing story of Jesus Christ is the story of the risen Lord present and powerful by the Holy Spirit, we must briefly consider the relationship between Christ and the Spirit in order to develop a Christology of the risen Lord in relation to the church. In the church, the Holy Spirit becomes the primary agent of God's activity. Looking back over the story of Jesus, we can see already the presence of the Spirit—as the divine agent of Mary's conception of Jesus, as the one who rests upon Jesus, guides him, empowers him, and raises him from the dead. So the Spirit does not suddenly at Pentecost make a first appearance in the gospel story. Yet the Spirit is doing something new at Pentecost by bringing into existence the church and empowering its witness.

Therefore, the relationship between the church and the Messiah is pneumatological—it is the work of the Holy Spirit not the work of humankind:

> It is not as if the church were a voluntary community of altruistic persons who thought it good to behave in the world as Jesus behaved; rather, it is a community gathered by the Holy Spirit and made participant in the life and work of the crucified and risen Jesus Christ. The *church* does not extend this representative life of Christ into a world in and to which the Christ himself is no longer present; rather, it is carried by the divine Spirit into the sphere of *the Christ's* representation.[11]

The relationship between the church and the Messiah is the work of the Spirit, but its ground and goal is Jesus Christ. Jesus himself indicated the ground of this work when he told his disciples that "the Holy Spirit, whom the Father will send in my name, will teach you all things and will remind you of everything I have said to you" (John 14:26). Likewise, the goal of the Spirit's work is to testify about Jesus Christ and bring him glory (John 15:26; 16:14).

Although the relationship between the church and the Messiah is initiated by the Spirit, with its ground and goal in Jesus Christ, the church is not merely a passive recipient of that work. As Reinhard Hütter comments on John 14:26:

> While the initiative clearly lies with the Holy Spirit, the activities of teaching and reminding presuppose, on the church's side, structures and practices of learning and remembering and ways of communally embodying that learning and remembering so that it can be passed on as that which the Holy Spirit has given and in the light of which new learning and remembering can take place.[12]

This active participation of the church in the life of Christ by the power of the Holy Spirit finds expression in doctrines and practices.

We may bring together three christological doctrines and three practices to understand more fully life in the risen Lord. This account as written may deepen that understanding, but in the end what really counts is the lived practice of the church in its real relationship to the Messiah through the power of the Holy Spirit. The three practices of the church we will consider are baptism, the eucharist, and foot washing. The first two need no preliminary explanation or defense, because their practice is widespread in the church. The third practice, much less common in the church, will be explained and defended later in my exposition. My purpose is not to give comprehensive accounts of these practices or resolve the numerous church controversies regarding them; my purpose is to display the profound connections between these practices and learning and participating in Christ. Although I will note numerous christological dimensions to these three practices, my focus will be on the way that baptism teaches Christ as victor, the eucharist teaches Christ as sacrifice, and foot washing teaches Christ as example.

Baptism and Victory

Many controversies swirl around the practice of baptism: What happens at baptism? Who should be baptized? How much water should be used? These controversies usually set the agenda for discussions of baptism. They are important questions, but they are not the only ways to approach the practice of baptism. In my discussion, I will try to set these issues aside in order to explore how baptism as a practice teaches us Christ.[13] Inevitably, I will make statements that more naturally support a position on the traditional issues. My intention is not to smuggle in a position on the controversies under the guise of another approach. My primary aim is to give a christological account of the practice of baptism. Secondarily, that account may set the traditional controversies in a different light that could, in another setting, help resolve the controversies.

In baptism, the church acts as the agent of the Triune God—Father, Son, and Holy Spirit. But we are baptized into Christ, and the efficacy of baptism, however we describe it, depends on the work of Christ. As we saw in part 2, Christ's work may be described through several images, all of which find some expression in the practice of baptism. The image that most fully captures the practice of baptism is Jesus as victor.

In the New Testament, Jesus' victory is located primarily in his crucifixion. Jesus Christ overcomes the world in his death by refusing the lies of the world and remaining obedient to the Father. When he was facing death, Jesus could have followed the way of the world and used his power to destroy his enemies; he could have played by the rules of the world's system of justice to avoid a guilty verdict. But he remained faithful to God, giving up his life in the world for life in the kingdom.

Jesus' resurrection reveals his victory over death and the world. It displays God's reversal of the world's verdict. It announces that the way of life led faithfully by Jesus even unto death simply *is* life that cannot be overcome by death. Jesus' victory is rooted in the reality of the kingdom of God. The power and truth of that kingdom are obeyed by Christ in his crucifixion and revealed by him in his resurrection.

When people are baptized into Christ, they are joined with him in his death and resurrection: "Or don't you know that all of us who were baptized into Christ Jesus were baptized into his death? We were therefore buried with him through baptism into death in order that, just as Christ was raised from the dead through the glory of the Father, we too may live a new life" (Rom. 6:3–4). This description of baptism precisely describes what I have called the image of Christ as victor. By participation with Christ through baptism, we too are victors over the world. By the practice of baptism, the church witnesses to the victory of Jesus Christ. By participation and practice we learn Christ more fully.

In our death and burial with Christ in baptism, we announce our obedience to Christ in faith. Just as Christ was faithful in and through his death, so we are faithful in baptism and joined to Christ's death. What we learn here is that it is not our own deaths that mark our victory over the world. Because we are born into the world as sinners, our own deaths in themselves have no power to overcome the world. But because Jesus Christ is not born of this world as a sinner, his own faithfulness in death is the victory over the world. Our victory over the world, then, is not seen in our own deaths but in our identification with Christ in baptism. Victory over the world is not something we achieve but something we receive. But we receive that victory by being in Christ. And if we are in Christ, then our lives are new.

In Christ, we die to the world. We bring to the waters of baptism all of our life in the world. We bring our love for power, our desire for prestige, our worship of self, and all other idols. In the waters of baptism, God puts that life to death; in the strongest language, we could say that God executes that old self. For this reason, Paul says, "May I never boast except in the cross of our Lord Jesus Christ, through which the world has been crucified to me, and I to the world" (Gal. 6:14). For those who have been crucified with

Christ, the lies and illusions of the world have no more power. And if the world has no more power over those who have been crucified with Christ, then death has no final power over those who have been raised to new life in Christ.

Of course, we still fall prey to the lies of the world and the fear of death. Forgetful of Jesus Christ, we fall back into the ways of the world. That forgetfulness does not change our essential being in Christ through baptism. Our task is to "live into our baptism." Our old life has been put to death and we have been given new life. Now we must grow up into that new life. Baptism is the concrete representation of the daily practice of the church renewing our life in Christ.

As we live into our baptism we learn more fully the meaning of Christ's victory over the world. In the early church, candidates for baptism underwent extensive preparation for baptism. This preparation involved learning the Christian understanding of the world that is put to death in baptism. The week before baptism was often devoted to exorcising the power of the world from the candidate's life. Today, this process takes place, if at all, after baptism. For us, baptism is the beginning of instruction in the Christian life. We discover the ways in which the world still rules us and the ways in which we still rebel against God. For us, baptism is also the form of instruction in the Christian life. The memory of our baptism and the renewal of our baptismal vows at each baptism teach us the way to overcome the world. When we are in Christ, the world has no essential power over us. The only apparent power it has is the power we grant it. In Christ, we find the lies and illusions of the world overcome and truth established. The way to victory is to repent of the world and confess our need for Christ.[14]

In baptism, we are incorporated into the story of the kingdom established and ruled by Jesus Christ. The church is the company of those who join with us and sustain us on the journey. In the church, we find the gifts of the Spirit that teach us the way the story is lived today by the power of the Holy Spirit. In the practice of baptism, Christ the victor teaches the church that we have been liberated from the world. That life is dead, and we are now free to witness to and serve the kingdom. In that practice, Christ also teaches us that we have come home. The kingdom is where we are intended by God to live; it is life, and in it we become truly human for the first time.

Eucharist and Sacrifice

Like baptism, the eucharist (communion, Lord's Supper) is the focus of many controversies: Who may celebrate the eucharist? How often should we celebrate it? What happens when we celebrate? Again, however, my concern will not be to adjudicate those controversies but to explore how the practice of the eucharist teaches us Christ and incorporates us into his life.[15]

In the eucharist, we learn more fully the meaning of Christ as sacrifice. Sacrifice is the center of the meal as we remember Christ's death on the cross. In connection with baptism and Christ as victor, we may say that "if baptism is the sacramental practice that initiates the journey of friendship with God, the eucharist is what provides sustenance along the way."[16]

In Christ's victory, we see the truth that God has freed us from captivity to the world. In his sacrifice, we see the truth that God has forgiven our rebellion and wiped away our guilt. In Christ as sacrifice, we learn that we ourselves are under the judgment of God. But we also learn that God has taken that judgment on himself so that we may be saved. Jesus Christ is the "judge judged in our place."

In the practice of the eucharist, the church learns Jesus Christ as sacrifice in memory, communion, and anticipation. In memory, we learn his life on earth, a life of sacrifice not just on the cross but from beginning to end. We learn that we are dying sinners whose only hope of life is the crucifixion of Jesus Christ. In communion with Christ through the eucharist, we are enabled by the Spirit to be present with the risen and ascended Christ, who intercedes for us: "Who is he that condemns? Christ Jesus, who died—more than that, who was raised to life—is at the right hand of God and is also interceding for us" (Rom. 8:34). We who are sinners in rebellion against God are transformed and our worship made acceptable to God. In anticipation, the eucharist teaches that Christ's sacrifice will be consummated in that great banquet of the perfected communion of the saints when Christ returns.

In the practice of the eucharist, we are sustained in the journey begun at baptism. This practice teaches us how to live into our baptism even as we live in the world:

> The reason why the eucharist may turn into condemnatory judgment is the fact that, despite our baptismal acceptance of the divine judgment on sin, we are still prone to sin. Nor, despite the forgiveness conferred on us sacramentally in our baptism, have we yet heard the final pronouncement of forgiveness at the last assize and entered to take our place at the meal of the kingdom.[17]

Baptism does not set us off on a journey on our own; it initiates us into Christ and the church. Only in Christ and his church can we continue that journey in faithfulness.

The continuing practice of the eucharist is the memory of Christ as the source of our life, communion with him as the sustainer of our life, and anticipation of him as the goal of our life.[18] As we "re-member" Christ in the eucharist, we become the body of Christ called to proclaim the kingdom by living in the world as he lived. When we commune with Christ in the eucharist, we realize our life hidden with Christ and the saints in heaven.

When we anticipate Christ's return in the practice of eucharist, we see before us the glory and the crown that await all those in Christ.

By celebrating the eucharist, the church learns Christ as sacrifice and is called as witness in its life to the kingdom of life that has come through that sacrifice. In the practice of the eucharist, Christ the sacrifice teaches the church that God has forgiven our sin and continues to do so. In that practice, he also teaches us that we have received pardon from God. Together, these teach us that we need not be weighed down by our sin, that through Christ we are free and able to serve God's kingdom without hindrance. Finally, in the eucharistic meal, Christ teaches us the *shalom* of God. We are invited to eat and drink at God's table; we are God's sons and daughters enjoying life in the kingdom as God's family.

Foot Washing and Example

If baptism and the eucharist are controversial because of the variety of their practice in the church, foot washing is controversial because of the relative absence of its practice in the church. A few traditions practice foot washing as an "ordinance" along with baptism and communion, among them, Mennonites, Church of Christ, Church of the Brethren, and Free Will Baptists.[19] Other traditions include a ceremony of foot washing in the liturgy for Maundy Thursday. I think that a case can be made biblically for the regular practice of foot washing, but the burden of the historical judgment of the church remains formidable: Foot washing is not of the same significance as baptism and the eucharist. My purpose here is not to argue the case for foot washing as an equal to baptism and the eucharist but to show that when and if it is practiced, foot washing teaches us Christ as example.

In Christ as example, the church sees the love of God made manifest to the world. Christ is not first an example of human devotion to God or love for God. The kingdom is always God's initiative and God's activity. But just as baptism initiates us into the story of the kingdom and the journey with Christ, and just as the eucharist sustains our faithfulness to the story and gives us strength for the journey, so foot washing teaches us the shape of that story and the path of that journey.

When Christ washed the disciples' feet, he did so on his last night with them. This act is the memory of his life with the disciples before his crucifixion and resurrection. He not only performs the act, he interprets it:

> You call me "Teacher" and "Lord," and rightly so, for that is what I am. Now that I, your Lord and Teacher, have washed your feet, you also should wash one another's feet. I have set you an example that you should do as I have done for you. I tell you the truth, no servant is greater than his master, nor is a messenger greater

> than the one who sent him. Now that you know these things, you will be blessed if you do them.
>
> John 13:13–17

In his life, death, and resurrection, Jesus exemplifies the concrete form of God's love for the world. Faced with a world in rebellion, the only way for God's saving judgment to be carried out is through the self-humiliation of God the Son. As John tells us, "Having loved his own who were in the world, he now showed them the full extent of his love" (John 13:1).

In Christ as example, we see the depths of God's love in his willingness to set aside his glory, power, and privilege to become human, to die, and to live again to save our rebellious race. The whole course of Jesus' life in this world is exemplified in his washing the disciples' feet.[20] John tells us that at the beginning of the act he "took off his outer clothing" (John 13:4). This is a sign of his willingness to set aside his glory to come as human. Then he no doubt stooped to wash the disciples' feet, signifying the attitude of a servant. And he not only washed the feet of those who were his own, he also washed the feet of Judas, who was not his own, exemplifying God's love for the world. In washing the disciples' feet, Christ as example gives himself away in service to others. But we must not miss the ground of this self-giving. John tells us that "Jesus knew that the Father had put all things under his power, and that he had come from God and was returning to God; so he got up from the meal . . ."—and washed the disciples' feet (John 13:3–4).

In his example of self-giving love, Christ did not serve from a position of weakness but of authority. His self-giving was not an act of self-destruction but an act of self-finding. There is no better commentary on the hymn to Christ in Philippians 2 than this act of foot washing. In it, Christ lays aside his glory and humbles himself in obedience to God, knowing that he will again be glorified. In this act and in the whole course of his life, Jesus teaches us that "whoever wants to save his life will lose it, but whoever loses his life for me will find it" (Matt. 16:25). This saying is true because it identifies the very life of the kingdom established and revealed by God in Jesus Christ.

In his act of foot washing, Jesus gives us a practice by which we may learn more of him as example. In this humbling act, we begin to learn what it meant for God to come in Christ to save the world. We learn that our acts of service and self-sacrifice in obedience to Christ's example are grounded not in our low status in the world but in our high status in the kingdom. We are weak in the world but strong in the kingdom. And it is in knowing that our lives are sustained by God for all eternity that we can give ourselves to the world in service to the kingdom of God established by Jesus the Messiah, who gave his life for the world.

In the practice of foot washing, Christ the example teaches us the depths of God's love. God the Son did not protect and preserve his glory; rather, he set it aside in love for the world. In the practice of foot washing, Christ teaches us that our alienation from God is overcome not by our raising ourselves to God but by God descending to us. Secure in this knowledge, we also learn in the practice of foot washing the power to serve in the world as Christ serves.

These three practices—baptism, the eucharist, and foot washing—bring the church into relationship with Jesus the Messiah. Baptism begins that relationship, the eucharist sustains it, and foot washing shapes it. The account I have given is not the only possible account. Baptism, for example, also teaches us Christ as sacrifice, as we are incorporated into his death by baptism. And it teaches us Christ as example, as it forms the rhythm of Christian life. The eucharist can teach us Christ as victor by reminding us that even now his death is efficacious in the forgiveness of sins and that in worship we are lifted into the presence of the risen Lord. It can teach us Christ as example by setting before us his sacrificial life. Foot washing, likewise, can teach us Christ as victor because he serves in the knowledge of the glory he has from God. And it can teach us Christ as sacrifice in the very form of sacrificial service that the practice embodies.

In these practices, then, the church is conformed to Christ. In the practices that conform it to Christ, the church "bodies forth" the kingdom of God proclaimed and embodied by him. In baptism, the church proclaims the value of the kingdom. The kingdom cost Jesus his life in the world and costs us ours as well. In baptism, we embody the giving up of life as we are buried with Christ in his death. And we embody the value of the kingdom in baptism as we are raised to life in the kingdom with Christ.

In the eucharist, we embody the perfection of the kingdom. The very elements of creation that sustain our life—food and drink—become the sustaining life of the kingdom, which is the perfection of creation. In the eucharist, as we confess our sin and need for God's cleansing, we embody the righteous perfection of the kingdom that will not allow any evil thing to corrupt its life. In this practice, as we anticipate the return of Christ and the great banquet, we embody the perfection of human longings in the kingdom—this future is our heart's true desire.

In the practice of foot washing, we embody the openness of the kingdom. Entry into the kingdom does not depend on human effort and achievement; no one can enter by virtue of power, privilege, or status. Everyone enters when he or she recognizes in the humbling, stooping form of Jesus, the Savior of the world. In the practice of foot washing, we lay aside all power, privilege, and status to serve in the world as Christ came to the world to open the kingdom to all, from the "greatest" to the "least," because all are loved by God.

Of course, this sketch could be drawn differently. For example, in the table fellowship of the eucharist, we embody the openness of the kingdom proclaimed by Jesus' table fellowship with sinners and outcasts. In baptism, we embody the perfection of the kingdom as our dying selves are buried with Christ and we are raised to the life of the kingdom. And in foot washing, we embody the value of the kingdom as we serve, secure in the knowledge that our lives are sustained by God.

Together, these practices bring us more fully into the reality of the kingdom as Christ is formed in us today. He has been crucified, he is risen and ascended, he has given us the Holy Spirit, and he is coming again. The church is that human community called by God to witness and serve that Messiah and his kingdom.

Conclusion

In the sending of the Spirit, the crucified, risen, and ascended Jesus Christ calls into being the church as the community of his disciples. In this community, his disciples are called to serve and witness to the kingdom of God. They carry out that mission as a people in the world but not of the world.

As a people who live in the time between the times of Christ's coming, and as a people whose life is in the world and in the kingdom, the church lives faithfully only by the power of Christ in the presence of the Holy Spirit. The church has no real life of its own; it is entirely dependent on God. The life that God sustains in the church is learned and embodied in the church by its practices. Our exploration of three of those practices central to the life of the church has revealed how we continue to learn Christ today.

The church is in the world today as those who know God and the kingdom that has come in Christ. Our task is to so know Christ that our lives bear witness to him and the kingdom so that others may come into the life of that kingdom, which will one day be the consummation of the salvation of all creation.

CONCLUSION

Jesus Christ is not merely a figure of the past. Therefore, our Christology cannot be confined to a study of the past. Jesus Christ is alive and active today in the kingdom, the world, and the church. Nevertheless, the church's final authority for discerning that work is the story of Jesus Christ recorded in Scripture by human beings through the trustworthy guidance of the Holy Spirit. For this reason, our study of the continuing work of Christ has directed us back to the earlier chapters on Jesus' life, death, and resurrection.

Today, the story of the Jesus who lived, died, and was raised continues in the kingdom, the church, and the world. The kingdom is the place where Jesus' perfect rule is realized. That kingdom is present—but not yet fully present—today. The world is the place where God's rule is rejected. Today, that rebellious world is sustained by the patient providence of God so that we may come to repentance and faith. The church is the place where God's love is known. Today, that knowledge and life is the message of salvation for all who become followers of the risen Lord.

When we confuse the kingdom, the world, and the church, our knowledge of God's love and our proclamation of the gospel also become confused. We untangle this confusion and return to faithfulness only by continually turning to Jesus Christ. The Holy Spirit is sent today as the agent of the kingdom, making its righteousness, peace, and joy real in our lives. The Spirit is sent into the world to judge the world and convict it of sin so that its illusions and death are exposed. The Spirit forms the church and guides it into Christ, taking the things of Christ and making them known to us today.

As we learn the kingdom, world, and church, we are drawn ever more deeply and fully into God's love for the world demonstrated and made effective in Jesus Christ. The story in which we participate by faith in Jesus Christ is not a story that we have made up or chosen. It is the story of God's redemption that chooses us. As we become participants in that story, our lives are changed. That change is embodied in the practices that make us participants in God's activity in the kingdom, church, and world. In that participation, we learn Jesus Christ more fully and witness to him more faithfully.

CONCLUSION

The good news that God loves the world in Jesus Christ is not the invention of human imagination or wishful thinking. It is the reality imposed upon us by God's actions in Jesus Christ. Disciples of Jesus Christ are called to live in the reality of that story and understand it clearly so that we can bear witness to God's love. To do so, we must know what Jesus himself said and did. As we have seen, the key to Jesus' words and deeds is the kingdom of God. To bear faithful witness to Jesus Christ, we must also know who he is. One of the keys to his identity is his fulfillment of the messianic expectations of Israel. As Jesus' disciples we must also know whose story we are telling in order to keep it straight. After much debate, the church was led by God to understand that the story of Jesus Christ is the story of God and humankind in perfect fellowship. In bearing witness to God's love, we are guided by the knowledge that Jesus Christ is fully human and fully divine.

To tell the story of Jesus Christ, we must also be guided by the images given by God that interpret the story for us. These images come into focus at the crucifixion of Jesus Christ, but they also illumine his entire life. Today, these images shine as light in the darkness of the world, teaching us to see rightly God, humankind, sin, and salvation in the light of the gospel.

As Christ's disciples live in him today, those lives are stretched between the kingdom, the world, and the church. But we live in the power and presence of the Holy Spirit, who forms our lives in practices that continue to teach us Jesus Christ.

In the introduction to this book, I lamented the fact that today most disciples of Jesus Christ know more about sports, hobbies, and their jobs than they know about Jesus Christ. I hope that through your study of this book that gap has been closed. But in the end, we come to know Christ not by reading a book but by living in him. Therefore, I conclude with a reminder that doctrine is for life. As we follow Jesus Christ, we come to know him more fully. We live in the midst of a world that has little or no understanding of God's love for the world in Jesus Christ. Our calling as his disciples is to make that love real in our lives so that the world may come to know Jesus Christ as the one in whom there is life everlasting. May it be so, to the glory of God.

NOTES

PART 1 INTRODUCTION

1. In another context, it might be appropriate to describe the gospel as a fairy tale. Frederick Buechner, *Telling Truth: The Gospel as Tragedy, Comedy and Fairy Tale* (New York: Harper & Row, 1977), makes good use of the category to illuminate the meaning of the gospel. My point is that the gospel is not make-believe.

2. See my description of worship as our participation in "the most real world," in Jonathan R. Wilson, *Gospel Virtues: Practicing Faith, Hope, and Love in Uncertain Times* (Downers Grove, Ill.: InterVarsity Press, 1998), 119–27.

3. "Farther up and farther in" is the joyous shout of the characters in the New Narnia; C. S. Lewis, *The Last Battle* (New York: Penguin Books, 1964).

4. This has been argued profoundly and persuasively by Hans W. Frei, *The Identity of Jesus Christ: The Hermeneutical Bases of Dogmatic Theology* (Philadelphia: Fortress Press, 1967, 1975).

5. A great deal of attention has been given to "story" and "narrative" in recent biblical studies, theology, and ethics. Biblical studies and ethics have made good use of story for their constructive work, but in doctrine much of the work remains methodological rather than substantive. That is, accounts of Christian doctrine have not made use of the insights gained from attention to story and narrative. My intention is to make use of those insights. Another who does so is James Wm. McClendon Jr., *Systematic Theology*, vol. 2, *Doctrine* (Nashville: Abingdon Press, 1994), 238–79.

6. For Dietrich Bonhoeffer, our inquiry into Christ and our theological reflection begin with the presence *here and now* of the person of Jesus, "the Christ present as the Crucified and Risen One"; Dietrich Bonhoeffer, *Christ the Center*, trans. John Bowden (New York: Harper & Row, 1960), 43. See also McClendon, *Systematic Theology*, 239–44.

Chapter 1

1. Today, many people are concerned with what Jesus really said and did—as if we have a better chance today of coming up with the right answers to this question two thousand years later, in a different culture, and not speaking the language of the New Testament. This "quest" for the "real," "historical" Jesus has been widely advertised, and many good responses have been given. In addition to the trustworthiness and authority of the New Testament is the question of the nature of the Gospels—what kind of literature are they? For what purpose were they written? How we answer these questions shapes our approach to the Gospels. In my judgment, the four Gospels were written to answer disciples' questions not historians' questions; the Gospels are "manuals of discipleship" not "chronicles of history." Applying the criteria of contemporary history to the Gospels is like trying to referee a football game according to the rules of soccer. That does not mean the Gospels are untrue; it simply means they were written to tell *disciples* how to live. Nor does this mean that the events narrated in the Gospels are unhistorical; it means that the Gospels were written not to prove that the events happened but to tell us the significance of the events for our lives as Christ's disciples. My approach to the Gospels will be that of a follower of Jesus Christ who believes that God guided the writing of the New Testament in such a way that the New Testament is trustworthy and authoritative.

2. The literature on the kingdom of God is voluminous. For a recent survey and bibliography, see Mark Saucy, *The Kingdom of God in the Teaching of Jesus in Twentieth-Century Theology* (Dallas: Word, 1997). While New Testament scholars have directed a great deal of attention to the kingdom of God, theologians have been less energetic until recently. For doctrinal explorations of the kingdom of God, see Wolfhart Pannenberg, *Theology and the Kingdom of God* (Philadelphia: Westminster Press, 1969); and *Systematic Theology*, 3 vols., trans. Geoffrey W. Bromiley (Grand Rapids: Eerdmans, 1991, 1994, 1998); the various works by Jürgen Moltmann, especially *The Way of Jesus Christ: Christology in Messianic Dimensions*, trans. Margaret Kohl (San Francisco: HarperSanFrancisco, 1990); and *The Coming of God: Christian Eschatology*, trans. Margaret Kohl (Minneapolis: Fortress Press, 1996). Stanley J. Grenz, *Theology for the Community of God* (Grand Rapids: Eerdmans, 2000) recognizes the significance of "the kingdom of God" but prefers "the community of God."

3. For example, George Pixley, writing from a commitment to liberation theology, gives a mixed report on the idea of the kingdom of God; see George V. Pixley, *God's Kingdom: A Guide for Biblical Study* (Maryknoll, N.Y.: Orbis, 1981).

4. Donald B. Kraybill, *The Upside-Down Kingdom* (Scottdale, Pa.: Herald Press, 1978), provides a wonderful, extended account of the kingdom with which I am in deep agreement. I use "right-side up" imagery to emphasize that the kingdom is the way God intended life to be lived and is indeed the only way to live. Any other "way of life" is death.

5. This account of the kingdom of God owes much to Julian N. Hartt, *A Christian Critique of American Culture: An Essay in Practical Theology* (New York: Harper & Row, 1967), 165–84. See my analysis of Hartt's account of the kingdom in Jonathan R. Wilson, *Theology as Cultural Critique: The Achievement of Julian Hartt* (Macon, Ga.: Mercer University Press, 1996), 51–83.

6. This matter of the kingdom's timing has caused great debate, particularly among conservative Christians. In some ways my account is an attempt to avoid that debate in an attempt to refresh the image of the kingdom. When pressed I would argue for the "already/not yet" scheme argued by George Ladd and others. See George Eldon Ladd, *The Presence of the Future: The Eschatology of Biblical Realism* (Grand Rapids: Eerdmans, 1974).

7. The wonderful, difficult book by Reinhard Hütter, *Suffering Divine Things: Theology as Church Practice,* trans. Doug Stott (Grand Rapids: Eerdmans, 2000), is an extended consideration of the implications of this actuality of God's work for the practice of theology.

8. Hartt, *Christian Critique of American Culture,* 231–73.

9. See Stanley J. Grenz, *The Millennial Maze: Sorting Out Evangelical Options* (Downers Grove, Ill.: InterVarsity Press, 1992). Grenz's work is helpful for understanding how evangelicals have thought about these issues. In this book, I am trying to change the way we think about the kingdom rather than simply give another answer to the same old questions.

10. Frederick Buechner, *Wishful Thinking: A Seeker's ABC,* rev. ed. (San Francisco: HarperSanFrancisco, 1993), 65.

11. To say that God became flesh is not to say that God became only partly human, that the flesh of humanity was the only part of humanity that God assumed. As we will see in chapter 3, that would be an error in our understanding of the story of Jesus. Rather, to say that God became flesh in Jesus Christ is in part to emphasize the concreteness of the incarnation over against a tendency to make it an abstract concept rather than an actuality.

12. Paul uses the term *flesh* to refer to our sinful nature, but he does not mean to condemn our materiality or to deny the created goodness of matter. It is our fallenness that is judged and condemned, not our physicality. However, theology, especially evangelical theology, has not done a good job of providing a theological account of our bodily lives. Consequently, we are vulnerable to worldly accounts of our bodies. For one of the few recent accounts, set within the Catholic theological tradition, see Mary Timothy Prokes, FSE, *Toward a Theology of the Body* (Grand Rapids: Eerdmans, 1996).

13. The crucifixion of Jesus Christ and the salvation it brings is the focus of part 2 of this book.

14. Philip J. Lee, *Against the Protestant Gnostics* (New York: Oxford University Press, 1987).

15. Among the many books on this topic, one of the most comprehensive is Ben Witherington III, *Women in the Ministry of Jesus: A Study of Jesus' Attitudes*

toward Women and Their Roles as Reflected in His Earthly Life (Cambridge: Cambridge University Press, 1984).

Chapter 2

1. For a brief survey of these offices, see Geoffrey Wainwright, *For Our Salvation: Two Approaches to the Work of Christ* (Grand Rapids: Eerdmans, 1997), 99–120.

2. The most influential account of the offices as "threefold" is John Calvin, *Institutes of the Christian Religion*, 2 vols., ed. John T. McNeill, trans. Ford Lewis Battles (Philadelphia: Westminster Press, 1960), I:494–503 (bk. II.xv).

3. One exception is James Wm. McClendon Jr., *Systematic Theology*, 123, where he notes the significance of the three offices "displayed in the narrative Jesus lived out." McClendon, however, does not go on to show how these offices are displayed.

4. My language of "before" and "after" is meant in a theological not chronological sense. The development and date of Deuteronomy is much debated. My account is independent of that debate.

5. The issues of law, covenant, temple, and sacrifice are hotly contested in New Testament studies today. I cannot untangle all the issues and resolve the debate. My own view is that our previous understanding of law, covenant, and temple has been amplified and corrected at many points but that the disagreement between Jesus and the religious leaders of his day was still enough to get him crucified.

6. While Jesus was hanging on the cross, "Those who passed by hurled insults at him, shaking their heads and saying, 'You who are going to destroy the temple and build it in three days, save yourself! Come down from the cross, if you are the Son of God.' In the same way the chief priests, the teachers of the law and the elders mocked him. 'He saved others,' they said, 'but he can't save himself! He's the King of Israel! Let him come down now from the cross, and we will believe in him. He trusts in God. Let God rescue him now if he wants him, for he said, "I am the Son of God"'" (Matt. 27:39–43).

Chapter 3

1. We will briefly study the history of the first three church councils below. For a history of these councils, see the various histories of Christian doctrine. One of the most detailed is Aloys Grillmeier, S. J., *Christ in Christian Tradition, Volume 1: From the Apostolic Age to Chalcedon (451)*, 2d rev. ed., trans. John Bowden (Atlanta: John Knox Press, 1975). A much shorter account that penetrates to the core of the debates is C. FitzSimons Allison, *The Cruelty of Heresy: An Affirmation of Christian Orthodoxy* (Harrisburg, Pa.: Morehouse Publishing, 1994). The original documents of these councils may be found in a variety of volumes. One of the best is John Leith, ed., *Creeds of the Churches: A Reader in*

Christian Doctrine from the Bible to the Present, 3d ed. (Louisville: Westminster/John Knox Press, 1982).

2. The doctrine of the Trinity has received considerable attention in recent years. Two very different and helpful historical treatments are T. F. Torrance, *The Trinitarian Faith: The Evangelical Theology of the Ancient Catholic Church* (Edinburgh: T & T Clark, 1993); and Catherine Mowry LaCugna, *God for Us: The Trinity and Christian Life* (San Francisco: HarperSanFrancisco, 1991).

3. For a further account of Adoptionism, see Allison, *Cruelty of Heresy,* 39–47 and 173–76.

4. Christians safeguard the beginning of the gospel in the activity of God through various means. One of the meanings of grace is that everything depends upon God. Another less well-known doctrine is the "preexistence of Christ." In relation to our questions, one of the effects of this doctrine is to rule out the belief that the story of the kingdom begins with humankind.

5. The precise relationship between Docetists and Gnostics is debatable, largely because of the paucity of original sources. Some treat the two as distinct groups; others regard "Gnosticism" as the larger category and "Docetism" as a description of their Christology. See the discussions by Allison, *Cruelty of Heresy,* 35–39 (Docetism) and 55–66 (Gnosticism).

6. See the incisive work of Lee, *Against the Protestant Gnostics.*

7. Today, we have several "gospels" written by Gnostics as counter-narratives to the canonical Gospels. Some argue that these Gnostic gospels (such as the "Gospel of Thomas") should be included in the canon and in our development of Christian doctrine. However, if that were to occur, the story of Jesus and the kingdom would be different from the story we have been studying to this point—it would be another "gospel" and another salvation. The exclusion of the Gnostics is rooted in profound theological convictions about the kingdom and our salvation. That judgment is not changed by the discovery of the Gnostic gospels.

8. Scholars debate the precise details of the relationship between the canonical Gospels and Gnosticism. Disagreement over the details does not change the larger fact that the New Testament asserts the full humanity of Jesus.

9. See my development of this comparison between Adam and Jesus in Jonathan R. Wilson, "Grace Incarnate: Jesus Christ," in *Grace upon Grace: Essays in Honor of Thomas A. Langford,* ed. Robert K. Johnston et al. (Nashville: Abingdon Press, 1999), 141–52.

10. Because Arius was condemned as a heretic, few of his writings have survived. This paucity of evidence contributes to lively scholarly debates. Arius probably had a deficient view of the humanity as well as the divinity of Jesus. Traditionally, Arius's denial of the divinity has been the focus and will be here.

11. These distinctions lead T. F. Torrance to observe that in Arianism "the Logos was regarded as neither properly divine nor properly creaturely"; Torrance, *Trinitarian Faith,* 118. I owe this reference to Telford Work.

12. If the incarnate Son and the Father are both fully divine, then this raises the question of how many gods Christians believe in. As this question was answered by the church, they were also led to the question of the divinity of the Spirit. A helpful recent exposition of the Christian belief in the Triune God may be found in Nicholas Lash, *Believing Three Ways in One God: A Reading of the Apostles' Creed* (Notre Dame: University of Notre Dame Press, 1993).

13. We do not know with precision the details of Apollinaris's position, but it is clear that he did not think the divine Logos became fully human.

14. John Leith, ed., *Creeds of the Churches: A Reader on Christian Doctrine from the Bible to the Present* (Garden City, N.Y.: Anchor Books, 1963), 35–36.

Part 2 Introduction

1. I have been helped to understand the role of images by Austin Farrer, *The Glass of Vision* (Westminster: Dacre Press, 1948); Julian N. Hartt, *Theological Method and Imagination* (New York: Seabury Press, 1977); John McIntyre, *Faith, Theology, and Imagination* (Edinburgh: The Handsel Press, 1987); Garrett Green, *Imagining God: Theology and the Religious Imagination* (San Francisco: Harper & Row, 1989); David J. Bryant, *Faith and the Play of Imagination: On the Role of Imagination in Religion* (Macon, Ga.: Mercer University Press, 1989); and my discussion of the "evangelical imagination" in Wilson, *Theology as Cultural Critique*, 145–51.

2. For a full history of the doctrine of the death of Christ, see H. D. McDonald, *The Atonement of the Death of Christ: In Faith, Revelation, and History* (Grand Rapids: Baker, 1985). For a consideration of the metaphorical language of atonement, see Colin E. Gunton, *The Actuality of Atonement: A Study of Metaphor, Rationality, and the Christian Tradition* (Grand Rapids: Eerdmans, 1989).

Chapter 4

1. The twentieth-century work that has done the most to reclaim the image of Christ as victor is Gustav Aulén, *Christus Victor: An Historical Study of the Three Main Types of the Idea of the Atonement*, trans. A. G. Herbert (London: S.P.C.K., 1931; New York: Macmillan, 1960).

2. There is a great deal of discussion today about God as a warrior. I will return later to the image of God as warrior, but I should note at this point that the climactic image of God and Christ in military terms is not warrior but victor. In Christ, God has already won the war. To the extent that contemporary discussions acknowledge this truth, they may increase our understanding of the gospel; to the extent that they neglect or suppress this truth, they may inhibit our understanding. Two helpful biblical studies are Millard Lind, *Yahweh Is a Warrior: The Theology of Warfare in Ancient Israel* (Scottdale, Pa.: Herald Press, 1980); and Tremper Longman III and Daniel G. Reid, *God Is a Warrior* (Grand Rapids: Zondervan, 1995). One book that seeks to recover warfare imagery in connection to spiritual conflict but insufficiently recognizes the theme of victory is Gregory A.

Boyd, *God at War: The Bible and Spiritual Conflict* (Downers Grove, Ill.: InterVarsity Press, 1997).

3. For further development of this theme, see Wilson, "Grace Incarnate," 141–52.

4. While I do not agree wholly with any one of them, several studies of Christ and the powers are helpful guides to our thinking here: the early work by Hendrikus Berkhof, *Christ and Powers* (Scottdale, Pa.: Herald Press, 1962); John Howard Yoder, *The Politics of Jesus: Vicit Agnus Noster,* 2d ed. (Grand Rapids: Eerdmans, 1994), 134–61; N. T. Wright, *Jesus and the Victory of God,* vol. 2, *Christian Origins and the Question of God* (Minneapolis: Fortress Press, 1996), 595: "Jesus declared that the way to the kingdom was the way of peace, the way of love, the way of the cross. Fighting the battle of the kingdom with the enemy's weapons meant that one had already lost it in principle, and would soon lose it, and lose it terribly, in practice."

5. Irenaeus, *Against Heresies,* III.18.7, *The Ante-Nicene Fathers,* vol. 1, ed. Alexander Roberts and James Donaldson (Grand Rapids: Eerdmans, 1977), 448.

6. For the notion of an incomplete symbol, especially in relation to images of the atonement, see McIntyre, *Faith, Theology, and Imagination,* 60.

7. Gregory of Nyssa, *Address on Religious Instruction,* 24, *Christology of the Later Fathers,* Library of Christian Classics III, ed. Edward Roche Hardy and Cyril C. Richardson (Philadelphia: Westminster Press, 1954), 301.

8. Aulén, *Christus Victor.* Marva Dawn has pointed out to me that my account of Luther may be misleading. For Luther, the "law" belongs to those powers that are good creations in rebellion against God. Jesus Christ does not defeat these powers, he redeems them. Satan, sin, and death, on the other hand, are enemies to be defeated, not redeemed.

9. Walter Rauschenbusch, *A Theology for the Social Gospel* (New York: Macmillan, 1917; Nashville: Abingdon Press, 1978), 257–58.

10. In fairness to Rauschenbusch, I must note his claim that "the Kingdom of God is divine in its origin, progress and consummation"; *A Theology for the Social Gospel,* 139.

11. The classic work of liberation theology is Gustavo Gutiérrez, *A Theology of Liberation: History, Politics, and Salvation,* trans. and ed. Sr. Caridad Inda and John Eagleson (Maryknoll, N.Y.: Orbis, 1973). Many works by many theologians have followed. A good, brief introduction is Leonardo Boff and Clodovis Boff, *Introducing Liberation Theology,* trans. Paul Burns (Maryknoll, N.Y.: Orbis, 1987).

12. See the story told by Karl Barth in the midst of his massive *Church Dogmatics* about an instance of the confession that "Jesus is Victor" by defeated demonic power. Karl Barth, *The Doctrine of Reconciliation; Church Dogmatics* IV/3.1, trans. G. W. Bromiley (Edinburgh: T & T Clark, 1961), 168–71.

13. Several works have helped me improve my vision of Christ as victor: P. T. Forsyth, The *Work of Christ* (London: Hodder and Stoughton, 1910); Barth, *Doc-*

trine of Reconciliation; F. W. Dillistone, *The Christian Understanding of Atonement* (Philadelphia: Westminster Press, 1968), chap. 3; Colin E. Gunton, *The Actuality of Atonement: A Study of Metaphor, Rationality, and the Christian Tradition* (Grand Rapids: Eerdmans, 1989), chap. 3.

14. I will develop this further in part 3.

15. Here many of us will be tempted to object—we have learned from the Christian tradition that human beings are not helpless victims of sin but active perpetrators of sin. At this point, it is important to keep the images distinct. According to the next image we will consider—sacrifice—human beings are perpetrators of sin, but according to this image—victor—humans are the victims of sin. As I will later argue, these differences are biblical and very important in pastoral circumstances. One of our lingering problems, especially in conservative Christianity, is that we conflate these images, privilege the image of sacrifice, and end up blaming victims when they are the object of sinful oppression and violence.

16. P. T. Forsyth, *The Justification of God* (London: Independent Press, 1948), 220.

Chapter 5

1. For example, in one of the most thorough evangelical expositions of the work of Christ, John Stott centers his account on a satisfaction theory of the image of sacrifice and subordinates the themes of conquest and example to the theme of sacrifice. See John R. W. Stott, *The Cross of Christ* (Downers Grove, Ill.: InterVarsity Press, 1986).

2. For a thorough survey, see Robert J. Daly, *Christian Sacrifice: The Judaeo-Christian Background before Origen* (Washington, D.C.: Catholic University of America, 1978).

3. The close connection among the images of Christ we are considering is evident in that this hymn to Christ's sacrifice is also put forward as an example for us to follow.

4. New Testament scholars have typically argued for one of the two meanings I will draw out. I see no reason to suppose that the hymn has only one reference in relation to Christ's sacrifice. One scholar who combines the views in a way slightly different from my account is N. T. Wright, *The Climax of the Covenant: Christ and the Law in Pauline Theology* (Minneapolis: Fortress Press, 1992), 56–98.

5. I have put "legal" in quotes because many questions may be raised about the legality of the proceedings in Jesus' case, even when measured by ancient Roman and Jewish law.

6. Anselm, *Why God Became Man*, in *A Scholastic Miscellany: Anselm to Ockham,* trans. and ed. Eugene R. Fairweather, Library of Christian Classics Ichthus Edition (Philadelphia: Westminster Press, 1956), 100–183.

7. For a thorough consideration of the criticisms, see John McIntyre, *St. Anselm and His Critics: A Re-Interpretation of the Cur Deus Homo* (Edinburgh: Oliver and Boyd, 1954).

8. Anselm, *Why God Became Man,* 176–81.

9. Calvin used a mixture of images, but penal substitution is the image that took root and flowered in the Calvinist tradition. See Calvin, *Institutes of the Christian Religion,* I:508–10 (bk. II.xvi.5).

10. Ibid., book II.xvi–xvii.

11. One of the most powerful recent accounts is J. I. Packer, "What Did the Cross Achieve? The Logic of Penal Substitution," *Tyndale Bulletin* 25 (1974): 3–45. In addition to the criticisms noted below, in the conclusion to part 2, I will consider the criticisms directed toward all images of atonement by some feminist theologians.

12. It is important to note that this criticism does not apply to all proponents of penal substitution. Calvin, for example, derives the work of atonement from God's love. *Institutes,* I:506–7 (bk. II.xvi.4).

13. Karl Barth, *Church Dogmatics,* IV/1.14, §59.2.

14. Although his account differs from mine in details, no one draws out this personal-moral world more evocatively than Forsyth, *The Work of Christ.*

15. L. Gregory Jones, *Embodying Forgiveness: A Theological Analysis* (Grand Rapids: Eerdmans, 1995).

16. Regarding the misuse of sacrificial imagery for Christian living, see the astute remarks by Yoder, *Politics of Jesus,* 112–33.

17. Here is one of the ways that the feminist critique of Christian sacrifice helps us develop a more careful account. When we are victims of sin, God does not delight in our sacrifice; rather, God fights for us as our warrior and liberator.

18. Here I find helpful the description of "the apocalyptic sufferings of Christ" in Moltmann, *The Way of Jesus Christ,* 151–212. To describe Christ's sufferings as "apocalyptic" is to locate them at the historic confrontation between the kingdom of God and the kingdom of the world(s).

Chapter 6

1. Friedrich Nietzsche (1844–1900), a German philosopher and son of a pastor, wrote many works, most of which contain an attack on Christianity. Nietzsche put the claim "God is dead" in the mouth of a "madman." Given Nietzsche's commitment to the "will to power," it is not surprising that one of his central objections to Christianity was its "active pity for all the failures and the weak"; *The Antichrist,* §2, in *The Portable Nietzsche,* ed. and trans. Walter Kaufmann (New York: Penguin Press, 1968), 570.

2. See the excerpts from this work in *A Scholastic Miscellany,* 276–97.

3. Ibid., 280–83.

4. Ibid., 283.

5. As I argue in the conclusion to part 2, we need the three images together to have a full portrait of the work of Christ. On this basis I would judge Abelard's account deficient because of what it rejects (the images of victor and sacrifice) not because of what it asserts.

6. Friedrich Schleiermacher, *On Religion: Speeches to Its Cultured Despisers,* trans. John Oman (German ed. 1799; reprint, New York: Harper & Row, 1958).

7. Ibid., 81.

8. Friedrich Schleiermacher, *The Christian Faith,* eds. H. R. Mackintosh and J. S. Stewart (2d German ed. 1830; reprint, Edinburgh: T & T Clark, n.d.).

9. Ibid., 451–65.

10. See the older work by Alexander Balmain Bruce, *The Training of the Twelve; or, Pages Out of the Gospels Exhibiting the Twelve Disciples of Jesus under Discipline for the Apostleship,* 2d ed. (Edinburgh: T & T Clark, 1877).

11. Several books have argued this over the years. Still one of the most helpful is Harry Blamires, *The Christian Mind* (New York: Seabury Press, 1963).

12. This is simply another instance of Nietzsche's "will to power" that found the "feebleness" of Christianity so offensive. What Christ as example teaches us is that we are all feeble. If God in Christ does not love the feeble, then we are all doomed. The lesson of history is that many prefer this doom to salvation by grace.

13. See my description of Christian education in Wilson, *Gospel Virtues,* 72–95.

14. See my attempt to recover the virtue of love and the practice of hospitality in ibid., 140–82.

15. Early in his career, in his opposition to liberalism, Barth had spoken of the "infinite, qualitative distance between God and man." Late in life, he wrote of *The Humanity of God* (Richmond: John Knox Press, 1960).

PART 2 CONCLUSION

1. My understanding of the kingdom of God has been significantly shaped by the Bible (of course) and by the work of Julian Hartt, especially *Christian Critique of American Culture,* 165–350.

2. Ibid., 345.

3. I will return to this theme in chapter 8, where I will argue that the very life of the church is empowered by these images and in turn witnesses to their truth; here I simply note the significance of the community for our proclamation of the images of Christ.

4. Joanne Carlson Brown, "Divine Child Abuse?" *Daughters of Sarah* 18, no. 3 (summer 1992): 24–28. The issue includes several responses to Brown that vary in their acceptence and rejection of Brown's argument.

5. Ibid., 28.

6. Ibid.

7. See the brief but profound account of the presence of Christ in Bonhoeffer, *Christ the Center,* 41–49.

Part 3 Introduction

1. This view has been most forcefully argued by George A. Lindbeck, *The Nature of Doctrine: Religion and Theology in a Postliberal Age* (Philadelphia: Westminster Press, 1984), and critiqued and developed by Hütter, *Suffering Divine Things*. For some brief remarks of my own along these lines, see Jonathan R. Wilson, "Toward a New Evangelical Paradigm of Biblical Authority," in *The Nature of Confession: Evangelicals and Postliberals in Conversation*, ed. Timothy R. Phillips and Dennis L. Okholm (Downers Grove, Ill.: InterVarsity Press, 1996), 151–62; and "The Gospel as Revelation in Julian N. Hartt," *Journal of Religion* 72, no. 4 (October 1992): 549–59.

2. As I noted in the introduction to this book, N. T. Wright follows a pattern very much like mine (kingdom-praxis, kingdom-stories, kingdom-symbols), though with differing emphases, in *Jesus and the Victory of God*.

3. For an account of faith as a way of knowing, see Wilson, *Gospel Virtues*, 49–71. See also the following works by Lesslie Newbigin: *Foolishness to the Greeks: The Gospel and Western Culture* (Grand Rapids: Eerdmans, 1986); *The Gospel in a Pluralist Society* (Grand Rapids: Eerdmans, 1989); and *Truth to Tell: The Gospel as Public Truth* (Grand Rapids: Eerdmans, 1991).

4. Three books that provide profound theological reflection on the resurrection are Paul S. Minear, *To Die and to Live: Christ's Resurrection and Christian Vocation* (New York: Seabury Press, 1977); Rowan Williams, *Resurrection: Interpreting the Easter Gospel* (New York: Pilgrim Press, 1984); and Moltmann, *The Way of Jesus Christ*, 213–73.

5. Jürgen Moltmann first drew my attention to this claim in *The Way of Jesus Christ*, 73–94.

Chapter 7

1. The role of righteousness and its relation to the law and faith in Christ has been the subject of much recent scholarly debate. My purpose here is not to adjudicate those debates in detail, though I will draw on some of that material.

2. Although I do not follow all of his interpretation here, N. T. Wright helpfully describes the "goodness" of the law in *The Climax of the Covenant*, especially 137–56. The differences between us are not disagreements but differing emphases and purposes.

3. This part of the story anticipates the next section on the peace of the kingdom, reminding us that the kingdom is not a schematic diagram of God's work but the complex reality of the continuing presence of Jesus Christ.

4. See the powerful exposition of Paul's "moral logic" in Richard B. Hays, *The Moral Vision of the New Testament: Community, Cross, New Creation: A Contemporary Introduction to New Testament Ethics* (San Francisco: HarperSanFrancisco, 1996), 36–46.

5. For a wonderful account of the fruit of the Spirit that goes into the kind of detailed exposition I cannot give here, see Philip D. Kenneson, *Life on the Vine: Cultivating the Fruit of the Spirit in the Christian Community* (Downers Grove, Ill.: InterVarsity Press, 1999).

6. Kenneson, *Life on the Vine,* does much to guide this process of discernment.

7. For an account of these disciplines, there is no better starting point than the work of Dallas Willard, *The Spirit of the Disciplines: Understanding How God Changes Lives* (San Francisco: Harper & Row, 1988); and *The Divine Conspiracy: Rediscovering Our Hidden Life in God* (San Francisco: HarperSanFrancisco, 1998).

8. See the discussion of "cosmic ecclesiology" in Hays, *The Moral Vision of the New Testament,* 62–66. Hays's "cosmic ecclesiology" is another way of describing the peace of the kingdom to which the church is called as servant and witness.

9. Ibid., 62–63.

10. I have put these terms in quotes to remind us that pacifism and just war can take many different forms. For an account of varieties of pacifism, see John Howard Yoder, *Nevertheless: The Varieties and Shortcomings of Religious Pacifism* (Scottdale, Pa.: Herald Press, 1971). For one account of just war thinking, see Paul Ramsey, *War and the Christian Conscience: How Shall Modern War Be Conducted Justly?* (Durham, N.C.: Duke University Press, 1963). Christian pacifism is committed to an understanding of the practice of kingdom-peace not because that practice will end war but because that practice witnesses to the peace of the kingdom. "Just war" thinking among Christians has traditionally also presumed the church's commitment to peace. In this tradition, war is just only when a series of stringent criteria are met as we go to war and as we fight a war. The stringency of these criteria displays the presumption that peace is the first commitment of the church.

11. One may think here of Jesus' parable of the talents (Matt. 25:14–30).

12. I am indebted to an unpublished paper by my colleague Bruce Fisk for clarifying the centrality of Christ's story as the ground for Paul's joy. See also the study by N. T. Wright, *The Climax of the Covenant,* 56–98.

13. Two books that drive this point home in very different ways are Hütter, *Suffering Divine Things;* and Marion Montgomery, *The Truth of Things: Liberal Arts and the Recovery of Reality* (Dallas: Spence, 1999).

14. The quotes come from the works cited in the previous note.

Chapter 8

1. Abraham Kuyper, quoted by Henry R. Van Til, *The Calvinistic Concept of Culture* (Philadelphia: Presbyterian and Reformed, 1972), 117.

2. To this point I have used quotation marks to signify that I am using "world" in a particular way. From this point on, as I specify my meaning, I will expect the reader to supply the quotation marks.

3. Francis Watson, *Text, Church, and World: Biblical Interpretation in Theological Perspective* (Grand Rapids: Eerdmans, 1994), 267.

4. Julian N. Hartt, *Toward a Theology of Evangelism* (New York: Abingdon Press, 1955), 69. My theological understanding of the world is significantly shaped by Hartt's exposition here and his fuller account in *Christian Critique of American Culture.* See my analysis of Hartt's understanding of "world" in Wilson, *Theology as Cultural Critique*, 113–42.

5. This point is forcefully made by Douglas Farrow, *Ascension and Ecclesiology: On the Significance of the Doctrine of the Ascension for Ecclesiology and Christian Cosmology* (Grand Rapids: Eerdmans, 1999). The ascension of Christ imposes on the church the question of his absence even as he is in some sense also present. This chapter is an attempt to make sense of this twofold conviction.

6. Hartt, *Toward a Theology of Evangelism*, 69.

7. Julian Hartt, *The Restless Quest* (Philadelphia: United Church Press, 1975), 49.

8. I have offered more specific critiques of North American culture in *Gospel Virtues* and *Living Faithfully in a Fragmented World: Lessons for the Church from MacIntyre's "After Virtue"* (Valley Forge, Pa.: Trinity Press International, 1997).

9. For an analysis of technology as rebellion against God, see Craig M. Gay, *The Way of the (Modern) World or Why It's Tempting to Live as If God Doesn't Exist* (Grand Rapids: Eerdmans, 1998), 70–129.

10. C. S. Lewis, *The Silver Chair: A Story for Children* (Baltimore: Penguin Books, 1953).

11. Ibid., 148.

12. Ibid., 151–52.

13. The role of the Queen and the issue of enchantment raise the question, To what extent have we created our own world and to what extent have we fallen under the spell of the enemy? The answer, which I will not develop here, is that it is always a mixture of the two. Whether we are enchanted or rebellious, the result is the same and our salvation from both comes though Jesus Christ.

14. See the exposition of a doxological reading of history rooted in Revelation by John Howard Yoder, "To Serve Our God and to Rule the World," in *The Royal Priesthood: Essays Ecclesiological and Ecumenical*, ed. Michael G. Cartwright, foreword by Richard Mouw (Grand Rapids: Eerdmans, 1994), 127–40.

15. See the wonderful account of Christian worship as the practice of messianic kingship in Marva J. Dawn, *A Royal "Waste" of Time: The Splendor of Worshipping God and Being Church for the World* (Grand Rapids: Eerdmans, 1999).

16. Yoder, "To Serve Our God," 130–31.

17. Alasdair MacIntyre, *After Virtue: A Study in Moral Theory*, 2d ed. (Notre Dame: University of Notre Dame Press, 1984), 29–35, 74–108.

18. Ibid., 29.

19. Ibid., 28.

20. Ibid., 108.

21. Wilson, *Living Faithfully in a Fragmented World,* 50. See my discussion of the manager, 49–51.

22. See the profound analysis of cultural anxiety in Hartt, *Christian Critique of American Culture,* 3–48.

23. See my description of this term in *Gospel Virtues,* 88–90.

24. The entire Book of Hebrews proclaims the messianic priesthood of Jesus.

25. For a telling indictment of unfaithful church management, see Philip D. Kenneson and James L. Street, *Selling Out the Church: The Dangers of Church Marketing* (Nashville: Abingdon Press, 1997).

26. Stanley Hauerwas, *The Peaceable Kingdom: A Primer in Christian Ethics* (Notre Dame, Ind.: University of Notre Dame Press, 1983), 99. See also, Yoder, "Why Ecclesiology Is Social Ethics," *The Royal Priesthood,* 102–26.

27. Lewis, *The Silver Chair,* 155–56.

28. Hartt, *Christian Critique of American Culture,* 80–81.

29. See the discussion in Gay, *The Way of the (Modern) World,* 245–70.

30. Hartt, *Christian Critique of American Culture,* 43–47.

31. Ibid., 49–61.

32. Ibid., 311.

33. Ibid., 87.

Chapter 9

1. The very term *church* is problematic today, because it has been adopted by so many—Church of Scientology, Church of the Inner Light, and so on, nearly into infinity. I will continue to use the term here because it is so much a part of our thinking. When I say church I mean the church of Jesus Christ—the "disciple community," as Douglas John Hall has termed it. For his most systematic account of the disciple community, see Douglas John Hall, *Confessing the Faith: Christian Theology in a North American Context* (Minneapolis: Fortress Press, 1996).

2. For my other less than systematic reflections on the church, see *Theology as Cultural Critique,* 82–112; *Living Faithfully in a Fragmented World;* and *Gospel Virtues.*

3. Hartt, *Christian Critique of American Culture,* 294. Hartt's discussion, 292–94, is a fuller defense than I can offer here of my claim about the "marks" of the church.

4. This paragraph is a slight rewording of my account in *Theology as Cultural Critique,* 95–96.

5. I describe this as the "intelligibility" of the kingdom in *Theology as Cultural Critique,* 79–80.

6. Julian Hartt, *Theology and the Church in the University* (Philadelphia: Westminster Press, 1969), 168: "If the church does not have local color, if it does not proclaim and body forth the Word in a response modulated by an acute awareness of the speciality of its immediate environment, the church is an invalid if

not a ghost. Really to be the church the congregation must preach the Word to *these* people."

7. One book that systematically disentangles the life of the church from Western culture is Rodney Clapp, *A Peculiar People: The Church as Culture in a Post-Christian Society* (Downers Grove, Ill.: InterVarsity Press, 1996).

8. See my discussion in Wilson, *Living Faithfully in a Fragmented World,* 9–23.

9. Hartt, *Christian Critique of American Culture,* 344.

10. Nathan Hatch, *The Democratization of American Christianity* (New Haven: Yale University Press, 1989); and Stanley Hauerwas, "The Democratic Policing of Christianity," *Pro Ecclesia* 3, no. 2 (spring 1994): 215–31.

11. Hall, *Confessing the Faith,* 185.

12. Reinhard Hütter, "The Church as Public: Dogma, Practice and the Holy Spirit," *Pro Ecclesia* 3, no. 3 (summer 1994): 334–61.

13. For a recent systematic treatment of baptism and the Christian life, see Wolfhart Pannenberg, *Systematic Theology,* vol. 3, trans. Geoffrey Bromiley (Grand Rapids: Eerdmans, 1998), 239–83.

14. For a complementary account of baptism as a practice, see L. Gregory Jones, *Transformed Judgment: Toward a Trinitarian Account of the Moral Life* (Notre Dame: University of Notre Dame Press, 1990).

15. For a systematic treatment of the eucharist, see Pannenberg, *Systematic Theology,* 283–336.

16. Jones, *Transformed Judgment,* 141.

17. Geoffrey Wainwright, *Eucharist and Eschatology* (New York: Oxford University Press, 1971), 82.

18. See the profound reflections on the future, past, and present of Christ in the eucharist in William T. Cavanaugh, *Torture and Eucharist* (Oxford: Blackwell, 1998), 222–52.

19. In the interest of full disclosure, I should note that Free Will Baptists brought me to Christ and first taught me Christ. To this day, my memories of foot washing powerfully shape my understanding of Jesus Christ and the Christian life. See my discussion of foot washing in Wilson, *Gospel Virtues,* 109–10, 137–38.

20. One scholarly monograph on the foot washing passage that has been published is John Christopher Thomas, *Footwashing in John 13 and the Johannine Community* (Sheffield: JSOT Press, 1991). In that monograph, Thomas argues that foot washing is concerned with post-baptismal sin in the Johannine churches. While there is much good information in Thomas's work, I think this central thesis is over-determined and speculative.

SUBJECT INDEX

SCRIPTURE INDEX

Jonathan R. Wilson (Ph.D., Duke University) is professor of religious studies at Westmont College. He is the author or editor of several books, including *Grace upon Grace* and *Gospel Virtues*.